Trade, Exchange Rate, and Growth in Sub-Saharan Africa

In this sophisticated yet accessible analysis of the open economies of Sub-Saharan Africa, Jean-Paul Azam analyzes international trade, exchange rate issues, and longer-term growth, taking due account of the distinctive features of African economies. In particular, he examines the informal as well as the formal institutional frameworks which prevail in different African countries and which affect their macroeconomic behaviour. Key issues explored include tariffs and quotas, membership of the CFA Zone, and currency convertibility or inconvertibility, as well as smuggling, corruption, parallel markets in goods and currencies, ethnic diversity, and redistribution. Case studies of important macroeconomic events are used to establish basic stylized facts from which the theory emerges, and special attention is paid to the consequences of macroeconomic events for the poor, via the food market or traditional redistribution mechanisms.

JEAN-PAUL AZAM is Professor of Economics at the University of Toulouse and the Institut Universitaire de France.

Trade, Exchange Rate, and Growth in Sub-Saharan Africa

JEAN-PAUL AZAM

CAMBRIDGE UNIVERSITY PRESS
Cambridge, New York, Melbourne, Madrid, Cape Town, Singapore, São Paulo

Cambridge University Press
The Edinburgh Building, Cambridge CB2 2RU, UK

Published in the United States of America by Cambridge University Press, New York

www.cambridge.org
Information on this title: www.cambridge.org/9780521684071

First published 2007

Printed in the United Kingdom at the University Press, Cambridge

A catalogue record for this publication is available from the British Library

Library of Congress Cataloguing in Publication data

Azam, Jean–Paul.
    Trade, exchange rate, and growth in Sub-Saharan Africa / Jean–Paul Azam.
        p. cm.
Includes bibliographical references and index.

ISBN–13 978–0–521–86536–4 hardback
ISBN–10 0–521–86536–0 hardback

ISBN–13 978–0–521–68407–1 paperback
ISBN–10 0–521–68407–2 paperback

    1. Africa Sub-Saharan–Commercial policy. 2. Africa,
Sub-Saharan–Commerce. 3. Foreign exchange–Africa, Sub-Saharan.
4. Informal sector (Economics)–Africa, Sub-Saharan. I. Title.

HF1611.A93   2006
382′.30967–dc22

Contents

List of figures and tables   page   vi
Preface   xi
List of acronyms and abbreviations   xvi

1   Introduction and overview   1

Part I   Unrecorded trade in goods and currencies   9

2   The welfare implications of unrecorded
     cross-border trade   11

3   Parallel trade and currency convertibility   45

Part II   Foreign exchange constraints   67

4   Dollars for sale: inflation and the
     black market premium   69

5   The public debt constraint in the CFA Zone   105

6   Currency crises, food, and the "Cola nut" effect   134

Part III   Longer-term growth in African countries   171

7   Exchange rate, growth, and poverty   173

8   Export crops, human capital, and
     endogenous growth   197

9   Ethnic rents and the politics of redistribution   213

General conclusion   239

References   240

Index   255

Figures and tables

Figures

2.1	Côte d'Ivoire: quarterly cocoa prices, 1983–1997	*page* 13
2.2	Screening importers, by type	25
2.3	Smuggling against a tariff	33
2.4	When smuggling drives out official trade	34
2.5	Smuggling against a quota	36
2.6	Smuggling out	37
2.7	When smuggling drives out official exports	38
2.8	Smuggling out subsized imports	38
2.9	Smuggling in an FTA	40
3.1	Arbitrage on the parallel market for the naira between Lomé (Togo) and Zinder (Niger), 1980–1989	49
3.2	Parallel market premium: Nigeria, 1987–1993	50
3.3	The clearing of the naira market	52
3.4	Tracking the inflow of BEAC notes into Niger using (3.3)	55
3.5	The simultaneous clearing of the labor and the export crop markets	58
3.6	Parallel exchange rate determination	62
3.7	Joint determination of e and p	64
4.1	Official and parallel exchange rates: Nigeria, 1979–1993	75
4.2	Inflation rate: Nigeria, 1979–1993	76
4.3	Parallel market exchange rate and CPI: Nigeria, 1979–1993	77
4.4	The parallel market premium: Kenya, 1964–1990	78
4.5	Official and parallel exchange rates: Kenya, 1964–1990	81
4.6	Indexation policy	84

4.7	Nominal anchor policy	86
4.8	The credibility issue	89
4.9	The conservative governor	90
4.10	Official and parallel exchange rates: Guinea, 1986:03–1996:05	92
4.11	Parallel market premium: Guinea, 1986:03–1996:05	94
4.12	The CPI and the official exchange rate: Guinea, 1986:03–1996:05	95
4.13	Rate of inflation: Guinea, 1986:03–1996:05	96
4A.1	Indexation policy	99
4A.2	Nominal anchor policy	100
5.1	TOT: Cameroon and Côte d'Ivoire, 1974–1992	107
5.2	TOT: Burkina Faso and Senegal, 1974–1992	108
5.3	Inflation rates: Cameroon and Senegal, 1974–1992	110
5.4	Inflation rates: Burkina Faso and Côte d'Ivoire, 1974–1992	110
5.5	Nominal exchange rate: Côte d'Ivoire, 1974–1992	111
5.6	GNP *per capita*: Cameroon, Côte d'Ivoire, Senegal, and Burkina Faso, 1974–1992	112
5.7	GNP *per capita* growth rates: Burkina Faso and Senegal, 1974–1992	113
5.8	GNP *per capita* growth rates: Cameroon and Côte d'Ivoire, 1974–1992	114
5.9	Determination of the solvency frontier *SS*	118
5.10	Imposing a ceiling on *R*	121
5.11	Debt/GNP ratio: Côte d'Ivoire, Senegal, Cameroon, and Burkina Faso, 1985–1992	124
5.12	Total reserves minus gold: Cameroon, Côte d'Ivoire, and Senegal, 1992:01–1994:03	128
5.13	Total reserves minus gold: Burkina Faso, 1992:01–1994:03	129
5.14	Impact of devaluation	130
6.1	Reserves ratio and real effective exchange rate: Madagascar, 1988:01–1997:05	139
6.2	Central bank credit to the treasury and inflation rate: Madagascar, 1988:01–1997:05	140

6.3   Joint determination of harvest-time and
        lean-season rice price   143
6.4   The real price of rice: Madagascar,
        1987:06–1997:05   145
6.5   The first-generation currency crisis model   150
6.6   A continuum of rational expectations equilibria   152
6.7   A second-generation currency crisis model   153
6.8   A third-generation currency crisis model   155
6.9   The dynamics of money balances in the
        third-generation model   156
6.10   Parallel exchange rate of the naira in US dollars
        and CFA Francs, 1991:01–1995:02   158
6.11   Equilibrium in the African goods market   162
6.12   Regional equilibrium and dynamics   165
7.1   Poverty and macroeconomic policy   174
7.2   Real GDP: Côte d'Ivoire, Senegal, Burkina
        Faso, Niger, Mali, Benin, and Togo, 1984–1998   177
7.3   Relation between public wages and public
        employment, 1987   178
7.4   Dynamic response to an expected formal
        sector wage cut   184
8.1   Conditions for manufacturing development   203
8.2   Transitional convergence   208
9.1   Ethnic rent and migration failure   218
9.2   Paying for peace   221
9.3   The redistribution/deterrence trade-off   226
9.4   The triangular redistribution game   228

Tables

2.1   The share of trade taxes in tax revenues,
        1988 and selected dates   *page* 12
4.1   Granger non-causality test between parallel
        and official rate   80
4.2   Augmented DF-tests, parallel/official rates:
        Guinea   92
4.3   Granger non-causality test, parallel/official
        rates: Guinea   93
4.4   Augmented DF- tests, inflation/official rates:
        Guinea   95

5.1   Growth rates in the CFA Franc Zone,
      1970–1993   109
7.1   Annual rate of change of the average
      wage in central government, 1993–1999   180
7.2   Côte d'Ivoire: contribution to poverty of
      different groups before and after the
      devaluation   189–190
7.3   Niger: contribution to poverty of different
      groups before and after the devaluation   193
7.4   Change in poverty incidence: Senegal,
      1994–2001   194

Preface

I went to Sub-Saharan Africa for the first time in 1985, as a visitor to the University of Abidjan. I had a good rapport with advanced students and young faculty there, and was struck by their passion for research in economics. Toward the end of my stay I gave a seminar on macroeconomics and presented a dynamic variant of IS-LM with rational expectations. They were very keen, and took in every word of my presentation, asking many pertinent questions: but my stay in Abidjan had been long enough to convince me that the type of macroeconomics that we do in Europe or the USA is almost completely useless for these countries. We take so much for granted when we model our economies: a labor market dominated by formal institutions, with resulting nominal wage sluggishness; a developed financial market with a well-defined interest rate; a democratic government, sensitive to electoral constraints, etc. We implicitly assume that the economy is well diversified, so that the terms of trade are relatively stable, and that the foreign exchange market is a large one, where anybody can buy or sell most of the currencies of the world. Most of these assumptions are unwarranted in many developing countries, and especially in Sub-Saharan Africa. I promised myself that I would devote my research to getting a better picture of the working of these economies. I tried for many years to produce such an "open economy macroeconomics for Africa," and this book is a reflection of that research agenda. It is neither a textbook nor a treatise, as many relevant issues are not discussed, and it reflects only my own research interest and field experience. Nevertheless its ambition is to attract some interest from advanced undergraduate and graduate students. I use many parts of it as a teaching resource; some of the material presented here has served as a basis for teaching in Abidjan, Antananarivo (at the central bank), Clermont-Ferrand, Louvain-la-Neuve, Namur, Ouagadougou and Toulouse. Nevertheless, I hope that some of my academic colleagues will also find some interest in it.

The focus of the book is clearly on applied theory, trying to offer analytical models that can help us to understand the functioning of these economies. Because the latter do not behave like western economies in all respects, it is crucial to base one's theorizing on an observation of the facts. Most of the chapters in the book therefore mix facts and theory, in the spirit of the "analytic narratives" method advocated by Bates *et al.* (1998). Some salient historical periods are discussed at length, because they help to identify some phenomena that are central to a proper understanding of the way these African economies behave. These stories are told with the help of an analytical model, stripped of any useless complications. I have been unable to produce a purely macroeconomic approach, and even less to produce a single model that can illuminate all the relevant issues at a glance. I tend to go back and forth between the macroeconomic and the mesoeconomic levels: in the case of African economies, it is sometimes useful to think in terms of small general equilibrium models, and sometimes to focus on more sectoral issues, in order to understand better some features which the economist trained in a western type of macroeconomics may find unusual.

The aim of these exercises is to come up with useful hypotheses, and not to establish the truth. Like most macroeconomic or mesoeconomic models, they all rest on some simplification, and do not do full justice to the complexity of the real world. Many of these hypotheses have been tested econometrically, but I only occasionally present all the empirical results here. In particular, there is a very rich empirical literature devoted to the growth performance of African economies which I leave completely outside the scope of this book, although it is obviously relevant in many respects: Collier and Gunning (1999) have produced a very exhaustive survey of this field. I do illustrate the relevance of many of the issues addressed here, using some of the data that helped me shape up my own ideas over the years. In most cases, I have not attempted to update the data used, taken from some of my previously published papers. They are often the result of some fieldwork, or at least country visits, and are adequate for discussing the historical episodes under scrutiny, without any need for updating the series. The ideas discussed do not seem to be too sensitive to the dates of the figures presented, in that similar stories seem to apply to other places at other times. The data presented aim only at giving the reader the flavor of the issues at stake, and not to give an accurate picture of the current state of the African economies. The historical episodes that are discussed provide a proving ground for putting the concepts to work; the latter remain the center of interest. This illustrates the beauty of case-based theorizing: while the data help us to imagine and then test the theory, the validity of the theory, if it is of value, extends far beyond the data set used.

However, I deliberately avoid any claim of universal validity for the results. On the contrary, one of the themes underlying this book is that countries differ from one another in several crucial respects. The fact that African economies differ from developed ones is an obvious claim of this book: I would not otherwise have devoted twenty years of my life to studying them. But the fact that African economies differ from one another also plays a prominent part. In particular, their institutional frameworks differ: although institutions are endogenous in the long run, they display enough inertia for them to influence the behavior of the different economies in the medium run. In the field of open economy macroeconomics for Africa, a crucial difference exists between the countries belonging to the CFA Zone (whose currency is almost completely convertible), and those that do not (whose currency is frequently inconvertible, and traded on a parallel market). This makes a significant difference as far as the conduct of macroeconomic policy is concerned. However, these differences are not relevant for all issues, and some useful generalization is possible for some questions. Economies are like fractal objects, whose details can sometimes be neglected when talking about "the big picture," while they need to be dealt with discretely when considering other issues.

This is a well-traveled book, as I visited most of the Francophone African countries, including Burkina Faso, Cameroon, Chad, the Comoros, Côte d'Ivoire, Guinea, Madagascar, Mali, Niger, and Senegal, as well as Morocco and Tunisia, north of the Sahara. I also went to Mozambique, when it was just coming out of isolation in 1987, and to several Anglophone countries: Ethiopia, Ghana, Kenya, South Africa, Zambia and Zimbabwe. My recurring visits to some of these countries have become the staple of my research activity. I have never been there as a tourist, except sometimes peripherally for a weekend, as most of these trips have been done either for teaching in universities, for participating in some African Economic Research Consortium (AERC) meetings, or for collecting data and insights for research or consulting contracts. This research therefore owes much to the many people whom I met in ministries, statistical offices, etc., and to various sources of funding. The latter include mainly the World Bank, the OECD Development Center, and the AERC. Many other sources of finance have been tapped occasionally (EU, UNICEF, UNDP, WHO ...), and I am grateful to all of them, without implicating their responsibility in any way. My debt to the AERC goes far beyond the financial support that I have received from time to time, as my intellectual debt to this wonderful network of researchers is enormous, beyond any possibility of repayment. Since my involvement in AERC began, in May 1991, I missed a biannual meeting, in Nairobi, or elsewhere, only in case of *"force majeure"* (as you say in English). The Center for the Study of African Economies (CSAE) in Oxford, where I have been a research associate since 1990, also gave me intellectual stimulus, as well as many opportunities for interacting with many fascinating people; several of my papers have been discussed at the lunchtime seminars there. The funding for my visits to Oxford came for a while from St Antony's College, where I had the privilege of being the Deakin Fellow for three years. More recently, I have used some of my research funding from the Institut Universitaire de France to pay for some visits to Africa, Oxford, and other fascinating places.

As a token of my appreciation, I wish to mention the names of those who taught me the most about African economies (without implicating their responsibility for my views): Chris Adam, Janine Aron, Melvin Ayogu, Robert Bates, Elliot Berg, Jean-Claude Berthélemy, Tim Besley, David Bevan, Catherine Bonjean, François Bourguignon, Stéphane Calipel, Gérard Chambas, Paul Collier, Cécile Daubrée, Lionel Demery, Shanta Devarajan, Magueye Dia, Nadjiounoum Djimtoingar, Ibrahim Elbadawi, Marcel Fafchamps, Augustin Fosu, Séraphin Fouda, Flore Gubert, Patrick and Sylviane Guillaumont, Jan Willem Gunning, Philippe Hugon, Tony Killick, Jean-Jacques Laffont, Jean-Michel Marchat, Allechi M'Bet, Christian Morrisson, Benno Ndulu, Gilbert N'Gbo, Tchétché N'Guessan, Dominique Njinkeu, Steve O'Connell, Kassey Odubogun (now Garba), Cathy Pattillo, James Robinson, Sandrine Rospabé, Ousmane Samba-Mamadou, Charles Soludo, Chris Udry, Kerfalla Yansané ... So many others have also contributed to shaping my ideas about African economies. Some of those cited above are no longer with us, but will continue to influence my work for a long time to come.

I owe my interest in monetary macroeconomics to the late Morris Perlman, at the London School of Economics (LSE), and my interest in growth and development to the late Henri Campan, in Toulouse. Both were great teachers, with a decisive influence on my subsequent research activity.

Special thanks are due to Jean-Philippe Platteau, whose invitation to teach a course on the topics of this book in Louvain-la-Neuve and Namur prompted me to develop the matters presented here in my own work, and to put it into its present shape. Some new material has been added to already published work when necessary, in all chapters, but especially in chapters 2, 3, 6, 7, and 9. Cathy Pattillo gave me the crucial impulse for submitting this manuscript for publication. I am very grateful, without implicating of course.

This book draws heavily on some of my previously published work, including Azam (1991a), (1991b), (1993), (1997), (1999a), (1999b), (2001a), (2001b), and (2004) and Azam and Besley (1989a). It also draws on Azam (1991c), Azam and Bonjean (1995), and Azam and Samba-Mamadou (1997), which have been published in French. I wish to acknowledge with gratitude the contributions of my co-authors, and also of the anonymous referees, with the usual caveat, for the parts of the book that draw on previously published work.

Acronyms and abbreviations

AERC	African Economic Research Consortium
BCEAO	Banque centrale des Etats de l'Afrique de l'Ouest
BEAC	Banque des Etats de l'Afrique centrale
CAISTAB	stabilization fund, Côte d'Ivoire
CAMU	Central African Monetary Union
CEE	Central and Eastern Europe
CEMAC	Communauté économique et monétaire de l'Afrique centrale
CES	constant elasticity of substitution
CET	common external tariff
CFA	Communauté financière en Afrique (WAEMU)
CFA	Cooperation financière en Afrique (CEMAC)
CILSS	Côte d'Ivoire Living Standard Survey
CPI	consumer price index
CSAE	Center for the Study of African Economies
ECOWAS	Economic Community of West African States
EMU	European Monetary Union
ESAM	Enquête Sénégalaise auprès des ménages
FGT	Foster, Greer, and Thorbecke
FMG	Malagasy Franc
FOB	free-on-board
FTA	free trade area
GDP	gross domestic product
IFI	international financial institution
ILO	International Labor Organization
IMF	International Monetary Fund
LARES	Laboratoire d'Analyse Régionale et d'Expertise Sociale
LDC	less-developed country
NGF	Nouveau Franc Guinéen (New Guinea Franc)

NIP	New Industrial Policy (Senegal)
NTB	non-tariff barrier
OCA	optimum currency area
QR	quantitative restriction
SAP	structural adjustment program
SOE	state-owned enterprise
TOT	terms of trade
UEMOA	Union économique et monétaire Ouest-africaine
WAEMU	West African Economic and Monetary Union
WAMU	West African Monetary Union

1 | Introduction and overview

1.1 Introduction

African countries often have weak formal institutions, which affect the working of their economies. Their fiscal administration, for example, is often powerless, and this results in an excessive taxation of foreign trade, the easiest flows to exploit, creating significant distortion. The latter gives rise to some rents that can be captured by various forms of rent-seeking, with competition between the agents of the government and others from the private sector. Corruption, fraud, and smuggling, are thus part of everyday life in African, as in so many other economies (e.g. the transition economies of Central and Eastern Europe, CEE). These are not mentioned here for the sake of attracting the attention of the reader with some exotic anecdotes; they shape the functioning of these economies in ways that a serious macroeconomic analysis should take into account. Failure to do so explains, for example, why we read some papers showing how international trade is inexplicably low between African countries whereas any fieldwork, either in warehouses or near the borders, would convince the observer that a lot of trade was going on. In this field, as in many others, statistics can be extremely deceptive, when they are not put in the right perspective by direct observation. I have seen bags of subsidized Nigerian fertilizers as far west as Senegal, and any traveler in West Africa will be familiar with the seemingly ubiquitous bottles of Nigerian petrol for sale at the roadside. Informal institutions to some extent substitute for the failing formal ones, and help this "parallel economy" to function.

I have a happy memory of an afternoon spent south of N'Djamena, in Chad, with my friend "Djim" in January 2001. It was a very hot day, and he took me to a restaurant run by a friend of his, very close to the Cameroonian border at N'Guéli. While we were sipping a cold "Flag" beer, sitting in the shade not far from the roadside, he drew my

1

attention to some strange couples, walking quite fast in the direction of the city. In each case, there was a lady walking in front, with an old blind man following her, holding her by the shoulder (there are many such victims of river blindness in Sahelian countries). These people had skinny faces, and very slim arms and legs, but the rest of their body looked obese. I then learned that they were transporting bags of sugar under their clothes, because the tax on sugar is lower in Cameroon than in Chad. Thanks to a fundamental aspect of the Sara traditional initiation rites, this trade offers a profitable occupation for old blind men in countries where most people have no social security. Among the Sara and other southern ethnic groups, one of the first things that young boys are taught at their initiation, is that they should never do any harm to handicapped people; when they grow older, some of them become customs officers, and would therefore never accost any old blind men, an immunity that extends to those helping them. By the time the "Flag" beer was finished, we had seen many such couples. Then we saw a crippled young man, sitting on a strange little car, briskly pushed by another young man. The car was made of a wooden box, painted green, fixed on four wheels, probably recycled from a baby landau, with a large handle for pushing it. Djim then told me that the local "brand C ..." beer factory benefited from a legal monopoly, while there was across the border, not far into the interior of Cameroon, another factory producing the same brand of beer in a more competitive environment. God bless the Sara initiation!

Because the opportunity cost of labor is so small for many people in Africa, some of them are prepared to spend a lot of time in arbitrage operations, to earn even a small margin. A lot of the trade that takes place between African countries is of this type, and never shows up in the official statistics. Trade statistics are also based on customs data, and are thus blighted by fraud. Because tariffs are not uniform, much activity at the customs is devoted to convincing the officer that what he sees is actually something else, with a much lower tariff rate. For a modest inducement, the trader and the officer can eventually agree to see the same thing. Even some recorded transactions are thus underestimated. One should never restrict one's attention to formal institutions, as the informal ones are every bit as important (see North, 1990).

Part I of this book seeks to shed some light on the economic consequences of this type of "hidden activity." Part II is devoted to short-run macroeconomics, focusing on foreign exchange and the constraints that stem from it, in economies that are more open than they look. Part III looks at longer-run issues, raising the issue of "pro-poor growth" when there is an informal sector, as well as that of the structural transformations that occur in the process of economic growth, when export crops are important. Lastly, it offers a general explanation for all the strange phenomena that have been met with in earlier chapters, such as corruption, smuggling, parallel markets, and other forms of unofficial transactions.

1.2 Overview

Chapter 2 begins by describing the "hidden trade" mentioned above, and gathers some of the observations that I have been able to put together over the years, or to pick up from others. It aims to bring out some of the stylized facts that must be taken into account when doing any open economy macroeconomics for African countries. Of course, not all the countries in Africa are exactly alike, and my experience has a definite West African bias. However, most of the stories that I have been able to collect from my fellow economists from Eastern and Southern Africa, whom I have met mainly through the AERC network, convince me that similar things are relevant for these countries, too. Think of the situation in Zimbabwe in 2005–6, where the official economy is crumbling under the rule of President Mugabe and the so-called "war veterans." There is scope for making a fast buck in parallel market activities, if you have the right connections. In many other African economies, market controls have on paper been lifted, in the wake of the liberalization movement that swept across the continent in the 1990s and early 2000s. However, as illustrated below, informal institutions such as corruption and fraud often fill the niche vacated by formal controls. Trade distortions depend as much on the behavior of customs officers as on the decisions taken by bureaucrats and politicians. Smugglers and other types of tariff evaders still have a bright future in Africa, as they do in many other parts of the world (see, e.g., Naylor, 1999).

These observations are then put into perspective using some traditional tools of trade theory to shed some light on the welfare consequences of unrecorded cross-border trade. Ironically, it turns out that borrowing the formal framework of Vinerian analysis of the customs union is particularly illuminating in this case. The analogy comes from the fact that smuggling can be analyzed as a form of partial, or preferential, trade liberalization, like the creation of a free-trade area (FTA). The welfare effect thus ends up being ambiguous, depending on the relative strength of the trade-diversion and trade-creation effects. However, the conclusion is that in general, the existence of parallel trade pushes the analysis in favor of trade liberalization and regional integration, as these policies tend to divert trade flows from the parallel to the official segment of the external market. In other words, smugglers have not yet completely performed the task of integrating regional markets.

Chapter 3 goes one step further, and embeds these "hidden activities" in a small general equilibrium model, in order to bring out some of the effects that a partial equilibrium analysis necessarily misses. There is in particular an interesting interaction between the parallel foreign exchange market and the goods market. Some background information is provided first on the parallel market for the naira, the inconvertible currency of Nigeria. Analyzing this in a general equilibrium setting shows how the convertibility of the local currency makes a significant difference for some key comparative statics effects. This sheds some light on the way in which some market institutions do significantly affect the predictable impacts of various economic policy measures, and should serve, along with other parts of the book, as a salutary warning against a "one-size-fits-all" approach to economic policy – which is, unfortunately, much too evident among some officers from donor agencies or international financial institutions (IFIs).

Part II takes the analysis further, in the direction of short-run open economy macroeconomics. It takes stock of some of the ideas developed in part I, and analyzes how these phenomena influence the conduct of monetary and exchange rate policies. Institutional differences again intervene.

Chapter 4 analyzes how the government can use the official segment of the foreign exchange market, when the currency is inconvertible, to covertly divert massive sums of money. A simple macroeconomic model is developed that sheds some light on the working of these parallel market economies. They are very different in Africa from those analyzed in Latin America by Dornbusch *et al.* (1983), where the parallel market is a "sideshow." In Africa, it is center stage, as the price level is in many cases in fact determined on this market. The parallel market premium and the rate of inflation are jointly determined, and the inflation tax is used to fund the subsidy that is implicit in the parallel market premium. The example of Nigeria is discussed at length, as this country offers a unique natural experiment based on the change in policy that occurred in 1986. This is done to test the macro economic impact of this diversion of potential tax revenues, depending on the behavior of the central bank. The latter can lead to some instability if it loses sight of the role of the official foreign exchange rate as a nominal anchor for the economy. A glance at Kenyan data suggests that, starting in the late 1970s, a similar problem existed for this country, as well. The case of Guinea is also discussed, showing that the central bank can stabilize the exchange rate and the price level if it chooses the right behavior. This is a tribute to my friend Kerfalla Yansané's skills as a central banker, although he hates my using him to epitomize the power of the "conservative central banker" in Africa *à la* Rogoff (1985), and I want to apologize for this here. I am doing it in a good cause, as I use this expression in a scientific sense.

An appendix to this chapter gives some microfoundations for the demand for money function used in chapters 4 and 6 of this book. It derives the required function from first principles, using Pontryagin's Maximum Principle in a variant of Sidrauski (1967) and Benhabib, Schmitt-Grohé, and Uribe (2002).

Chapter 5 examines the second type of constraint that emerges from the external sector, in the case where the national currency is convertible. In Africa, this is mainly the case for the CFA Zone, and its main features are described. Convertibility reduces the ability of the government to divert money through the official market channel and it opens the way for some external constraints. The particular institutions of the CFA Zone give some leverage to the former colonial power (France), for better or worse. However, the most important external constraint facing this group of countries is foreign debt. This is where the disciplinary force restraining the government comes from. This is discussed in chapters 5 using a dynamic model for structuring the narration of the events that led to the 1994 devaluation of the CFA Franc. This case shows that external pressure can lead to misguided policies – in this instance, the suspension of the external convertibility of CFA Franc bank notes. This triggered a spectacular currency crisis which made a devaluation unavoidable.

Chapter 6 considers the lessons to be learned from episodes of African currency crises. Although they rarely hit the headlines, they have a lot to teach us. These episodes can take place without involving the financial market; unfortunately, for the poorest, the food market provides the assets that can best bear the effects of a flight against the local currency. The example of Madagascar is discussed in particular, to show how rice paddy can sometimes be a very lucrative asset to hold. A short theoretical section sketches the main points of the three "generations" of currency crisis models, suggesting that the case studies approach is probably the most fruitful one to adopt for analyzing these events. The CFA Franc crisis is then discussed again, in order to illustrate the working of the African brand of the so-called "Tequila effect." This refers to the Mexican crisis of 1994, whose contagion spread to its neighbors in Latin America. There is an "effect" which provides the transmission channel whereby a shock on the CFA Franc can be passed on to the naira, in neighboring Nigeria. The Cola nut is produced in the forest zone, where it is not greatly consumed, except by migrants, and is consumed in the Sahelian zone, where it is not produced. It is thus a good symbol of the links that exist between the different economies of the region.

Part III looks at longer-run issues. Chapter 7 looks at medium-run matters, showing that, as expected, the 1994 devaluation of the CFA Franc triggered a recovery in the growth rate in the CFA Zone countries. What was not expected was that some deepening of poverty occurred, together with the recovery in growth, documented by looking at data from Côte d'Ivoire and Niger. A simple analytical model is presented to explain this somewhat counter-intuitive observation, and it rests on the stratification that is typical of African labor markets. Formal sector workers are much richer than others, and they often run additional businesses in the informal sector. An expected cut in their purchasing power – in the wake of a future devaluation, for example – leads them to cut their consumption and invest temporarily in their informal sector businesses for the sake of consumption smoothing. The resulting increase in capital intensity has a temporary positive effect on informal sector wages. When the expected cut occurs, they begin gradually to run down their assets, creating a negative effect on informal sector wages.

Chapter 8 looks at a still longer-run issue, characterizing the structural changes that occur in an economy where export crops – as they are in most African economies – are paramount in the early phase of development. At a later stage, the accumulation of human capital becomes the dominant engine of long-run growth. This is done using the "Côte d'Ivoire" model of endogenous growth; it assumes that the economy is open to the free immigration of labor and the perfect mobility of capital. The limiting factor is local human capital. This model displays an interesting transitional dynamics, where export revenues play an active role, while the asymptotic steady-state growth path depends entirely on the efficiency with which human capital is created. This model sheds some light on the type of economic convergence that should be observed in Africa. High growth rates are observed in thriving crop-exporting economies, and the challenge is to use these resources to develop the local human capital efficiently. Later, as the economy diversifies, the growth rate slows down, as the economy becomes more reliant on the accumulated human capital.

Chapter 9 provides an explanation for some of the inefficient behaviors or institutions described in earlier chapters. It traces the fundamental problem to ethnic polarization, and the resulting risk of conflict that it entails. It then shows that redistribution in favor of politically excluded groups is a fairly efficient way to prevent political violence and civil war. Redistribution can be performed using different channels, ranging from corruption and patronage to publicly provided education and health care.

1.3 Conclusion

Most of the chapters in the book have a focus on the observation of one particular event, such as the devaluation of the CFA Franc which took place in January 1994, the adjustment policy adopted by Nigeria during 1986, or the speculative attack against the Malagasy Franc which took place in May 1994. These major macroeconomic events are difficult to analyze by statistical methods, because they are so infrequent, and pose a significant challenge to the professional macroeconomist. The latter must therefore equip herself with simple analytical models in order to recognize such events when they occur, and to draw some useful implications from them. My experience as a consultant has taught me that decision-makers are convinced only by hearing simple stories based on relevant case studies. The type of clarity required to do this comes from the implicit use of simple models that help to structure the narration. The aim of this book is to convey this truth to the reader.

PART I

Unrecorded trade in goods and currencies

2 | The welfare implications of unrecorded cross-border trade

2.1 Introduction

Most developing countries do not have the administrative capacity for raising tax revenues in an efficient way. Foreign trade turns out to be one of the easiest taxes to exploit, since traded goods have to pass through easily monitored points, such as seaports, train stations, or airports. Customs officers thus play a major role in collecting fiscal revenues for the government, and sometimes for themselves, as "informal levies." This is especially true in Africa, where taxes on foreign trade often amount to about half the total tax revenues. Table 2.1 illustrates this point by showing the ratio of trade-related taxes to total tax revenues in selected Sub-Saharan countries in the 1980s.

Many attempts have been made to change this situation, but the need to collect fiscal revenues is delaying reform. For example, between 1997 and 2000 the West African Economic and Monetary Union (WAEMU) adopted various reforms aimed at harmonizing the taxation of trade flows among its members, and at creating a common external tariff (CET), while removing tariffs on most intra-WAEMU trade. However, various escape clauses were put in place allowing countries to introduce temporary new taxes, which have in many cases become permanent.

All these levies bear generally more heavily on imports and on export crops, and create significant distortion. They provide some protection to firms that produce import substitutes and thus create, in many cases, an anti-export bias. Moreover, the figures in table 2.1 are an under-estimate for some countries. For example, oil-rich Nigeria levies more than 60% on the profits from oil exports as royalties, which appear under the heading of corporate tax, and not as a trade-related tax. A similar effect occurs, *mutatis mutandis*, in uranium-exporting

This chapter draws on Azam (1998).

11

Table 2.1. The share of trade taxes in tax revenues, 1988 and selected dates, %

		1988	Previous dates
Cameroon	:	18.4	29.0 (1981–3)
Congo	:	32.3	17.0 (1978–80)
Côte d'Ivoire	:	42.3	46.3 (1980–2)
Gambia	:	77.9	78.8 (1976–8)
Ghana	:	37.9	37.1 (1981–3)
Kenya	:	2.1	22.3 (1979–81)
Niger	:	n/a	40.0 (1978–80)
Nigeria	:	17.5	19.4 (1976–8)
Senegal	:	37.7	38.5 (1980–2)
Uganda	:	46.7	55.8 (1981–3)
Zaire	:	46.9	35.8 (1980–2)

Note: n/a = Not available.
Sources: 1988: Tanzi (1992); Previous dates: Tanzi (1987).

Niger. In the case of Cameroon, the royalties on oil exports have been kept out of sight for a long time, deposited in a US bank account at the discretion of the president, so that they are also not included in the figures given in table 2.1. Similarly, importers often pay bribes in order to avoid paying the full amount of the necessary customs duties (Daubrée, 1996). This is again a kind of tax on foreign trade, even if it does not show up in the government budget.

Exports are also often taxed in Africa by a marketing board or a stabilization fund. This type of levy is not included in table 2.1, although it sometimes amounts to a significant percentage of the border price. This was the case for a long time in Côte d'Ivoire, where the stabilization fund known as CAISTAB was in fact capturing a large share of the export proceeds. This lasted until the fall in international prices for coffee and cocoa in the late 1980s (Ridler, 1988; Schiller, 1989; Azam and Morrisson, 1994). Figure 2.1, from McIntire and Varangis (1999), represents the series of the producer price of cocoa in Côte d'Ivoire, as well as the free-on-board (FOB) price. The difference between the two was levied either by CAISTAB or directly by the state. It then transpired that most of the money levied on producers through CAISTAB had not been invested in liquid assets that could be easily sold in order to raise funds to compensate

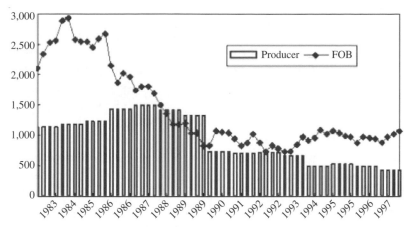

Figure 2.1. Côte d'Ivoire: quarterly cocoa prices, 1983–1997, 1990 US $/mt
Source: McIntire and Varangis (1999).

farmers for the price fall, as a proper stabilization fund should have done. The stabilization fund was thus able to stabilize prices only when they were going up on the world market, and not when they were going down. The FOB price was below the producer price for only a short period at the end of the 1980s. It is thus reasonable to regard these levies as taxes, most of the time, although they do not appear explicitly in the government budget. The cocoa and coffee sector in Côte d'Ivoire was liberalized in 1999, but was captured again by president Gbagbo and his close supporters in the mid-2000s.

In addition to these explicit or implicit taxes one may add the effect of exchange rate over-valuation, especially in countries where a parallel foreign exchange market is active. The premium on foreign currencies can be interpreted as a tax on the export proceeds that are surrendered at the official exchange rate, and as a subsidy on official imports. In some countries, such as Nigeria, the government is a net seller of foreign exchange to the private sector. This is true also for many other African countries, if only because of aid money. In such cases, the government sells the foreign currencies from oil exports and international aid at a discount through the central bank, which enables it to transfer some money to some privileged agents who have access to these sales (Odubogun, 1994; Azam, 1995). Chapter 4 in this volume develops this analysis in detail.

However, trade taxes and exchange rate over-valuation are not the only reason for cross-border trade and smuggling, as African governments often used quantitative restrictions (QRs) instead of tariffs. The reason why non-tariff barriers (NTBs) have been so popular in Africa has to do with the political economy of resource redistribution. A quota imposed on the import of a particular good creates two types of rents, which are in some respects equivalent to a tariff (McKinnon, 1979). First, it creates a wedge between the border price and the consumer price, which is pocketed by the importer. Second, quotas create some monopoly power for import-substituting firms, as they prevent external competition. By a selective quota policy the government is thus unobtrusively able to redistribute some resources in favor of some privileged groups. From the government's point of view, this way of diverting resources from the budget has the definite advantage of reducing the possibility for the parliament or the Bretton Woods institutions to control their use, and has similarities with the sale of foreign exchange at a discount through the central bank described above. But it may be socially costly if real resources are invested by rent-seekers to capture the benefits of these distortions. Krueger in her classic (1974) paper has illustrated the social cost of competitive rent-seeking, as rent-seekers have an incentive to invest resources in the competition until the value of the rent is dissipated. QRs have been widely replaced by tariffs in the wake of IMF structural adjustment programs (SAPs), but reappear from time to time in some countries. Since 2000, Zimbabwe has suffered heavily from this type of QR imposed on imports. Usually, at least to some extent, traders find various ways of sidestepping the problems raised by these trade taxes. Smuggling and deliberate misinvoicing are extremely common in Africa, and the countries represented in table 2.1 contain many well-known cross-border trade partners. Smuggling between the Gambia and Senegal is a very active business, to the extent that official imports of sugar in the Gambia, on a *per capita* basis, are probably at world record levels, most of it being smuggled to Senegal in order to avoid the heavy protection granted there to this sector. Many other goods are involved in the Gambia–Senegal cross-border trade, which has been studied by Daubrée (1996). Smuggling is also widespread between Côte d'Ivoire and Ghana where cocoa and manufactured goods are smuggled across the border in one direction or the other, depending on the changing pattern of trade taxation (May, 1985; Azam and Besley, 1989a). In the late 1970s and the early 1980s, cocoa crossed the border between Ghana and Côte d'Ivoire. It was estimated that about 50,000 tons of cocoa were smuggled out of

Ghana in 1978–9, out of a production level of 265,000 tons (Franco, 1981); May (1985) gives slightly lower estimates. Azam and Besley (1989b) in a regression analysis found a significant impact on official sales of cocoa by the Cocoa Marketing Board (Cocobod) of the price difference of the cocoa producer price between Côte d'Ivoire and Ghana, evaluated at the parallel market exchange rate. May (1985) has estimated that in Ghana in 1982 the parallel market activity, involving both illegal imports and exports, was equal to 32.4% of official GDP. Although the marketing system has been liberalized to some extent in Ghana, the implicit tax rate on cocoa exports was still around 50% at the end of the 1990s (McIntire and Varangis, 1999). Since September 2002, the territory of Côte d'Ivoire has been split between the government's side and the "New Forces" (originally called the rebels). Crossing the line between the two sides is extremely difficult, and many traders have reopened the old smuggling routes via Ghana and Burkina Faso. During the worst days of the Idi Amin or Obote regimes in Uganda, coffee was smuggled out through the Kenyan border and in the days of the Mengistu regime it was illegally exported from Ethiopia into Kenya (Kidane, 1993). The proceeds from these illegal exports were partly used to finance some imports of manufactured goods, and partly for capital flight. The cross-border trade between Nigeria and its neighbors, considered below, responds to the same type of incentives.

The present chapter gives examples of the type of parallel activity that is going on in Africa, and hints at the consequences. Because of my biased research interest, a lot of emphasis is put on the relationships between Nigeria and its neighbors, all of which belong to the CFA Zone. Cross-border trade between Nigeria and its immediate neighbors (Benin, Cameroon, and Niger) was analyzed thoroughly in 1993, 1994, and 1995, through various surveys (Herrera and Massuyeau, 1995; LARES, 1995; Mahamadou and Boukary, 1995). The aim was to track the impact of the devaluation of the CFA Franc that took place in January 1994, which provided some valuable clues on the working of the illegal trading networks.

2.2 Trade between Nigeria and its neighbors (Benin, Cameroon, and Niger)

Parallel trade between Nigeria and its neighbors, all belonging to the CFA Franc Zone, has been studied for a long time. Grégoire (1986) presents a geographical and sociological analysis of the cross-border trade between Niger and Nigeria, together with the parallel market for the naira (the Nigerian currency). He focuses on the city of Maradi in Niger, close to the border with Nigeria, which is the main trading center for the smugglers. This town started to make a fortune during the civil war in Nigeria, beginning in 1967, as the northern part of the country was cut off from international trade. The main advantage of the city of Maradi is that it is, on the Niger side, the main Hausa city near the border, and not far from Kano, the heartland of the Hausas, south of the border. This ethnic group is split between Niger and Nigeria, as the border was determined by a long bargaining process between France and Great Britain in the colonial era, without any account being taken of the Hausa people themselves. The common ethnic roots make trade easier, with cattle, cloth, cowpeas, English cigarettes, and Nigerian fuel the traditional mainstays of trade. Daubrée's (1995) analysis of price differentials for a large basket of goods has shown that the market of Maradi is more integrated with that of Kano in Nigeria than with that of Niamey, the capital city of Niger; she shows that the co-movement of the prices of several consumer goods is tighter between the markets of Maradi and Kano than between the former and the markets of Niamey.

Trade in goods and assets

Nigeria and its neighbors, including Cameroon and Niger presented in table 2.1, trade many goods across their common borders. This includes Nigeria-made Peugeot cars, in addition to more traditional items such as cowpeas, English cigarettes, etc. (Azam, 1991a, 1991b; Daubrée, 1995). In this case, the parallel market for foreign exchange plays a crucial role, as the parts for making the cars are paid for at the official exchange rate, while the cars are then sold at the parallel market exchange rate. As the premium on foreign exchange on the naira market can be quite substantial (about 80% on average in the early 1980s), this amounts to a large input subsidy, which makes Nigerian-made Peugeot cars more competitive than those made in France. (This system was *de facto* abandoned in February 1995.) In the case of Nigeria, the over-valuation of the local currency has also triggered some fake exports from neighboring countries, with massive over-invoicing. Niger, for example, had for a while an agreement with

Nigeria whereby some cattle were exported to Nigeria, with the proceeds being purchased by the central bank in Niger at the official exchange rate. Traders would export a couple of sick cows into Nigeria, for example, in order to get a receipt for a large sum of nairas, which they in fact bought on the parallel market, for eventual sale at the official exchange rate at the central bank. This was a simple way of pocketing the parallel market premium, which was widely used in Niger.

In the 1980s, this intense activity of border trading was not well understood when the SAP was conceived for Niger, so that its influence was under-estimated. In particular, the collapse of the naira in the parallel market, where it lost more than 80% of its value in terms of CFA Franc during this period, led to a real appreciation of the CFA Franc in Niger, resulting in a strong deflationary influence (Azam, 1991a, 1991b). This did not help the adjustment process. This trading activity has more recently been disturbed by the monetary policy pursued by the central banks of the CFA Zone. In particular, when the Banque centrale des Etats de l'Afrique de l'Ouest (BCEAO) and the Banque des Etats de l'Afrique centrale (BEAC) decided to suspend the convertibility of CFA Franc bank notes outside the two CFA Franc monetary unions in August 1993, there was a panic flight against the CFA Franc in Nigeria. This triggered substantial imports into Nigeria from all the neighboring countries (Herrera, 1994; Grégoire, 1995; Azam, 1997). In particular, cattle ("assets on the hoof," Azam, 1991b) was exported from Cameroon when Nigerians moved their portfolio away from CFA Franc into other inflation-proof assets (Herrera and Massuyeau, 1995). The sale of cattle on the Adoumri market (Cameroon), a central place for cross-border trade, went up by 46% just after the suspension of the external convertibility of CFA Franc bank notes, compared to August 1992. In August and September 1993, the price of cattle went up by 20% in this market. Cattle from Chad and the Central African Republic transited through this market; the price of the naira in nearby Garoua (Cameroon) doubled overnight (Herrera, 1994). Cattle, and hides, and skins, are also the main exports of Niger into Nigeria. This thoughtless decision to suspend the external convertibility of CFA Franc bank notes entailed the loss of many assets in CFA countries, illustrating vividly how far bureaucrats at the central banks (and elsewhere) were from understanding the importance of cross-border trade with Nigeria, and the resulting international role of the CFA Franc as a "hard currency," an inflation-proof asset for Nigerians and other non-CFA country residents. Chapter 5 develops the analysis of this event in more detail.

The devaluation of the CFA Franc that took place in January 1994 also had a significant impact, as did the policies adopted by the Nigerian president General Abacha, who seized power around the same time. Abacha decided to repress the free working of foreign exchange bureaux, and to fight against the parallel forex market, which had been *de facto* legalized earlier; the legal sale of foreign currencies was again centralized at the central bank. This had a negative influence on the value of the naira on the parallel market, so that although the CFA Franc was devalued by 100%, the price of the naira went up by only about 70%. This suggests that the cost of General Abacha's policies was equivalent to a loss of about 30% of the naira's market value. Then, in February 1995, the foreign currencies market was *de facto* unified in Nigeria, removing some of the incentives for smuggling.

The setting in Benin

Although cross-border trade is often called "informal trade," it is in fact well organized, and more and more data are now available about its structure and pattern. Hashim and Meagher (1999) have presented a vivid description of the informal institutions involved, mainly based on a monographic study of trade in goods and currencies in Kano, in Northern Nigeria. Benin is the closest CFA country to Lagos, the economic capital city of Nigeria. It has therefore an especially important role for trade between Nigeria and many of the countries of the region. It has been called the "Warehouse State" (LARES, 1995), because such an important part of its economic policies, and in particular its trade policy, is determined by the government's determination to make cross-border trade as easy as possible for Beninese traders. There are basically three main routes in this trade (LARES, 1995). The southern route links Lagos to Cotonou, the capital city of Benin, and its main seaport. The goods follow either the coastline road, which is the most natural route to follow, or are shipped on the lagoon between Cotonou and Badagri in Nigeria, a route preferred when customs officers are too active on the alternative route. From Benin, it is then straightforward to transport the goods to neighboring Togo, Ghana, and Burkina Faso in the north. There is another route that links Lagos to Ibadan and Shaki in Nigeria, and then across the border into central Benin or, further north, into Burkina Faso via Babana (Nigeria) and Kandi (Benin). Despite their higher transportation cost, the northern routes remain competitive with the southern route because there is almost no customs activity along the border. Smuggling and fraud are very easy.

The goods imported into Benin are either manufactured goods or petroleum products, which are very cheap in Nigeria. In order to estimate the amount of fraud that is involved in this trade, customs data have been compared systematically with those from the LARES survey (LARES, 1995), conducted in the main warehouses of Lagos and some other Nigerian cities. For many goods, the fraction that is actually declared at the customs is less than 10% of the actual traded flow. For example, between October 1993 and February 1994, 3,453 bicycle tires went through the warehouses as being exported to Benin, but only 291 of them were reported in the customs books. Similarly, while 1,614 truck tires went through the warehouses, only twelve went explicitly through customs. For batteries, the corresponding figures were 25,205 and 355, respectively. For some other goods, fraud did not involve such a large fraction of the trade flow. For example, for corrugated iron sheets and radios, the customs data showed 2,072 and 4,174, respectively, while the warehouse data showed 4,134 and 7,928, respectively. For pipes, it seems that most of the flow was declared at the customs, as the numbers were 1,643 and 1,809, respectively.

A similar exercise was performed in Niger in 1993 (Mahamadou and Boukary, 1995), with comparable results. Petroleum products imported officially amounted to 1,780 million CFA Francs, while the survey data showed 2,836 million CFA Francs; electrical appliances imported from Nigeria showed up as 70 million CFA Francs in the official records, while they amounted to 1,025 million according to the survey; wheat flour amounted to 415 million CFA Francs in the official data, and to 1,604 in the survey data, etc. However, smuggling across the Niger–Nigeria border is regarded as a fairly dangerous business, especially near Zinder (Niger), as bandits are almost more active there than customs officers. Traders do not travel in isolation, but organize convoys; this makes them easier to catch by the customs officers, who prefer collecting bribes than fines. In Maradi, transport is smoother, as many small traders cross the border, transporting goods that are stored in nearby warehouses.

Benin is a small oil producer, with no refinery. It exports its crude oil, and imports refined petroleum products. A parastatal called Sonacop is in charge of this trade, and levies very high taxes on it. For premium fuel, the price is thus multiplied by 2.7, for standard fuel by 2.9, and for diesel fuel by 2.1. This creates a strong incentive to import fuel from Nigeria, where by world standards it is very cheap. The official price difference between the two countries for fuel fluctuated between a minimum ratio of 4 to one of 20 in 1992. Moreover, there is a system of pan-territorial pricing, through the subsidies paid by the "Equalization Fund Management Board" which, *de facto*, subsidizes the transportation of fuel up to the Beninese or Cameroonian borders. Beside a network of 3,500 fuel stations, Nigeria has thousands of informal stations with hand pumps. Beninese traders thus face no problem for getting the fuel that they want. Nigerian traders carry the fuel from Ibadan or Lagos by trucks up to smaller towns near the border; these traders are grouped in partnerships that help them finance their purchases, and own the warehouses. Beninese traders come and get the fuel in these Nigerian small towns, and transport it across the border, using small trucks or vans. Normally, they transport the fuel by 200 litre barrels. In the central part of Benin, women also do a large part of this trade on foot, transporting three or four 10 litre cans on their head. Other traders use bicycles, transporting some 100 litres on them. In the south, many cars or buses have been transformed, with their tanks expanded in order to transport larger quantities of fuel across the border. Small boats transporting up to 300 50-litre cans are used along the lagoon from Badagri to Cotonou, mainly at night. The retail trade in Benin takes different forms, including some petty trade where people sell fuel by the bottle along the streets of most towns, and even along the earth roads. According to a LARES estimate, more than 50,000 people are involved in the fuel business in Benin, including 35,000 of them in villages. Smuggling of fuel into Cameroon is also an important part of cross-border trade.

Benin has no manufacturing industry to speak of so that most of its exports into Nigeria are re-export of transit trade, in other words exports of trading services. The only exceptions are cotton and cement. A similar situation prevails in Niger. Second-hand cars are banned in Nigeria when they are more than five years old, so that they make a very profitable transit trade through Cotonou. Rice, flour, sugar, and concentrated tomatoes also play a large role in this trade. The quantity of rice that transited in Benin before being re-exported into Nigeria has been estimated at 211,000 tons in 1993 and 164,000 tons in 1994. In order to understand the importance of this trade for Benin, these figures must be compared with local consumption, which is about 60,000 tons. The cigarette trade is the hallmark of traders from Niger, who transport them from Cotonou through their country, and then either south to northern Nigeria, their main outlet, or north to Libya. English cigarettes are especially valuable in this trade. Customs duties are paid on the way into Benin. Wax cloth and second-hand tires are also traded with Nigeria. Thanks to the external convertibility of the CFA Franc, which remains valid for all international transactions except for bank notes, Beninese banks also provide Nigerian businessmen with financial services, and are active in helping them invest their funds in London or Switzerland. This entails a non-negligible demand for CFA Francs as a vehicle for capital flight from Nigeria. A similar system is at work in Cameroon, Chad, and Niger.

Recent events

Trade between Benin and Nigeria was significantly affected by the devaluation of the CFA Franc in January 1994, and by the simultaneous reforms adopted by General Abacha. The naira went up only by 60–70%, after a short-lived peak just after the 100% devaluation. It started to fall again from July 1994, falling below its pre-devaluation rate in October. It then reached a stable value from November 1994 to April 1995, as analyzed in more detail in chapter 6.

The devaluation of the CFA Franc and the strong inflation that took place in Nigeria (100% in 1994, mainly in the second semester), resulted in a fall in the demand for Nigerian goods in Benin. A fair estimate of the rate of this fall in imports is about 30% (LARES, 1995). This resulted not only from the devaluation and macro-economic stabilization in Benin, but also from the strikes that hit the oil sector in Nigeria over the summer of 1994. As far as non-petroleum goods were concerned the fall in the imports from Nigeria was about 51% during the first semester of 1994; the fall in trading flows affected both imports and exports, because of the Nigerian recession. The Nigerian government also adopted a series of liberalization measures in February 1995, lifting QRs on rice imports and cutting some tariffs. As a result, some trade flows were diverted to the official market. However, some other tariffs – for example, on wheat and on sugar – were increased. Simultaneously, Benin cut some levies on various imported goods involved in the transit trade, in order to maintain its smugglers' competitiveness. The imports of fuel also went down, as the Nigerian government decided to increase the price of petroleum products. The price of standard fuel went from 0.7 nairas per litre to 3.25 in November 1993 and from 3.25 nairas per litre to 11 in October 1994; this resulted in a drastic cut in the incentive to smuggle fuel across the border, making the life of the Beninese parastatal much easier.

Interestingly, this fall in import flows was accompanied by a large cut in the trading margin for most goods. The price of Nigerian goods should have increased by at least 100%, in view of the depreciation of the currency on the parallel market and of the inflation rate in Nigeria; however, the price of these goods delivered in Benin went up by only about 70%, even after correcting for the general fall in the quality of the goods imported (LARES, 1995). A similar effect was observed in Cameroon (Herrera and Massuyeau, 1995). This positive correlation between the fall in volume and the fall in the price margin suggests strongly that the supply curve for imports into Benin is upward-sloping, at least in the short run. The theoretical models presented in this chapter and chapter 3, as well as that in chapter 6, examine this issue in more detail, showing its importance for the analysis of the welfare effect of smuggling.

More and more people and institutions are coming to realize how important is the welfare cost of trade distortions, and many efforts have been made in several African countries to try and reduce their incidence. However, most of these reforms have a definite administrative bent, the reformers being content when they have changed some regulations or laws regarding foreign trade. Section 2.3 aims to illustrate how deceptive such an approach can be: most regulatory trade reforms can be undone immediately by an increase in corruption at the customs. This is brought out using a very simple game-theoretic model.

2.3 Will tariff cuts reduce trade distortion?

A limited survey performed by Oji (2005) in Nigeria nicely illustrates the origin of trade distortion in African countries. A questionnaire was presented to various agents, including mainly importers, working in the Lagos wharf area, and a few other people working in the port area. The bottom line of the study is that a large fraction of these people prefer using the port of Cotonou to that of Lagos: 52% prefer Lagos, 40% use Cotonou, and 8% use both. The reasons advanced for preferring Cotonou, despite the additional distance, are corruption (63.3%), lack of infrastructure (25.9%), and bureaucracy and delays in customs clearance. On average, imported goods are cleared in Cotonou in twenty four hours, and in between seven working days and three months in Lagos. About 34% of the respondents took two weeks to get the imported goods cleared, 29.5% one month, and only 15.5% were done in one week. In order to correct this situation, the government of Nigeria is analyzing the possibility of simply forbidding the use of Cotonou's port for big containers. One may guess that smugglers are really hoping for this type of response. Only 23.7% of the respondents think that tariff reduction is addressing the right problem regarding the cost of importing into Nigeria. A glance at the data provides some additional support for this view. Between 1986 and 1994 the average tariff rate was 33.53%, and the ratio of trade to GDP was 12.99%. For the 1995–2000 period, the average tariff rate fell to 26.7% while the ratio of trade to GDP fell to 11.76%: not a big fall, but one that should be seen as a warning by those who believe that cutting tariff rates will trigger a strong positive response in trade flows.

The following model is admittedly conceived to be provocative. Assume that an importer is purchasing a good in the world market, which can be sold in the domestic market at the price of 1. Assume also that this good is subjected to a tariff θ, so that the importer's pecuniary benefit is $1- \theta$ if he goes through the official channel. Furthermore, assume that the customs officers are known to harass those who go through the latter channel, imposing an additional cost by inflicting on them a level h of harassment. The latter can be measured in terms of days lost at the customs, or of various forms of intimidation. Assume that the officers' commitment capacity is such that no importer can ever hope to go through the official channel without being harassed in such a way. Moreover, assume that there are two types of importers, differing by the extent of the damage that the harassment h is inflicting on them. When they see an importer, the customs officers cannot tell whether he has a high stake α_H or a low stake α_L in expediting his customs clearance. However, it is assumed that these officers know the probability distribution of the two types, with λ denoting the probability of the low type. The importer's profit net of harassment cost is then as follows, if he goes through the official channel:

$$\pi^T = 1 - \theta - \alpha h, \alpha \in \{\alpha_L, \alpha_H\}, \alpha_L < \alpha_H, \text{prob } \alpha_L = \lambda. \qquad (2.1)$$

The importer has another possible choice, namely to pay a bribe b, also called an "undefined levy," and sidestep all the hassle. Then, his profit is:

$$\pi^B = 1 - b. \qquad (2.2)$$

It is useful to think of this setting as the result of an implicit contract (see Bolton and Dewatripont, 2005, for a rich introduction to contract theory). The importer is faced with an implicit contract stipulating: "If you go through the official channel and pay the tariff θ, then I will inflict on you a level of harassment h; by contrast, if you pay the bribe b, then you will go through without hassle."

The importer will therefore agree to pay the bribe rather than the tariff if the following participation constraint holds:

$$b \leq \theta + \alpha h. \qquad (2.3)$$

This expression brings out very nicely the fact that the customs officers are playing on the two alternatives open to the importers. By harassing those who want to pay the tariff, they create some room for asking higher bribes from those who accept to play in the informal way. Figure 2.2 helps to understand how the threat of harassment induces the high-stake importers to pay the bribe. The participation constraints of the two types of importers are represented in the $\{b,h\}$ space by the two upward-sloping lines. These represent the maximum bribe that each type of importer will agree to pay, as a function of the level of harassment forthcoming in case of no payment. Point B represents a $\{b,h\}$ combination such that each importer is induced to reveal his type. The α_H importers pay the bribe, while the α_L importers are not willing to do so, and prefer to go through the official channel,

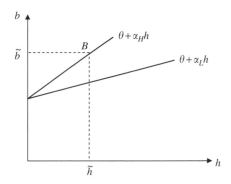

Figure 2.2. Screening importers, by type

pay the tariff θ, and get harassed to an extent $\tilde{h}$. The revelation principle of contract theory tells us that we can restrict our attention to such an outcome (Bolton and Dewatripont, 2005). In this particular application, it requires that λ be "small enough."

Of course, harassing the importers also imposes a cost on the officer, denoted ωh. It takes a lot of his time and of his energy to perform this activity. However, these harassment efforts are rewarded by the bribes paid by the participating importers, supposed to give the customs officers a level of utility $u(b)$, $u'(b) > 0$, $u''(b) < 0$. The latter will thus choose the $\{b^*, h^*\}$ pair with a view to maximize their expected utility, i.e.:

$$\max_{b,h}(1 - \lambda)u(b) - \lambda\omega h,$$
$$\text{s.t. } b \leq \theta + \alpha_H h. \tag{2.4}$$

Using the first-order condition of this program, one can derive the chosen $\{b^*, h^*\}$ pair, which reads:

$$b^* = u'^{-1}\left(\frac{\lambda\omega}{(1 - \lambda)\alpha_H}\right), \tag{2.5}$$

and:

$$h^* = \frac{b^* - \theta}{\alpha_H}. \tag{2.6}$$

Equation (2.5) brings out the main point of this exercise, namely that the trade distortion affecting the high-stake importers, i.e. those who do not pay the tariff, is independent of the tariff rate. Equation (2.6) shows that the trade distortion affecting the low-stake importers will depend on the tariff rate. This can be used for computing the average trade distortion, which is easily found to read:

$$\Delta = (1 - v)b^* + v\theta, \qquad (2.7)$$

where:

$$0 < v = \frac{\lambda(\alpha_H - \alpha_L)}{\alpha_H} < 1. \qquad (2.8)$$

Hence, the average trade distortion can be written in this simple model as a linear combination of the tariff rate and the bribe, while (2.8) suggests that the weight of the tariff rate might be quite a small number, in particular if the stakes of the different types of importers are not too far apart and if the share of the low-stake importers is small. Equation (2.7) suggests that even a tariff rate of 0 would not necessarily remove all trade distortion, if customs officers were still present at the border point – for example, just to control any import of prohibited goods such as weapons or drugs.

Hence, once the response of the customs officers' behavior to a tariff cut is taken into account, tariff cuts do not look really like a panacea for liberalizing trade and integrating regional markets. In this model, they have very little impact on trade distortion. Of course, the precise result found in (2.6) is model-dependent, and it would be easy to modify its specification to get either an increase or a decrease in the level of trade distortion affecting the high-stake importers as a response to the tariff cut. The specification adopted here is deliberately provocative, but is simple enough to make the main point, namely that the distance between tariffs cut and trade liberalization is probably longer than many realize. This suggests that parallel markets will thrive as long as official imports have to go through customs, even if the official tariffs are reduced. Corruption seems to be a much tougher nut to crack than tariffs on the way to trade liberalization.

Section 2.4 aims first to analyze whether cross-border trade and mis-invoicing are an efficient way of getting around the distortions entailed in trade restrictions. As shown below, the answer to this question depends on whether tariffs or quotas trigger the smuggling, and whether it involves resource costs or just transfers such as bribes and fines. As suggested in particular by Johnson (1987), a Sierra Leonian working at the IMF, the welfare analysis of cross-border trade bears close resemblance to the classical Vinerian analysis of the FTA (Robson, 1987). I develop this insight systematically to see if the analysis sheds any light on the case for trade liberalization in Africa. Is there any room left for liberalizing, or can it be said that smugglers have done the entire job? This question has been raised by Roemer (1987), Azam (1990), and Barad (1990); trade policy in Africa is also increasingly being discussed within the framework of regional integration and policy coordination (Foroutan, 1993). I discuss below how the existence of cross-border trade changes the analysis of an FTA within the traditional Vinerian framework. Establishing an FTA may be considered as a way to create some official trading activity that competes with the smugglers. Lastly, I raise the issue of the effect of smuggling on the efficacy of exchange rate policy.

2.4 Alternative models of smuggling or misinvoicing costs

In their seminal paper, Bhagwati and Hansen (1973) assume that smuggling involves a cost difference as compared with official trade. Neglecting any cost of official trade, they model the (extra) cost of smuggling as a real resource cost, captured by assuming that a constant fraction of the goods being smuggled is lost. This results in a constant-returns-to-scale supply curve of smuggled goods, so that official and parallel trade cannot in general coexist in their model. One observes either official trade, if the unit smuggling cost is too high given the distortion imposed on trade, or official trade is driven out by smuggling, in the opposite case. However, in the real world, official and non-official trade often occurs simultaneously: hence the expression "parallel trade,"

In order to model the simultaneous activity of the official and parallel trades, two main routes have been followed. I now discuss them briefly.

Increasing marginal cost of smuggling

The first is based on the assumption of an increasing marginal cost of smuggling. Azam and Besley (1989a), Devarajan, Jones and Roemer (1989), O'Connell (1992b), Kamin (1993), and Daubrée (1994,

1995), among others, discuss this assumption. In this framework, a
typical parallel trader seeks to maximize his trading profit:

$$\pi(p - p^*) = \max_Q (p - p^*) Q - c(Q). \qquad (2.9)$$

In this problem, the analysis is simplified by assuming that the
smuggler being studied is only an importer. The volume traded is
denoted Q, while p and p^* denote, respectively, the local price of the
good and its international price. The extra cost of smuggling is
denoted $c(Q)$, assumed to be increasing and convex, while the unit
cost of official trade is set to zero.

The first-order condition for this problem can be written:

$$p = p^* + c'(Q). \qquad (2.10)$$

The right-hand side of (2.10) is the marginal cost of smuggling, being
the sum of the price of the good across the border, plus the marginal
cost of transporting it and selling it inside the country. Then, in competitive equilibrium, it must be equal to the price of the good sold in the
local market. If official and unofficial trade are simultaneously active,
and have access to the goods on the international market at the same
price, then we must also have the following arbitrage condition:

$$p = (1 + \tau)p^*, \qquad (2.11)$$

where τ is the tax rate on officially imported goods, or the tariff
equivalent of the QR on imports. Combining (2.10) and (2.11) shows the
crucial role of this tax rate in determining the level of smuggling activity:

$$c'(Q) = \tau p^*. \qquad (2.12)$$

It is obvious that (2.12) cannot hold in general if the smuggling
technology has constant returns to scale so that $c''(Q) = 0$, unless
there is a "cover effect," discussed below.

Equation (2.10) makes it clear that the quantity smuggled is an
increasing function of the price difference $p-p^*$: By differentiating,
one gets:

$$dQ = (1/c'') \, d(p - p^*). \qquad (2.13)$$

The case of an exporter can be analyzed in a similar way, as seeking
to maximize:

$$\pi^X(q^* - q) = \max_X (q^* - q)X - c(X). \qquad (2.14)$$

Here, q represents the local price of the good being smuggled out,
q^* its price on the international market, and X the quantity exported.

The first-order condition can then be written as:

$$q^* - c'(X) = q. \tag{2.15}$$

The left-hand side can be interpreted as the inverse derived demand for the good, which in a competitive equilibrium must be equal to its price. Differentiating (2.15) would then give X as an increasing function of $q^* - q$, in a way close to (2.13).

These two examples assume, for the sake of simplicity, that the marginal costs of exporting or importing are independent of each other. Azam and Besley (1989a) discuss the case of economies of scope in smuggling, whereby the marginal cost of smuggling in is a decreasing function of the quantities of goods smuggled out. This is a simple way of modeling the fact that the transportation technology usually implies that some vehicle must be driven back, after being used for exporting some goods. The marginal cost of transporting something on the return trip is therefore lower, as the vehicle would need to be driven back anyway, even if empty. The same reasoning can be applied *mutatis mutandis* when the main trip is the importing one, ensuring symmetry of the argument.

O'Connell (1992b) emphasizes that assuming decreasing returns to scale at the level of the individual smuggler is not enough to explain why official and unofficial trades are simultaneously active. The supply curve might then be perfectly elastic with free entry, each smuggler trading a very small amount. O'Connell solves the problem by assuming some externality – such that, for example, the congestion of discrete smuggling routes increases the probability of being caught by the customs officers when too many smugglers take them. He also discusses the alternative assumption of barriers to entry, resulting in the number of smugglers being fixed. Then, the upward-sloping supply curve results as well.

Because of indivisibilities and credit market imperfections, the latter assumption may be quite realistic in some cases, at least in the short run. For example, a very juicy smuggling activity in the late 1980s was the illegal import of a famous English brand of cigarettes across the Niger–Nigeria border, when Nigeria was trying to protect its cigarette-makers by a ban on their imports (Azam, 1991a, 1991b). According to a very reliable source, a banker whom I invited for dinner in Niamey, there were precisely fourteen traders involved in this trade. This suggests that some barriers to entry were operating; one must assume some kind of Bertrand competition, or that the number of incumbent smugglers was rather large, for (2.10) or (2.15) to hold.

The "cover" effect

The second route for explaining the simultaneous existence of official and parallel trade has been presented by Pitt (1981, 1984), who assumes that official trade provides a "cover" for the smuggler, so that some goods are traded in the open in order to cloak the undeclared part of the trade. Then, even with constant returns to scale, the two types of trade can coexist. To see this, denote Q^F and Q^S the quantities that are declared and undeclared, respectively. Denote τ the tax rate on official imports, including any effect of the parallel market premium on foreign exchange. Then, the trader's profit function becomes:

$$\pi(p, p^*, \tau) = \max_Q (p - p^*)Q^S + (p - (1 + \tau)p^*)\, Q^F - C(Q^S, Q^F).$$
$$(+)\ (-)$$
$$(2.16)$$

Denoting C_S and C_F the partial derivatives of $C(-)$ with respect to Q^S and Q^F, respectively, the first-order conditions can be written as:

$$p - p^* = C_S > 0, \tag{2.17}$$

and

$$p - (1 + \tau)p^* = C_F < 0. \tag{2.18}$$

These two equations can be combined to yield:

$$p^* < p < (1 + \tau)p^*. \tag{2.19}$$

This implies that the declared units of the imported good are sold at a loss on the local market, which is compensated by the profit made on the sale of the undeclared units of the good. This result also implies that the consumer surplus is higher with smuggling than without it, as we show below, under this assumption.

To determine the quantities imported Q^S and Q^F, we can jointly solve (2.17) and (2.18) if there are decreasing returns to scale. Otherwise, in the case of constant returns to scale, with the function $C(-)$ being homogeneous of degree one, C_S and C_F are homogeneous of degree zero in their two arguments, so that (2.8) and (2.18) can determine the ratio Q^S/Q^F only as a function of $\{p, p^*, \tau\}$. One must then bring into the analysis the demand function, say $D(p)$, as done below, for determining the values of Q^S and Q^F.

Under the assumption of constant returns to scale in the smuggling business, one can simultaneously solve (2.17) and (2.18) and get the following reduced-form price equation:

$$dp = (1/(C_{SS} - C_{FS})) \, (((1 + \tau)C_{SS} - C_{FS}) \, dp^* + C_{SS}p^*d\tau). \quad (2.20)$$

In this equation, the various subscripts denote the corresponding second derivatives, taking into account the homogeneity property of the $C(-)$ function. It is natural to assume $C_{SS} > 0$ and $C_{SS} > C_{FS}$. Then (2.20) states that any increase in p^* or in τ is passed on to the consumer, but not necessarily one-for-one. In particular, the impact of an increase in p^* is larger than 1.

In the discussion of the welfare effect of smuggling that follows in the next section, it is important to specify whether the costs involved are only a kind of transfer (bribes, fines...), or involve some real resource costs. Let us now discuss this issue.

The nature of the cost of smuggling

Devarajan, Jones, and Roemer (1989) assume that the cost difference between official and unofficial trade involves only transfers such as bribes or fines. Denoting $0 \leq q \leq 1$, the probability of being caught smuggling and f the fine (or the bribe) per unit of smuggled good, their assumption may be written:

$$C(Q^S, Q^F) = q(Q^S, Q^F)fQ^S.$$
$$(+) \; (-) \qquad (+) \; (-) \qquad\qquad (2.21)$$

Then, the direct cost of smuggling is only a transfer from the smuggler to the government or to the customs officer.

O'Connell (1992b), Kamin (1993), and Daubrée (1994, 1995), following the classic paper by Bhagwati and Hansen (1973), however, assume that the smuggling cost difference involves some real resource cost, namely the use of some quantity of labor. This is rather surprising in Kamin's model, which aims only at describing mis-invoicing. Daubrée (1994, 1995) combines the two approaches, assuming both transfers and resource costs.

Deardorff and Stolper (1990) challenge this view, arguing that unofficial trade involves less resource cost than official trade. They argue that transaction costs on the official market are extremely important in African countries. Because of bureaucratic behavior, getting goods cleared through the customs may be a very costly activity, involving both labor time and bribes aimed at accelerating the process, and bureaucratic delays at the customs can also be very damaging when the goods involved are perishable. Smuggling is then an efficient way of reducing real resource costs, by taking a faster route that avoids the customs. This is an important point affecting the impact of smuggling on welfare; however, Deardorff and Stolper's assumption does not answer the question of what may explain the simultaneous activity of official and unofficial trade.

2.5 The welfare effect of smuggling and trade liberalization

For the sake of simplicity, I discuss here only the case of imports without a local substitute (it would be straightforward to add a sector producing import substitutes). I then extend the analysis to discuss the case of exports. Besides the nature of the smuggling costs, discussed above, the welfare effect of smuggling depends on the type of distortion that triggers it. As is customary in the international trade literature, I discuss welfare only in terms of consumer, producer, and government surplus, taken together. As we all know, many distributional issues have to be added in order to provide a fully convincing welfare analysis. I first analyze the case where official trade does not provide any cover effect, before turning to the case corresponding to Pitt's specification.

The import side

Figure 2.3 illustrates the case where the trade distortion is created by a tariff or bribe, and when both official and unofficial imports are non-zero. The demand curve for the imported good is labeled D, while the upward-sloping curve describes the supply of the smuggled good, corresponding to (2.10). In this case, smuggling only diverts trade from the official market to the parallel market, using the classic Vinerian terminology. At best, this trade-diversion effect leaves welfare unaffected only if the real resource cost difference between official and unofficial trade is zero. If any real resource cost is involved,

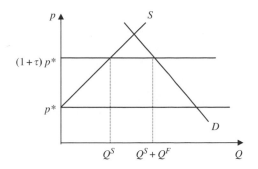

Figure 2.3. Smuggling against a tariff

then welfare goes down. If the smuggling costs are made up only of resource cost, then the welfare loss entailed by smuggling is measured by the triangle below the S curve, to the left of Q^S, and between p^* and $(1+\tau)\,p^*$. This welfare loss must be added to the usual dead-weight loss of the tariff, measured by the area of the triangle below D, to the right of $Q^S + Q^F$, and between p^* and $(1+\tau)p^*$, in order to measure accurately the welfare loss entailed by the tariff. Insofar as smuggling is the automatic response of the private sector to the imposition of a tariff, the welfare loss implied by smuggling must also be blamed on tariff protection.

Notice that smuggling entails a fall in the tax revenues of the government equal to $\tau p^* Q^S$. Hence, in this case, smuggling may reduce both social welfare, as seen above, and the welfare of the government, as measured by its tax revenues. It therefore reduces drastically the appeal of the tariff, from both a welfare and a public finances point of view. Taking due account of smuggling should thus reduce the attractiveness of tariff protection for African governments, and make the case for trade liberalization more appealing.

In this case, it is straightforward to show that trade liberalization increases welfare. This can be seen graphically using figure 2.3, by shifting downwards the $(1+\tau)p^*$ line. The areas of the two relevant triangles shrink, showing a positive welfare effect. Notice that a part of this welfare improvement comes from the diversion of a trade flow from the parallel to the official segment of the market, if smuggling entails any real resource cost. Hence, in the case where the smuggling activity is triggered by a tariff, and where both official and unofficial trades are simultaneously active, the existence of smuggling strengthens the case for trade liberalization. However, it is not certain

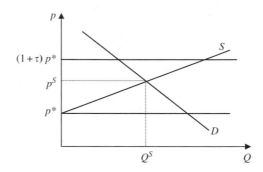

Figure 2.4. When smuggling drives out official trade

that the tax revenues of the government go up as the tax rate goes down, while the tax base goes up. The outcome depends on the elasticities of $D(-)$ and of S.

Figure 2.4 illustrates the case where the trade-creation effect is positive. Official trade has been driven out, and welfare may have increased, if the real resource cost of smuggling is low enough not to offset the benefit of the trade-creation effect. The domestic price of the imported good is now $p^S < (1+\tau)p^*$. As official trade has vanished in this case due to smuggling, the government loses the tax revenue that the tariff would entail in the absence of smuggling.

Trade liberalization, understood as a cut in the tariff rate, could thus be beneficial to both the consumer and the government. If τ is cut by a large enough percentage, so that $(1+\tau)p^*$ now falls strictly below p^S, then consumption of the good goes up, with the consumer surplus moving in the same direction, while the tax collected by the government goes up as well. In this move, only the smugglers lose something, as some trade is diverted from the parallel to the official market, as in the previous case. This may entail an additional welfare improvement if there is any real resource cost in smuggling. However, from a political economy point of view, this suggests that one should expect smugglers to be the most active lobby against trade liberalization.

We would basically get the same diagram as figure 2.4 with Pitt's specification discussed above, except that the S curve would be replaced by a horizontal line located between p^* and $(1+\tau)p^*$. The main differences are that, with Pitt's assumption, the case of figure 2.3 is not relevant, whereas the case of figure 2.4 prevails while official trade is not driven to zero. As shown above in (2.20), the market price

p is an increasing function of the tariff rate τ, so that the case for trade liberalization is unambiguously favorable here.

These examples show that the welfare impact of smuggling is ambiguous when it is triggered by a tariff. The impact is probably negative when there is no "cover" effect, if the two types of trade are simultaneously active, and if there is some resource cost difference in favor of official trade. At best, there is no impact, unless official trade is driven out. In the latter case, the outcome is ambiguous, and depends crucially on the nature of the smuggling cost. If the latter mainly involves expected transfers, à la Devarajan, Jones, and Roemer (1989), then smuggling makes a positive contribution to social welfare. Otherwise, the trade-creation effect might be offset by the real resource cost of smuggling. But the assumption that smuggling drives out official trade from the market completely seems a bit unrealistic – or, to say the least, not very common in the real world.

Pitt's assumption makes a positive diagnosis more likely, as such an outcome may result even when smuggling does not drive out official trade, as it provides a "cover" for the latter. In other words, cheating at the customs, which is the most common interpretation of Pitt's model, is probably more beneficial for the society as a whole than smuggling narrowly defined as importing goods without going through the customs at all.

There is no ambiguity when the smuggling activity is triggered by a quota, as shown in figure 2.5, where Q^R represents the quota. Sometimes, the QR has a bearing on the foreign exchange needed to make the purchase abroad. A given amount of foreign currency is allocated for a type of imports over a given period of time. It has the same effect as a quota. If the latter is binding, in the absence of smuggling, then smuggling necessarily improves welfare, by expanding the quantity sold and reducing its price. Let p^R denote the resulting price. In this case, any partial trade liberalization, defined as an increase in Q^R, is bound to improve welfare, without necessarily reducing the value of the rent. It all depends on the elasticity of demand and the elasticity of the smuggling supply curve. Hence, the privileged importers who benefit from the quota rent, if they perceive the demand curve as highly elastic, will not necessarily oppose this type of liberalization.

These contrasted results have an important (although not unexpected) policy implication. During the era of adjustment since the

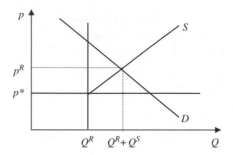

Figure 2.5. Smuggling against a quota

early 1980s, the Bretton Woods institutions have tried their best to convince African governments to lift the QRs that they used to impose on imports of many goods. As a transitional measure, the governments were advised to replace the quotas first by an equivalent tariff. Our analysis in figure 2.5 suggests that such a move has no welfare effect if the tariff-inclusive price is set at p^R. The main effect is to transfer the value of the quota rent from the importers to the government, who will now get it as tax revenues. Obviously, if the government fixes the tariff rate so that the new tariff-inclusive price is above p^R, then welfare goes down, as smuggling expands, if the latter entails any resource cost. However, this can hardly qualify as trade liberalization.

The export side

Let us now turn briefly to the analysis of unofficial exports. Figures 2.6 and 2.7 describe the case where the producer price is below the world price. In Africa, this mainly happens when a marketing board or a stabilization fund controls the official trade of an export crop. For the sake of simplicity, I deal with the case where no domestic demand for the good exists. This would be a widely unrealistic assumption for Ethiopian coffee, for example. However, it is straightforward to include a domestic demand in the analysis, so that the export supply function needs to be interpreted only as the net export function, or the excess of domestic supply over domestic demand.

The world price is denoted q^*, and τ denotes the (equivalent) tax rate. The supply curve is labeled X, while X^S and X^F denote the

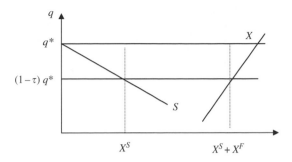

Figure 2.6. Smuggling out

unofficial and the official quantities exported, respectively. The curve labeled S is the derived demand for unofficial exports, corresponding to (2.15) above. In figure 2.6, both official trade and smuggling are non-zero, and we can see that smuggling has no welfare effect if it entails no real resource cost. If, on the contrary, all the smuggling cost is made up of real resources, then the welfare loss entailed by smuggling is measured by the triangle above S, to the left-hand side of X^S, and between $(1-\tau)\,q^*$ and q^*. If the cost of smuggling is partly made up of transfers, and partly of real resources, then, only that fraction of this triangle that corresponds to the share of real resource cost should be counted as a welfare loss. If one regards smuggling as the automatic response of the economy to the export (explicit or implicit) tax, then its resource cost must be added to the triangle below X, to the right-hand side of $X^S + X^F$, and between $(1-\tau)\,q^*$ and q^*, in order to measure the total welfare loss entailed by the export tax. The case for trade liberalization can be discussed *mutatis mutandis* as above. Cutting τ increases total exports and official exports, while it reduces smuggling. The area of the two triangles representing the welfare losses entailed by the export tax shrinks, increasing the welfare of the producer, and may also increase the welfare of the government, if the relevant elasticities are right.

When the smugglers are able to drive out the official trade, as in figure 2.7, then we get the same ambiguous result as above. The trade creation effect is positive here, so that it is possible that it offsets the resource cost of smuggling and delivers an increase in welfare. If there is no real resource cost, then welfare is unambiguously increased.

Another typical case of exports involving smuggling in Africa is that of re-export of subsidized goods. For example assume, as in figure 2.8,

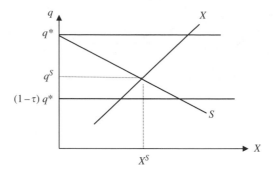

Figure 2.7. When smuggling drives out official exports

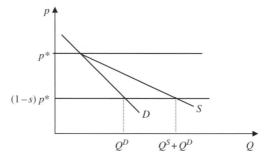

Figure 2.8. Smuggling out subsized imports

that an importable good can be bought in the world market at the price p^*, and can be sold in the domestic market at the price $(1-s)\,p^*$. This is typically the case when there is a parallel market for foreign exchange. If the good under study can be imported at the official exchange rate, and re-exported at the parallel exchange rate, then the parallel market premium works like an import subsidy. A quantity Q^D will be consumed domestically, while an additional quantity Q^S will be imported by the country for re-export by smugglers at the non-subsidized price p^*. If smuggling involves only real resource costs, the welfare loss is measured by the triangle above S, to the left-hand side of $Q^D + Q^S$, and between p^* and $(1-s)\,p^*$. In West Africa, this type of re-export is well known, involving Nigerian fertilizers or Algerian drugs.

This section has shown that, although the welfare impact of smuggling is generally ambiguous, unless one gets into detailed assumptions about the cause of the distortion and the nature of the smuggling cost, its existence usually strengthens the case for trade liberalization. This analysis is restricted to across-the-board trade liberalization; section 2.6 shows that the same conclusion is found when only selective trade liberalization is analyzed.

2.6 Smuggling and the case for regional integration

The classical Vinerian analysis of regional integration can be easily extended to include smuggling. I restrict the analysis to the creation of an FTA, where two countries agree to have no tariff at all bearing on trade between them, while the importing country keeps a tariff against the rest of the world. Figure 2.9 represents the case where initially the country has a tariff bearing on all imports, and where official and unofficial trades exist side by side. Assume that initially the trade-diversion effect of smuggling is dominant, as in figure 2.3, with a negative welfare effect if there is any resource cost entailed by smuggling.

Assume now that the country under study creates an FTA with a neighboring country. The two countries can trade among themselves with no tax or tariff being levied, while a tariff with the rest of the world is kept by the importing country. Define $T(p, p^*)$ as the net export function by the second member country of the FTA. In figure 2.9 the curve labeled $S + T$ represents the import supply function comprising both smuggling and official imports from the FTA member country. I have represented the case where the selective liberalization provided by the creation of the FTA may be enough for improving welfare. The curve labeled $S + T$ intersects the demand curve at a point below $(1 + \tau) p^*$, so that the trade-creation effect is positive. In this case, the smugglers and the union member country supply all the imports, and no more direct official trade with the world market, at the tariff-inclusive price, takes place. Hence, the government raises no funds through the tariff. Notice also that the creation of the FTA in this case entails some trade diversion from the parallel to the official market, with a positive welfare impact insofar as smuggling implies any real resource cost.

This example shows that smuggling strengthens the case for regional integration, understood here as the creation of an FTA, in the following sense. Assume that the neighboring country is not large enough to offer an export function such that the trade-creation effect

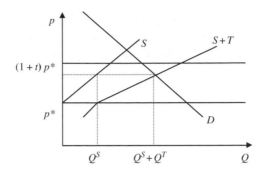

Figure 2.9 Smuggling in an FTA

dominates the trade-diversion effect at the prevailing tariff-inclusive price, in which case regional integration is detrimental. Smugglers can then complement the exports from the member country in such a way that any other trade flow with the rest of the world is driven out. The trade-diversion effect can then be dominated by the trade-creation effect, even if the opposite outcome would prevail in the absence of smuggling. Nevertheless, the other case – where the opening of trade to imports from the neighboring country is not enough to drive out any other direct official trade with the rest of the world, despite a positive level of smuggling – is also possible. This suggests that the FTA should be created by involving large enough countries to drive out the rest of the world from the import market, with the help of the smugglers. Otherwise, the welfare effect would be negative.

However, the creation of an FTA is not the only relevant type of regional integration in Africa. Foroutan (1993) has even shown that this has not been a very successful endeavor in Africa. On the contrary, monetary integration has been more successful, with the experience of the CFA Franc Zone and of the Rand Zone. Let us now analyze how smuggling bears on the desirability of monetary integration.

2.7 Smuggling and the case for monetary integration

Monetary integration is generally understood as the fixing of the exchange rate among a group of countries, or the adoption of a common currency (de Grauwe, 1992). The issue of the optimum currency area (OCA) is an active research topic which lies to a large extent outside the scope of this chapter. Nevertheless, some aspects can be discussed in the context of cross-border trading.

The classic discussion of the OCA is based on the factors that reduce the effectiveness of the exchange rate as a tool for affecting relative prices between two countries. The exchange rate plays two different roles in any economy, which Corden (1993) has labeled the "nominal anchor approach" or the "real target approach." This refers, respectively, to the possibility of stabilizing the price level by fixing the exchange rate, and to the possibility of affecting the real exchange rate by changing the nominal exchange rate. There is usually a trade-off between these two functions of the nominal exchange rate, as shown notably by Devarajan and Rodrik (1992) in the case of the African CFA Zone member countries. Fixing the exchange rate provides credibility to the government for fighting inflation, but does not allow for accommodating external shocks, while the possibility of devaluing in response to an external negative shock creates a credibility problem, with an inflationary impact. The more effective the nominal exchange rate is for affecting the real exchange rate, the more costly it thus is to fix it as a means for controlling the price level. On the contrary, if the nominal exchange rate is not a very powerful tool for affecting the real exchange rate, then the opportunity cost of using it as a nominal anchor is reduced.

I can now show that the existence of smuggling flows, by increasing the tradability of some goods, makes the real exchange rate less sensitive to the nominal exchange rate. In order to do that I use again the first model analyzed above, where there is no "cover" effect, with simple changes made in order to make explicit the role of the exchange rate. Let us first assume that the world price of all goods is fixed and equal to 1. Then, denote e the nominal exchange rate, so that $p^* = e$. Assume that there is no smuggling concerning some goods, called the tradable goods, while some other goods are not tradable at the margin, because of QRs. Let p again denote their domestic price. Assume that smuggling concerns these imperfectly tradable goods, and thus increases their tradability at the margin. This is typical of African economies, where there are very few genuinely non-tradable goods, while many goods are subject to QRs, or other trade distortions, and are involved in cross-border trade.

Then, assuming that $c'(Q^S) = p^* \gamma(Q^S)$, the first-order condition (2.10) can be written as:

$$p = p^*(1 + \gamma(Q^S)) = e(1 + \gamma(Q^S)). \qquad (2.22)$$

Inverting (2.22) yields the following smuggling supply function:

$$Q^S = Q^S(e/p), Q^{S'} < 0. \qquad (2.23)$$

This equation simply states that a depreciation of the real exchange rate, by reducing the gap between the border price and the local price of the imperfectly tradable good, reduces the incentive to smuggle.

Define the price index as the following function, assumed to be increasing in its two arguments, differentiable, and homogeneous of degree one:

$$v = v(e, p). \qquad (2.24)$$

Then, equilibrium in the market for these imperfectly tradable goods requires:

$$D(e/p, M/v) = Q^S(e/p), \qquad (2.25)$$
$$(+) \quad (+) \qquad (-)$$

where $D(\cdot)$ is the domestic excess demand function for this good and M is the quantity of money. This equation simply states that in equilibrium smuggling puts up the excess of domestic demand for this good over the domestic supply. Differentiating (2.25), holding M constant, yields:

$$\frac{d\log p}{d\log e} = \frac{D_e - Q^{S'} - D_M v_e pM/v^2}{D_e - Q^{S'} + D_M v_p p^2 M/ev^2} < 1. \qquad (2.26)$$

The lower this elasticity, the more effective is a devaluation, i.e. the more an increase in e can affect e/p. Looking at (2.26) shows that the more active is the smuggling sector, captured here by a higher $|Q^{S'}|$, the closer to 1 this elasticity becomes. In other words, if cross-border trade is not very active, so that a change in relative prices does not trigger any strong reaction by the smugglers, then a change in the nominal exchange rate is passed on only partly to the price of imperfectly tradable goods. The devaluation is then quite effective. On the contrary, if cross-border trade is very active and responsive to relative price changes, then any change in e is to a large extent passed on to p, so that the nominal devaluation entails a weak real devaluation. In the limit, as $Q^{S'}$ becomes infinite, the degree of effectiveness falls to zero, as any change in e is entirely passed on to p.

Therefore, as smugglers increase the degree of tradability of imperfectly tradable goods, the nominal exchange rate loses its efficacy as a means to affect the real exchange rate e/p. Hence, in this case, it becomes more interesting to use the nominal exchange rate as a nominal anchor, irrespective of its impact on the real exchange rate, which is very weak. On the contrary, by reducing the scope for internal shocks to affect relative prices, the enhanced tradability of the goods brought about by smuggling increases the power of the exchange rate as a tool for controlling inflation. However, the use of the exchange rate as a nominal anchor is not an easy task, as a credibility problem can arise. Joining a monetary union is one of the best responses to the credibility constraint (de Grauwe, 1992). In other words, unrecorded cross-border trade should be taken into account in the design of a currency area.

2.8 Conclusion

This chapter has first motivated the analysis by giving descriptive information on the type of cross-border trade that is going on in West Africa, with special emphasis on the trade between Nigeria and its neighbors. The results of various surveys performed in the warehouses of the traders near the borders have been described, and actual import data compared with customs data. In some cases, the differences are striking; this strongly suggests that one should not pay too much attention to official trade statistics in this area. The descriptive sections have also shown how various policy changes have affected cross-border traders.

A very simple model of corruption at the customs was then used to discuss the true meaning of trade liberalization. This model suggests that cutting tariff rates might be ineffective unless corruption were simultaneously reduced. The subsequent sections systematically developed the welfare analysis of cross-border trade and regional integration. The analysis turns out to be extremely akin to the classical Vinerian theory of regional integration. I first showed that the welfare effect of smuggling depended on what type of distortion triggered it, and on the nature of the cost difference with official trade. If these costs are only some sort of transfers, like expected bribes or fines, then smuggling does not reduce welfare, and may well even have a positive contribution, if the trade-creation effect is positive. If there is any real resource cost involved, then the welfare effect is more uncertain. A necessary condition for a positive welfare effect when smuggling is triggered by a tariff, in the case where official trade does not provide any "cover" effect, is that official trade is driven out. But this is not a sufficient condition if the real resource cost involved offsets the benefit from trade creation. When smuggling is triggered by QRs, smuggling necessarily increases welfare. Therefore, when due account is taken of smuggling, quotas turn out to be less damaging than suggested by the usual analysis that neglects it, while tariffs are more damaging, because of the diversion of trade from the official market to the parallel market that they entail. However, this result does not hold if the resource cost difference between official and unofficial trade is negligible, as argued by Deardorff and Stolper (1990). In that case, smuggling is never harmful.

In this framework, trade liberalization never reduces welfare, and in most cases actually improves it. This is because a cut in tariff or a relaxation of a quota leads to some trade diversion from the parallel market to the official market, which should entail a lower resource cost. Similarly, partial trade liberalization, such as the creation of an FTA with some neighboring country, is most likely to have a positive welfare effect, provided that the trade-creation effect is dominant. This occurs when trade within the FTA, added to the smuggling flow, adds up to a large enough level of trade to drive out any official direct trade with the rest of the world. This is an important caveat in view of the attempt made by the member countries of WAEMU to reform their trade relations since 1997. A CET was adopted in July 1998, and steps were taken to remove tariffs on intra-WAEMU trade in January 2000. However, official trade is low inside the Zone, and the success of the reform will depend on the behavior of the parallel trade flows.

Lastly, I showed that the existence of smuggling made the case for monetary integration stronger. The reason for this finding is that lots of non-tradable goods in Africa are not intrinsically non-tradable but are made so at the margin by QRs. Insofar as smuggling increases the tradability of these goods, it makes the exchange rate less powerful as a tool for affecting the real exchange rate, and a more powerful instrument for controlling inflation. Fixing the exchange rate within a monetary union may thus be the right choice to make in small open economies where parallel markets are pervasive, as in most African countries.

3 | *Parallel trade and currency convertibility*

3.1 Introduction

Unrecorded cross-border trade is sometimes a response to a distortion affecting not the goods market but the foreign exchange market. If the parallel market for foreign currencies is illegal, then you cannot import goods legally unless you have a foreign exchange allocation from the official market. This was mentioned in chapter 2, and treated as a different form of QR bearing on trade flows. This cannot happen when the currency is convertible. On some occasions, as a transitory measure, some governments have introduced an "own-funds scheme," whereby importers have been granted an import license without having to get their foreign exchange from the official market. This is a partial sort of convertibility, analyzed by O'Connell (1992a). However, whether the currency is convertible or not creates deeper differences between two economies affected by parallel trade. The aim of this chapter is to bring out some of these, emphasizing the different responses to some standard policy tools that may result.

The countries of the CFA Zone have long benefited from their membership of this grouping in terms of long-term growth performance (Devarajan and de Melo, 1987a; Guillaumont, Guillaumont, and Plane, 1988). This did not impair their ability to adjust to some short-run shocks, at least until the terms of trade (TOT) crash in the late 1980s (Devarajan and de Melo, 1987b; Devarajan and Rodrik, 1992). This was partly due to the convertibility of their currency, which helped them to stay open even in the face of some negative external shocks. By contrast, many other African countries have responded to balance of payments problems by imposing QRs on imports and foreign exchange controls, in order to compress their imports. They thus add a monetary distortion on top of the standard

This chapter draws on Azam (1991 c), with a quite different analytical model, and Azam (2000).

trade distortions; at times, cumulative shortages have resulted, leading to economic implosion. Berthélemy, Azam, and Faucher (1988) have documented this process in the case of Madagascar and Mozambique, and Mozambique is also discussed by Bevan, Collier, and Gunning (1990). Under these circumstances, parallel markets often develop, and help to improve supplies to consumers. However, this type of macroeconomic shock is not the only reason for interfering with external trade, and thus triggering the development of parallel markets. In the CFA Zone, it is mainly trade distortions that trigger this type of response. To be relevant, the impact of convertibility must thus be analyzed in a second-best world where trade distortions are already in force. This is done below, using a very simple extension of the general equilibrium model presented in Azam and Besley (1989a) and Azam (1991c). Its comparative statics allows us to simulate the effects of various policy measures commonly implemented as part of SAPs.

The internal aspect of convertibility can be distinguished from its external aspect, and is the focus of the present analysis. It refers to the fact that any agent from an economy having a convertible currency can freely purchase or sell foreign currencies in the official market; external convertibility exists when this currency is widely accepted by foreign partners. In Africa, it seems that the backing of a foreign power is required to ensure such acceptance, as in the heyday of the CFA Zone, while there are many instances of internal convertibility.

From a macroeconomic point of view, the main difference between the convertible or inconvertible currency concerns the way in which the parallel foreign exchange market clears. When the currency is inconvertible, the flexible adjustment of the exchange rate on the parallel market ensures that the country's balance of payments in the parallel market is in equilibrium at each point in time. No central bank intervenes to support a preferred exchange rate. The econometric analysis of the determinants of the parallel market exchange rate has been done within this framework by Azam and Besley (1989a), for Ghana, and Azam and Daubrée (1991), for the cases of Nigeria, Zaire, and Ghana. By contrast, the parallel balance of payments does not need to be zero when the currency is convertible, irrespective of whether the exchange rate is fixed or flexible. Even when the official rate is flexible, the parallel balance of payments may not be zero, provided that the official rate has the same absolute value, with the opposite sign.

Section 3.2 shows that this property of a convertible currency holds even if the parallel trade is with a country whose currency is inconvertible. In other words, it shows that you can earn convertible currencies by trading with a country whose currency is itself inconvertible. What is required is that the arbitrage operations of the exchange brokers create a link between the different convertible-currency countries involved in the market. The surplus obtained by one convertible-currency country in its trade with an inconvertible-currency country is then balanced by a deficit with at least another convertible-currency country involved in the same market. It implies a flow of convertible currency from the deficit to the surplus country. This is quite difficult to observe, but a feel for it can be obtained by looking at flows of bank notes. This is done below by looking at the flow of BEAC bank notes, issued in the Central African Monetary Union (CAMU), into Niger, which belongs to the West African Monetary Union (WAMU).

3.2 The naira market as a link between the two CFA monetary unions

The efficiency of African traders and their ability to overcome the problems raised either by a hostile natural environment or by government intervention is strikingly illustrated by the functioning of the parallel market for foreign exchange. I have some data for the case of the Nigerian currency in the 1980s, which I now discuss. However, the relevance of parallel markets for foreign exchange is far from being restricted to this country over that period. Since the decision was taken in August 1993 to suspend the external convertibility of their bank notes, under the influence of the French treasury, such markets now affect even the CFA Zone member countries. The predictable speculative attack that this decision triggered, which is discussed at length in chapters 5 and 6, inflicted two huge costs. The first is the loss of reserves, estimated at US$ 610 million during the second half of 1993, for the CFA Zone as a whole. This is a huge amount of foreign exchange, equivalent to more than three years' US aid for the whole continent of Africa. The second is the emergence of a parallel market for foreign exchange in the CEMAC region, with all the ensuing costs related to rent- seeking. The parallel market differential between the two CFA Francs is now estimated to be 10%, after having occasionally reached 30%, allowing for a lot of arbitrage profit, as financial

transactions are allowed at par. Zimbabwe is also a striking example of
a country where the parallel market is currently thriving. In fact, since
2000, most goods have two prices, one in US dollars and one in
Zimbabwean dollars, which do not look comparable at the official
exchange rate. In fact, the official rate in late November 2002 was 55
Zim dollars to the US$, while the parallel one was 1,800 Zim dollars to
the US dollar. I have never personally witnessed such a large premium
elsewhere. This refers only to the buying price, while the threats
expressed by the government against parallel changers seem to entail a
sizable spread. Additional threats conveyed by newspapers reduced the
buying price to 1,000, and then 1,400, in early December. In mid-
October 2005, the official rate was 26,000 Zim dollars to the US dollar,
and the parallel rate was about 100,000 Zim dollars to the US dollar. The
depreciation of the Zimbabwean dollar between these two dates was
incredibly fast but, in percentage terms, the parallel market premium is
much smaller at the latter date. The most impressive fact is the pile of
bank notes that you need to carry when you go to the restaurant ...

The integration of the naira market

Figure 3.1 illustrates the impressive arbitrage performance of the naira
market between Lomé (Togo) and Zinder (Niger) over the period
1980:08–1989:02. These two cities are more than 1000 km apart, as
Lomé is on the coast while Zinder is on the northern border of Nigeria,
quite far east on the road to Lake Chad. The two series are mostly very
close to each other; the only period where a significant deviation can be
observed is 1984:04–1984:09, when the Nigerian army was attempting a crackdown on smuggling in the north of the country.

  The very good spatial arbitrage taking place on this parallel market
is demonstrated clearly in (3.1). It regresses the percentage deviation
of the Zinder parallel market naira exchange rate from that in Lomé
on a constant and a dummy variable for the military intervention
along the northern border:

$$DEV = 0.006 + 0.37ARMY,$$
$$(2.11) \quad (7.13) \tag{3.1}$$

$$N = 103, \quad R^2 = 0.82, \quad DW = 1.89, \quad F(2, 101) = 457.14,$$
$$\text{White-}F(2, 101) = 45.23.$$

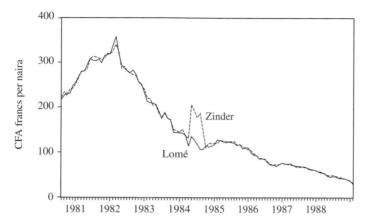

Figure 3.1. Arbitrage on the parallel market for the naira between Lomé (Togo) and Zinder (Niger), 1980–1989
Source: Computed from confidential BCEAO data.

The variable *ARMY* is a dummy variable that takes the value 1 during the military intervention along the northern border, from 1984:04 to 1984:09, and zero otherwise. The number of observations is N, and the first three statistics presented are self-explanatory. The fourth is White's heteroskedasticity test, which shows that the variance of the deviation has also been affected by the army intervention. The auxiliary equation on which this test is based is:

$$r^2 = 0.001 + 0.015 \ ARMY,$$
$$(1.46) \quad (6.73)$$

(3.2)

$$N = 103, \quad R^2 = 0.31, \quad DW = 2.46, \quad F(2, 101) = 45.24$$

where r^2 is the squared residuals from (3.1).

The t-statistics in parentheses below the coefficients are White's heteroskedasticity consistent ones. Equation (3.1) clearly shows that, apart from the temporary shortage of nairas in the north due to the army's intervention, the market is strikingly well integrated, with an average discrepancy below 1%, despite the natural and social obstacles met by the traders on the ground.

The foregoing exercise thus illustrates how government intervention, here with the army, is the main cause of occasional malfunctioning of markets in Africa. African traders can handle even relatively mild interventions such as the loosely enforced ban on private dealings in foreign currencies. The parallel market for the naira emerged because of the predatory behavior of the Nigerian government on the official foreign exchange market. It was thus an illegal market, at least during several periods, which nevertheless displays one of the crucial marks of efficient functioning, namely spatial arbitrage. It is only when the army intervenes massively that the inefficiency is restored, enabling officials to pocket additional arbitrage profit. Otherwise, the only arbitrage failure is due to the restricted access to the official market, which played a crucial part in the Nigerian clientelist political system, before February 1995, when a significant reform occurred.

Figure 3.2 shows the premium driving a wedge between the parallel market price of the US dollar and the official one. Comparing figure 3.1 and 3.2 should convince the reader that the second one does not depict a true market phenomenon. Azam (1999a, and chapter 4 in this volume) shows how this foreign exchange market was used by the government for more than a decade to divert large sums of money from government revenues in a covert way, as these sums were diverted before being registered in the government budget. The simple trick is to record the official inflow of foreign currency, originating mainly in the royalties of the oil exports and occasionally in aid inflow, at the official exchange rate. It is then distributed through a fake auction to selected people who can then dump it on the parallel market, and pocket the premium. Odubogun (Garba since her

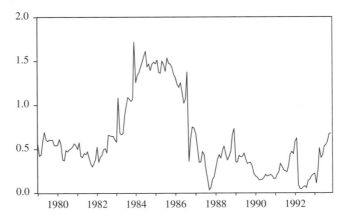

Figure 3.2. Parallel market premium: Nigeria, 1987–1993
Note: 1.0 = 100%.
Source: Azam (1999a).

marriage) has provided a very useful institutional analysis of this mechanism (Odubogun, 1995; Garba, 1997). The irony is that international agencies, including the World Bank and the IMF, were insisting that their agents sold their US dollars on the official market, thus inadvertently fueling the diversion process. Moreover, the official market discount entails a loss on the taxes bearing on foreign trade. Official imports, for example, are registered at the official exchange rate, up to some fraud, and are thus under-taxed relative to their true market value. This is a "shadow transfer" to official importers, which was probably unintended by the government.

The parallel market premium has at times been enormous, well above 100% in the first half of the 1980s, for example, as can be seen from figure 3.2. The sums diverted via the official market, including a sizable share of oil revenues, can be estimated to have occasionally reached some 4% or 5% of GDP. Azam (1999a, and chapter 4 in this volume) shows how this process can fuel large inflationary pressures because of the missing revenues. The system was, however, significantly improved by various reforms between February 1995 and 1997, described by Komolafe (1998).

Beside the budgetary and inflationary costs of this diversion of (potential) public revenues, the main social cost is probably that it involved some of the most talented members of the Nigerian elite in a very profitable rent-seeking activity: they would be employed in a socially more profitable way had they invested their talents in entrepreneurship (Shleifer and Vishny, 1998).

The balance of cross-border trade in Niger

This good spatial integration of the naira market has some interesting implications for the quantitative analysis of hidden trade and capital flows, some of which have been exploited in Azam (1991a, 1991b). One can think of the naira market as being a regional market, where all the neighboring countries are active. As the naira is inconvertible, its parallel market has to clear by price adjustment; no central bank intervenes to peg the exchange rate. Hence, from Nigeria's viewpoint, this market clears. However, all the other countries participating in the naira market can run a surplus or a deficit, provided that the rest of the market participants have a net balance of the same magnitude with the opposite sign.

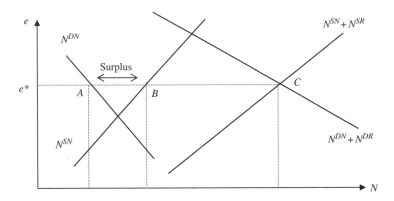

Figure 3.3. The clearing of the naira market

Figure 3.3 illustrates this reasoning, describing the flows of demand and supplies of naira over a given period of time – say, a "Hicksian week." These are not stock demands and supplies, representing an existing quantity of nairas and the demand for them at a point in time, as would be the case, for example, in portfolio analysis. The flow demand and supply curves reflect the transactions technology, which requires, for example, that imports from Nigeria must be paid in naira, while exports to Nigeria must be paid in CFA Francs or any other convertible currency. These curves thus represent quantities of nairas that are changing hands. The exchange rate – say, the CFA Franc price of the naira – is measured on the vertical axis, while the flows of naira are measured on the horizontal axis. The downward-sloping curves represent the demands by residents from Niger (N^{DN}) and the sum of the latter and the demand for naira by the rest of the world ($N^{DN} + N^{DR}$). In Niger, for example, the demand for naira is the sum of imports from Nigeria, investment in Nigeria by residents from Niger, and increases in naira balances held by the latter. The same interpretation holds for the rest of the world. The negative slope reflects the fact that an increase in the price of the naira reduces the competitiveness of Nigerian products and, for given expectations, reduces the expected capital gains on assets denominated in naira. The upward-sloping curves N^{SN} and $N^{SN} + N^{SR}$ are the supply curves of naira, being the sum of exports to Nigeria, foreign investment by Nigerians in Niger or other neighboring countries, and reduction in naira balances held. The positive slope reflects the increased profitability of exports into Nigeria, and the reduced attractiveness of naira-denominated assets.

Because of the good arbitrage performance illustrated in figure 3.1, the market is unified at the regional level. The equilibrium exchange rate e^* is found where total demand equals total supply, at point C. In the case presented at figure 3.3, this market equilibrium involves an excess of supply from Niger, measured at point B, over demand by Niger, measured at point A. Niger thus runs a surplus in its operations with Nigeria in this case. Notice that this equilibrium also implies that the rest of the world runs a deficit in its operations with Nigeria. Its supply of naira, measured by BC, is smaller than its demand, measured by AC. This deficit is the mirror image of Niger's surplus. If arbitrage did not function properly, then the price of the naira would be lower in Niger, and higher in the rest of the market. When there is no impediment to competition among exchange brokers, the price difference so created would trigger some profitable arbitrage operations. The brokers would transfer the unwanted naira from the border markets of Niger to the other places where there is a positive excess demand. If transaction costs are low enough, and if competition reduces the brokers' profits to a minimum, then the same price approximately rules everywhere in this market. We have seen above that this is the case in the naira market, with impressive arbitrage between Lomé and Zinder. The flow of naira from the surplus country to the deficit ones necessarily entails a flow of convertible currencies in the opposite direction. This is what the brokers use for buying the naira where they are cheap or for selling them where they are dearer, to get the hard currency.

The foregoing description of the arbitrage operations going on in the naira market is a simple application of a standard reasoning of elementary microeconomics. However, it yields an interesting prediction, namely that a CFA Zone country running a surplus in its cross-border operations with Nigeria should witness an inflow of convertible currencies. This is a difficult phenomenon to observe accurately. I have, however, been able to generate some imperfect observations of this flow, using the inflow of bank notes issued in the BEAC Zone (Cameroon, Chad, etc.) into Niger during the 1980s. In those days, the BEAC CFA Franc used to exchange one-for-one with the BCEAO CFA Franc. However, the former were not legal tender in the shops of the then WAMU (now WAEMU, West African Economic and Monetary Union). Hence, traders who had acquired BEAC bank notes from their cross-border operations would bring them to a bank in order to exchange them for BCEAO bank notes. This latter transaction would be recorded, and would enter the calculation of the official balance of payments of the country. This was before the suspension of the external convertibility of these bank notes that took place in August 1993, which is discussed at length in chapter 5. I had the privilege to obtain this series for the 1980s in Niger, despite the traditional secrecy of the central banks.

The theoretical discussion above suggests that a country such as Niger should have an inflow of convertible currency whenever it runs a surplus on its parallel balance of payments with Nigeria. However, it is difficult to measure the inflow of foreign currencies into Niger; there always exist some gross inflows of various currencies, while the prediction is about the net inflow. On the other hand, there are only a small number of significant actors in the naira market: Benin, Cameroon, Chad, and Niger. One might thus expect that most currencies involved in such flows would be bank notes from these countries. Of course, some more sophisticated payment means are sometimes involved, such as checks on some banks in Cotonou or Yaoundé, but this should not greatly concern Niger, which is much poorer. Cameroon and Chad belong to the BEAC Union, while Benin and Niger belong to the BCEAO. Only the bank notes from the BEAC will end up in the banks, while the others are legal tender in Niger. An interesting working hypothesis is thus that Niger should witness an increased inflow of BEAC bank notes whenever its parallel balance of payments increases.

Figure 3.4 shows the series of bank notes from the BEAC side purchased by the central bank in Niger, mainly in the branches of Maradi and Zinder, over the 1980s, expressed in logarithms. It also shows the tracking of this series that is achieved by the fitted value from the very simple regression equation (3.3). The latter regresses the log of the inflow of BEAC bank notes on the fiscal deficit expressed as a percentage of GDP. In view of the very small number of observations (10), there is no point in trying to estimate a richer equation. Nevertheless, it is very clear that the adjustment program which started in 1983, involving a significant cut in the fiscal deficit from 11.3% to 8.7% of gross domestic product (GDP), had a sizable impact on the inflow of BEAC bank notes. A better fit can be obtained by using an autoregressive-distributed-lag specification, as described in Banerjee *et al.* (1993). However, the small number of observations

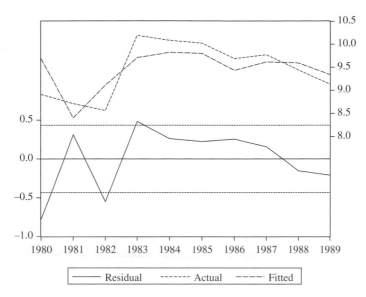

Figure 3.4. Tracking the inflow of BEAC notes into Niger using (3.3)

makes the latter unconvincing.

$$\log BEACnotes = 11.7 - 0.23 \; Deficit/GDP$$
$$(15.17) \, (2.97)$$

(3.3)

$$N = 10, \quad R^2 = 0.52, \quad DW = 2.09, \quad F = 8.80 \; (p = 0.018).$$

Equation (3.3) suggests that Niger was able to earn convertible currencies in its parallel trade with Nigeria thanks to the arbitrage operations of the exchange brokers in this market. The SAP adopted in 1983 most probably resulted in an increase in Niger's surplus in its cross-border trade with Nigeria.

This descriptive analysis brings out some striking stylized facts, which need to be taken on board in a model aiming at identifying the specific difference that currency convertibility makes in a parallel market economy. The crucial factor is probably that the balance of payments on the parallel market does not need to be zero all the time in an economy with a convertible currency. By contrast, when the currency is inconvertible, the price level and the exchange rate are jointly determined simultaneously to clear the goods market and the market for the local currency. This entails some differences in the comparative statics predictions of the model, which are derived below.

3.3 The model

Paradoxically, a money-less model is enough to make this point. By "money-less" economy, I mean here what used to be called an "inside-money" economy (Patinkin, 1965). The stock of government money is zero, but private agents do issue money, whose aggregate stock is also zero: the claims of some private agents are the liabilities of others. In this setting, agents who sell goods earn tokens which entitle them to buy goods during the same period. These tokens are convertible if you can, for example, sell goods on the parallel market, and then spend your tokens on the official market. Otherwise, they are inconvertible.

There are three representative agents in this model: households produce some export crops and consume imported goods; smuggling firms import and export goods by parallel channels; the government taxes official transactions, fixes the official exchange rate, and imposes QRs upon imports, in the last case discussed below.

The smuggling firm

The smuggling firm imports a quantity of the consumption good c^S, which it buys on the foreign market at a price in foreign currency normalized to 1, and it sells it at the local price p. It also exports a quantity of the export crop x^S, which it buys locally at the price q, for selling it abroad at the foreign price q^*. All the foreign exchange used in these transactions is acquired or surrendered on the parallel currency market, at the exchange rate e, if the local currency is not convertible. Otherwise, the foreign exchange market is unified, by definition. The official exchange rate, which determines the price of the imported goods in the absence of a quota on the official market, is E. The smuggling activity has a real resource cost in this model, captured by a labor requirement function, as in Daubrée (1995). The quantity of labor required for trading c^S and x^S by the parallel channels is:

$$\ell^S = z(x^S, c^S) \tag{3.4}$$

where $z(.)$ is strictly increasing and convex.

The nominal profits of the smuggling firm are thus equal to:

$$R = \max\left((eq^* - q)x^S + (p - e)c^S - wz(x^S, c^S)\right). \tag{3.5}$$

Denoting partial derivatives by a subscript, the first-order conditions for this problem are:

$$eq^* = q + wz_x(x^S, c^S),$$ (3.6)

and:

$$p = e + wz_c(x^S, c^S).$$ (3.7)

The selling price must thus cover the buying price plus the smuggling cost. We met similar conditions in chapter 2. From (3.6) and (3.7), by taking the total differentials and rearranging the terms, one can derive the following functions governing the trade flows by parallel channels. Because the function z (.) is strictly increasing and convex, these two functions are increasing in their two arguments, assuming that there are positive economies of scope in smuggling ($z_{xc} \leq 0$):

$$x^S = x^S \left(\underset{(+)}{\frac{eq^* - q}{w}}, \underset{(+)}{\frac{p - e}{w}} \right),$$ (3.8)

and:

$$c^S = c^S \left(\underset{(+)}{\frac{eq^* - q}{w}}, \underset{(+)}{\frac{p - e}{w}} \right).$$ (3.9)

The representative household allocates its labor time, normalized to 1, between producing the export crop and working for the smuggling firm. In the former occupation, returns to scale are constant, and units are chosen so that labor productivity is also equal to 1. The crop is sold at price q, if at least a part of it is sold in the official market. Figure 2.6 in chapter 2 illustrates a similar case. It is clear that the two types of occupation must be paid at the same price, in an interior equilibrium. Then we have $w = q$. Figure 3.5 shows how the markets for labor and for the export crop clear simultaneously in this case. It is similar to figure 2.6, with slight differences of interpretation. The quantity exported by official channels is determined residually, and is denoted x^F. This equilibrium means that the total labor income of the household may be written as:

$$w\ell^S + q(1 - \ell^S) = q.$$ (3.10)

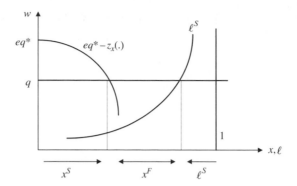

Figure 3.5. The simultaneous clearing of the labor and the export crop markets

One can easily derive from the above that the official sales of the export crop are governed by the following function:

$$x^F = x^F \left(\frac{eq^* - q}{q}, \frac{p - e}{q} \right)$$
$$(-) \qquad (-)$$

$$= 1 - z\left(\frac{eq^* - q}{q}, \frac{p - e}{q} \right) - x^S\left(\frac{eq^* - q}{q}, \frac{p - e}{q} \right). \tag{3.11}$$

As mentioned in chapter 2, Azam and Besley (1989b) have estimated an econometric equation to explain the official exports by the Ghanaian Cocoa Marketing Board from the 1960s to the 1980s; they find a significant negative impact of the price difference for cocoa in Côte d'Ivoire and Ghana, compared using the parallel market exchange rate. Equation (3.11) provides a neat explanation for such a result.

Using Hotelling's Lemma for signing the partial derivatives, now define the real profit function of the representative smuggling firm as:

$$\psi\left(\frac{eq^*}{p}, \frac{p - e}{p}, \frac{q}{p} \right) = \frac{R}{p}.$$
$$(+) \quad (+) \ (-) \tag{3.12}$$

This way of writing the arguments of this profit function allows us to find unambiguously the signs reported in parentheses below the arguments. Denoting the partial derivatives by a numerical subscript, and using again Hotelling's Lemma, it is easily checked that they are: $\psi_1 = x^S$, $\psi_2 = c^S$, and $\psi_3 = -x^F$. However, this clearly leaves some ambiguity for some individual effects. It is of some interest to check the following partial derivatives:

$$\frac{\partial \psi}{\partial e} = \frac{q^* x^S - c^S}{p}, \tag{3.13}$$

and:

$$\frac{\partial \psi}{\partial p} = \frac{qz}{p^2} - \frac{e}{p^2} \frac{\partial \psi}{\partial e}. \tag{3.14}$$

They both depend on the balance of cross-border trade. If the representative smuggling firm exports more than it imports then the depreciation of its national currency increases its profits. The opposite sign is found when the balance of cross-border trade is in deficit. A similar ambiguity affects the impact of increases in the price of the imported consumer goods. There is a positive effect, as the goods are sold at a better price, given the other prices, but this impact is undermined by another effect, which depends on the trade balance. Only when the latter is in deficit or in equilibrium do we get an unambiguous positive impact.

The representative household

Assume that the representative household is infinitely lived, or else is a dynastic family whose successive generations are linked by some altruism. Denoting c its consumption at date t, $u(c)$ the instantaneous utility derived from it, where $u(.)$ is strictly increasing and concave, and k its capital stock, this household seeks to maximize:

$$\max \int_0^\infty u(c) e^{-rt} dt, \tag{3.15}$$

subject to:

$$dk/dt = rk + q/p + \psi(.) - c. \tag{3.16}$$

In these two equations, r represents both the real rate of interest and the rate of time preference, assumed equal to ensure existence of an optimum steady state. Moreover, I normalize the initial value of the capital stock to zero: $k(0) = 0$.

Applying Pontryagin's Maximum Principle, one can easily derive the following optimality conditions:

$$u'(c) = \lambda, \tag{3.17}$$

$$d\lambda/dt = 0, \tag{3.18}$$

and

$$\lim_{t \to \infty} \lambda k e^{-rt} = 0, \tag{3.19}$$

where λ is the Lagrange multiplier attached to constraint (3.16).

From (3.17) and (3.18), it follows that c is constant at all future dates, and can thus be treated parametrically in the dynamic analysis. As q/p and $\psi(.)$ are also constant, it follows that the dynamics generated by (3.16) is explosive, as the change in k is an increasing function of k. All the divergent trajectories fail to fulfill the transversality condition (3.19), and the only acceptable trajectory has:

$$k = 0, \forall t. \tag{3.20}$$

It follows that consumption is equal to:

$$c = q/p + \psi(.). \tag{3.21}$$

The aim of this exercise is to bring out the fact that the comparative statics predictions are affected by the institutional framework – more precisely by whether the currency is convertible or not.

The case of tariff-driven smuggling

Contrary to Azam and Besley (1989a), Azam (1991c), and Daubrée (1995), I assume here that the parallel trading activity on the consumption goods market is triggered by a tariff, at an *ad valorem* rate τ, rather than by a quota. This is probably a more appropriate assumption for many African countries, after two decades of SAPs. Assuming that official trade is positive, the price of the imported good on the local market is:

$$p = (1 + \tau)E. \tag{3.22}$$

In the convertible case, e and p are both determined by E, with $e = E$ and $p = (1 + \tau)E$. Then the smuggling profit function may be written as:

$$\psi\left(\frac{q^*}{1+\tau}, \frac{\tau}{1+\tau}, \frac{q}{(1+\tau)E}\right). \tag{3.23}$$

It is then easy to derive the following two comparative statics results, holding q and q^* constant:

$$\frac{\partial c}{\partial E} = \frac{-qx^F}{(1+\tau)E^2}, \tag{3.24}$$

and

$$\frac{\partial c}{\partial \tau} = \frac{-qx^F - E(q^*x^S - c^S)]}{(1+\tau)^2 E}. \tag{3.25}$$

Hence, while devaluation has an unambiguous negative impact on consumption, as it reduces labor income, the impact of the change in the tariff rate is ambiguous. It is negative if the cross-border trade balance is in surplus or in equilibrium, but may become positive when there is a large deficit. The increase in the tariff makes smuggling more profitable, with a positive income effect on consumption. In a country such as Niger over the period discussed above, partial trade liberalization, involving a cut in the tariff rate, would thus have a positive effect on consumption, as its cross-border trade balance is in surplus. The loss in the rent on the imported consumption good is more than offset by the increased purchasing power of labor incomes. However, the countries in deficit, belonging most probably to the BEAC side, where the observed inflow of bank notes was coming from, might have suffered from such a policy reform at that time.

When the currency is inconvertible, a new constraint must be taken into account in the comparative statics analysis – namely, that the balance of cross-border trade is kept in equilibrium at each point in time by the adjustment of e, in this money-less economy without capital flows. The following equation must thus hold:

$$q^*x^S = c^S. \tag{3.26}$$

It follows that the impact of the devaluation, given by (3.24), is unchanged while the impact of a change in the tariff rate is now:

$$\frac{dc}{d\tau} = \frac{-qx^F}{(1+\tau)^2 E}. \tag{3.27}$$

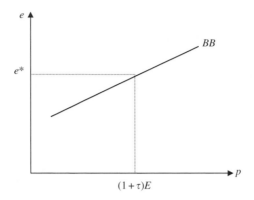

Figure 3.6. Parallel exchange rate determination

It is thus unambiguously negative. In other words, from the point of view of the household's welfare, a partial trade liberalization is unambiguously beneficial when the currency is inconvertible, while it might be detrimental when the currency is convertible.

Moreover, (3.26) implies that the price level and the parallel market exchange rate are jointly determined for maintaining cross-border trade balance equilibrium. This determines the BB locus in figure 3.6. Differentiating (3.26), using (3.8) and (3.9), and the fact that $w = q$ in equilibrium, yields:

$$\frac{\partial e}{\partial p} = \frac{c_2^S - q^* x_2^S}{c_2^S - q^* x_2^S + q^* (q^* x_1^S - c_1^S)}. \tag{3.28}$$

This derivative is positive provided that the economies of scope are not too strong. In this case, x_2^S and c_1^S are small enough. It may also be either larger or smaller than 1, but is likely to be less than 1 unless economies of scope are quite strong. Equation (3.28) gives the slope of the balance of cross-border trade equilibrium locus. The $\{e, p\}$ pairs located above it correspond to a surplus, assuming again that the economies of scope are not too strong. Azam and Besley (1989a) and Azam (1991c) generalize this analysis to the case of a truly monetary economy with capital flows, where a similar relationship also holds. It does not tell us anything about the direction of causality. If smuggling is triggered by a tariff, as assumed here, with (3.22) holding, then E is the driving force, which determines p, and then e via (3.26). Otherwise, if the case of figure 2.4 from chapter 2 holds, with a tariff high enough to drive official trade out, or the case of figure 2.5, where a quota is in force, then e and p are jointly determined, as in Azam and Besley (1989a) and Azam (1991c). Let us now focus on the case of QRs on official imports.

The case of a quota

Throughout the 1970s, and up to the mid- or the late 1980s, many African governments imposed substantial QRs on imports, either with a view to respond to recurrent balance of payments deficits, or to create scarcity rents allocated to politically sensitive people. Only a small number of countries, mainly in central and southern Africa, are still affected by this type of policy. Nevertheless, the temptation to impose such a trade regime is always present, despite its harmful effects. Zimbabwe is one recent example, being affected by significant shortages in 2002, and again in 2005.

Denote c^R the quota imposed by the government on official imports. Then, the goods market must clear by price adjustment:

$$c = c^R + c^S. \tag{3.29}$$

Assume that the quota rent $(p - E)c^R$ is handed over to the representative household. In the real world, such an allocation is motivated by distributional issues, which can be neglected in a macroeconomic framework. Then, using (3.21), and substituting for $\psi(.)$, yields:

$$\frac{q}{p} + \frac{eq^* - q}{p} x^S + \frac{p - e}{p} c^S - \frac{q}{p} \ell^S + \frac{p - e}{p} c^R = c^R + c^S. \tag{3.30}$$

Taking the labor-cum-export crop market equilibrium condition into account, this expression simplifies to:

$$\frac{qx^F - Ec^R}{p} + \frac{e(q^* x^S - c^S)}{p} = 0. \tag{3.31}$$

The first term on the left-hand side is the difference between the official sales of the export crop by the household and the cost of buying the consumption good on the official market, net of the redistributed quota rent. This is the balance of official dealings by the household. Equation (3.31) says that the sum of the balance of official dealings and that of cross-border trade must be zero. In this money-less economy, this is just a reflection of Walras' Law. Therefore, if the local currency is inconvertible, so that (3.26) holds, the imported

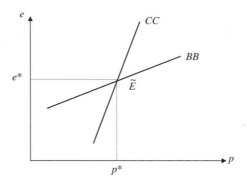

Figure 3.7. Joint determination of e and p

good market equilibrium condition (3.31) is achieved by simultaneous adjustment of e and p, ensuring:

$$qx^F\left(\frac{eq^* - q}{q}, \frac{p - e}{q}\right) = Ec^R. \tag{3.32}$$

Define the CC locus by the set of $\{e, p\}$ pairs such that (3.31) holds. This is the goods market equilibrium locus. A simple geometric argument shows that it has probably a positive slope, which is steeper than that of BB, or may be a negative slope. Start at point $\tilde{E}$ in figure 3.7, assumed to be the general equilibrium point, and move along the BB locus to the right. Then, as p and e are increasing simultaneously, providing incentives to smuggle more, official sales go down. This assumes again that economies of scope are not too strong. Thus, consumption demand goes down, and p must decrease to restore goods market equilibrium. Now, fix p and move upwards from $\tilde{E}$. We know that the cross-border trade balance is in surplus above BB, so that the increase in e has a positive income effect on consumption demand. This is partly offset by the negative impact on official sales of the export crop, itself mitigated by the effect of economies of scope. The net impact is thus plausibly positive on consumption demand, leading to excess demand. The slope of CC is then positive, and steeper than that of BB. If the negative impact on official sales was dominant, its slope would be negative, without changing the comparative statics predictions derived below. Azam and Besley (1989a) derive a similar diagram.

Now, the general equilibrium of the model is a pair $\{e^*, p^*\}$ belonging to both BB and CC, i.e. in point $\tilde{E}$. Its location in this space depends on two policy instruments, namely E and c^R. A devaluation of the official exchange rate – i.e. a rise in E – or a partial liberalization – i.e. a rise in c^R – both shift the CC locus leftwards, without affecting the BB locus. In both cases, the driving effect is the fall in the quota rent, brought about by the increase in the official price of the good (in the former case), or by the fall in its selling price (in the latter one). This is deflationary, and entails an appreciation of the local currency in the parallel market. Smuggling activity is reduced, while official crop sales go up. The total impact on private consumption is positive, as the loss on the quota rent is more than offset by the increase in real labor incomes.

The comparative statics predictions are quite different if the local currency is convertible. Then, the BB locus can be forgotten, as convertibility makes a non-zero balance of cross-border trade possible. Moreover, the exchange rate is now unified, with $e = E$. The CC locus is now slightly different, as its equation is:

$$qx^F - Ec^R + E(q^*x^S - c^S) = 0. \tag{3.33}$$

The impact of a partial trade liberalization, with fixed E, is not drastically different: the CC locus shifts to the left, but the deflationary impact is not amplified by a fall in e, as in the previous case. However, it is the impact of the devaluation that makes a difference. The equilibrium moves upwards along an unchanged CC. If it still has a positive slope, then the devaluation has a positive impact on the price of goods, contrary to the case of the inconvertible-currency economy. However, CC might now be downward-sloping, in which case the difference is less striking.

3.4 Conclusion

This chapter has shown that it makes a difference when an economy with a thriving parallel market has a convertible currency or not. Particular attention has been devoted to the description of the working of the naira market in West Africa. The data presented allow us to show that this market is well integrated, thanks to the arbitrage operations of the exchange brokers. It has also been shown that this integration allows convertible-currency countries, such as the CFA Zone members, to run a surplus or a deficit in their balance of cross-border trade with an inconvertible-currency country, such as Nigeria.

They might thus earn some hard currency via their cross-border trade with an inconvertible-currency country. However, what is earned by one country in such a way is necessarily lost by another, as the market for the inconvertible currency as a whole must clear.

I have discussed a very simple model, of a money-less economy, which takes these stylized facts on board. Even this stripped-down model shows that whether the currency is convertible or not does affect the comparative statics results. In particular, the model shows that while a partial trade liberalization is beneficial for the representative household in this economy when the currency is inconvertible, it may have a detrimental effect when the currency is convertible, and the balance of cross-border trade has a large enough deficit. This effect is channeled by the fact that trade liberalization reduces the rent earned by the smugglers on the imported consumption good, while the fall in their price increases the purchasing power of labor incomes. When the balance of cross-border trade is in equilibrium, the latter effect is dominant, as the loss of rent on imports is precisely offset by the gains on cross-border exports, thanks to the equilibrating adjustment of the parallel exchange rate. However, when imports are much larger than exports, as can happen with a convertible currency, the lost rent may become the dominant effect.

This model has also been discussed for the case where the parallel market activity is triggered by QRs on imports, rather than by a tariff. The parallel market exchange rate and the price level are thus jointly determined if the currency is inconvertible. In the resulting general equilibrium, devaluation has a deflationary effect, because of the reduced quota rent distributed to the households, and the currency appreciates on the parallel market. If the currency is convertible, then the opposite effect on the price level is possible.

Of course, this model is too simple to be applied imediately to the real world, but it is a good basis for building up one's intuition about these parallel market economies. Chapter 4 goes deeper into the analysis, by bringing money explicitly into the model.

PART II

Foreign exchange constraints

4 | *Dollars for sale: inflation and the black market premium*

4.1 Introduction

The government of Nigeria used to sell its dollars in the official market at a sizable discount, compared to the parallel market exchange rate, to a small number of selected intermediaries (Odubogun, 1995, Garba, 1997). For example, in 1988, US\$ 2,910 million were sold by the central bank, out of a total of US\$ 5,229.2 million of exports (including US\$ 4,924.9 of oil exports), while the parallel market premium was on average 33.7% (Odubogun, 1995). About US\$ 1 billion was thus given up that year. The share of the foreign exchange transactions taking place in this way decreased substantially after February 1995; I focus on the previous period, which provides a natural experiment for assessing the impact of a policy that is common to many African countries. The premium on foreign currencies transacted in the parallel market is often interpreted as a means for taxing private exporters, with a view to implicitly subsidizing government imports (Pinto, 1989). In the case of Nigeria, as well as in the case of many other African countries, this diagnosis needs to be revised, as the government is selling at below market price the dollars that it gets from oil exports and aid money. Aid money is currently negligible in Nigeria. Oil accounts for 98% of the export revenues of the country, and the government has retained the ownership of at least 60% of the capital of the foreign oil companies operating there. Roughly speaking, this translates into a similar share of the oil export

This chapter draws heavily on Azam (1999a). Some of these ideas have been presented in seminars in Dakar, Nairobi, Oxford, Paris, and Toulouse. I wish to thank the participants for their comments, without implication. Special thanks are due to Patrick Asea, Oumar Diakité, Ibrahim Elbadawi, and Kassey Garba. I wish also to thank former Governor Yansané for discussing these ideas with me, as well as the AERC for financial support and for the stimulating atmosphere, with the usual disclaimer. Valuable comments by two anonymous referees are also acknowledged.

revenues. The government is thus giving up significant potential resources, often worth several percent of GDP, by selling these dollars below the market price.

In fact, the government thus reserves for its own use a discretionary budget that enables it to allocate "covert" subsidies to selected agents by controlling the use of these dollars sold by the central bank in such a way. Access to this so-called "auction" is severely controlled, and restricted to "authorized dealers" (Odubogun, 1995, Garba, 1997). Odubogun (1995) provides convincing evidence that the foreign exchange sold by the central bank is in fact rationed, suggesting that the "auction" does not clear the official market. The ruling price on this market is largely controlled by the government. Consequently, some potential revenues never appear in the government budget, and contribute to enlarging the fiscal deficit. I discuss below why the government should choose such a pricing behavior for its foreign currency revenues. As the monetary financing of the deficit is the only available solution (except very recently, when the government managed to float some bonds in the capital market) a direct link between the rate of the discount granted by the government on its sales of foreign currencies, through the central bank, and inflation results.

The case of Nigeria before 1995 just described is only an extreme example of a phenomenon that is very common in Africa. In most African countries, the government is the main provider of foreign exchange, either via aid money that often amounts on average to more than 10% of GNP, or via the export revenues from a primary sector that is largely controlled by the government through some parastatals. In Mozambique in 1993, for example, net disbursement of official development assistance amounted to 79.2% of GNP, while the corresponding figure for Tanzania was 40%, and for Guinea-Bissau 40.3% (World Bank, 1996). A large share of the mining sector, of which the government has retained ownership in most African countries, is the most common provider of foreign currency, and the government must sell a significant share to fund its domestic expenditures. I also discuss the case of Guinea, where bauxite is the dominant source of foreign currency for the government. Marketing boards and stabilization funds used to perform a similar task in countries where agricultural exports were the main source of foreign exchange (see, e.g., Ridler, 1988; Schiller, 1989), but many of these have now been dismantled. Parallel markets are less pervasive in Africa today, after the SAP phase, as many countries have liberalized their foreign exchange market and removed many trade restrictions that diverted trade flows into the parallel market. However, some important countries (Ethiopia, Nigeria, Zimbabwe) still show a significant premium. Even the CFA Franc from CEMAC now has a parallel market for its bank notes, after the suspension of their convertibility in August 1993.

Notice that it is almost axiomatic that the government will be a net supplier of foreign exchange in an economy with an active parallel market for foreign exchange: if the parallel market exchange rate is more favorable than the official exchange rate to the exporters, or the other agents that bring foreign exchange into the country, then the government must acquire its desired foreign exchange by violating the rule of voluntary trade; otherwise exporters would sell their export revenues at the higher parallel market rate. This reasoning can be easily extended to the case where there is a cost for participating in the parallel market, without basically changing the prediction. The case where the government is a net buyer of foreign exchange on the official market, while there is a positive premium to be earned in the parallel market, is thus not economically interesting.

This fact makes the analysis of foreign exchange markets in African countries quite different from the usual ones that can be applied to other continents, and gives to the official exchange rate a very clear fiscal role. In particular, it precludes the use of the analysis presented by Dornbusch *et al.* (1983), where the emergence of the parallel market is a response to capital account inconvertibility, and does not concern trade flows. Here, as explained in part I of this volume, it is the official market which is, in Dornbusch *et al.*'s own terms, "a sideshow" (Dornbusch *et al.*, 1983, p. 25), as the parallel market rate is the one which affects prices, and is thus center stage. The present chapter aims to analyze the macroeconomic consequences of this type of behavior, by showing how the premium on foreign currencies on the parallel market and the fiscal deficit combine to determine the dynamics of inflation. The analytical model used is a very simple variant of the type of model initiated by Sargent and Wallace (1973), where the interplay between the monetary financing of the fiscal deficit, the demand for money, and rational expectations determines inflation. The model is adapted, like those by Lizondo (1987), Edwards (1988), Kharas and Pinto (1989), and Pinto (1989), in order to take into account the parallel market for foreign exchange. However, unlike the latter, I explicitly model the fiscal effect of the premium. Pinto (1989) verbally emphasizes this fiscal effect, but does not really model it; moreover, he misleadingly restricts his discussion to the issue of whether or not the government is a net seller or buyer of foreign exchange. The fiscal impact of the premium, and the ensuing impact on the money supply, is in fact more complex, as what really matters is to know what fiscal revenues and expenditures are indexed on the official exchange rate or on the parallel market exchange rate, respectively (Kaufman and O'Connell, 1992). For example, customs duties are paid in domestic currency but are indexed on the official exchange rate. The government is therefore in fact granting a tax discount to importers by evaluating imports at the official exchange rate instead of the higher parallel market rate. It is thus conceivable that the government may be a net seller of foreign currencies while having a deficit on its budget that is indexed on the official rate. I show in the appendix (p. 99) that this case drastically changes the main policy conclusion. On the other hand, I simplify the model by neglecting currency substitution in private portfolios, which does not play a central part in deriving the main results. This issue is discussed by Dornbusch *et al.* (1983), Lizondo (1987), Edwards (1988), Kharas and Pinto (1989), and Pinto (1989).

This very simple model, presented in section 4.3, sheds some light on the evolution of inflation in Nigeria during the 1980–93 period. Like many other less-developed countries (LDCs), Nigeria has pursued a policy of import substitution and market distortion from its independence in 1960 until the adoption of a SAP in 1986. Many regard the latter as a relative success, mainly because positive growth has resumed (Bevan, Collier, and Gunning, 1992). Various aspects of the policies pursued before and after 1986 are discussed by Pinto (1987, 1989), Azam and Daubrée (1991), Egwaikhide *et al.* (1992), Robertson (1992), Faruqee (1994), and Odubogun (1995).

However, a neglected aspect of the change in Nigeria's macroeconomic performance is the increase in the rate of inflation and in its volatility after the adoption of the SAP; this is discussed in section 4.2. Nigeria remains a moderate-inflation country during the period under study, as defined by Dornbusch and Fischer (1993). Nonetheless, its consumer price index (CPI) increases faster after 1986, at a pace that seems to accelerate; this phenomenon is illustrated in section 4.3. The interpretation offered here blames this slippage on the change in the rule followed by the central bank for determining the official exchange rate. Before 1986, the price of the dollar at the central bank was fixed without any link to the parallel exchange rate or the price level. An impressive premium sometimes resulted from this, as shown by figure 3.2 (p. 50). After 1986, one can observe a *de facto* indexation of the official exchange rate: the government does not let the premium become too large, by adjusting the official exchange rate in response to changes in the parallel market rate. The case of Kenya is briefly presented at section 4.3, using yearly data, and shows that a similar behavior was probably adopted in 1976.

Although this move makes the government's fiscal operations more transparent, it also removes a nominal anchor from the economy (Bruno, 1991; Dornbusch and Fischer, 1993). Hence, even in a parallel market economy, the official exchange rate may play a crucial role in the determination of the price level. Of course, it is the parallel rate that directly affects the price level, as predicted by basic principles, either if there are QRs bearing on imports, or if official trade is driven out by too high a tariff (Azam and Besley, 1989a, chapters 2 and 3 in this volume). The official rate is generally infra-marginal in such an economy. Both Chhibber and Shafik (1991) and Younger (1992) confirm econometrically the weak link that exists between the official exchange rate and the price level. They use data on Ghana, over a period when exchange controls and QRs on imports were pervasive (until 1988 or 1986, respectively). These results show that a devaluation of the official exchange rate has no systematic effect, or only a very weak one, on the price level at any given time horizon. However, it is not correct to infer from this observation, as these authors do in the case of Ghana, that the official rate does not affect prices. In fact, the parallel rate is a powerful transmission mechanism between the official rate and the price level, even if it is a complex one, as shown by the model presented in section 4.4. The latter allows us to contrast the properties of the rational expectations equilibria resulting from the two opposing methods of pricing foreign currencies described above – the nominal anchor approach, on the one hand, and the backward indexation approach, on the other. It suggests that the former is definitely superior to the latter for controlling the rate of inflation. However, it raises an interesting problem of credibility, in view of the benefit that the government can reap from a surprise increase in the rate of inflation and in the parallel market premium; this issue is discussed in section 4.5.

Section 4.6 illustrates with the case of Guinea the main policy conclusion of this chapter, namely that the official exchange rate can be profitably used as a nominal anchor of a typical African economy, provided that a low rate of crawl is selected, whose management is delegated to an independent central bank with a conservative governor, *à la* Rogoff (1985).

4.2 Exchange rate policy and inflation in Nigeria, 1980–1993

Figure 4.1 shows the series of the official and the parallel exchange rates over the period 1979–93, in logarithms. Examination of these series[1] shows that the parallel market exchange rate has a more homogeneous behavior over this period than the official one. Before 1986, the latter has a very little growth relative to the parallel rate. After 1986, on the other hand, the two rates have much closer profiles. The official rate seems to follow the parallel one most of the time, although with a lag.

This is confirmed by econometric analysis, and the assumption that the growth rate of the parallel market rate does not Granger-cause the growth rate of the official rate is rejected over this sub-period, with an F-test of 3.06 (with 12 lags). The reverse hypothesis, according to which the official rate does not Granger-cause the parallel rate, is also rejected, with an F-statistic value of 2.00. On the contrary, over the preceding period, these two assumptions can be accepted, with F-tests of 0.35 and 0.56, respectively.

The following pair of dynamic equations, of the error-correction type, also describes this behavior of the central bank, over the 1986:07–1993:11 period. The negative numbers in parentheses after the estimated coefficients represent the number of lags, while those presented below the coefficients are the usual t-ratios. N is the number of active data points, after taking into account the different lags and

---

[1] The data used come from the following sources:
Nigeria
– Parallel market exchange rates: *Picks' Currency Yearbook* (various issues); *World Currency Yearbook* (various); Ogiogio (1993)
– Official exchange rate: Central Bank of Nigeria (quoted by Ogiogio, 1993)
– CPI: *International Financial Statistics* (IMF) (several editions)
Kenya
– *World Currency Yearbook* (various issues)
Guinea
– Banque Centrale de la République de Guinée (internal sources)

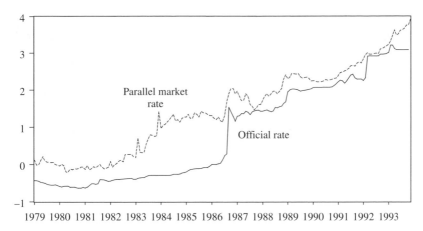

Figure 4.1. Official and parallel exchange rates: Nigeria, 1979–1993, logarithmic scale

differencing operations. It shows, on the one hand, that the parallel market exchange rate e^P affects the official one e^F, both via the error-correction term $z(-1)$ and via the short-run impact term $\Delta \text{Log } e^P(-1)$. On the other hand, it shows in (4.2) that during this period the official rate has no impact at all on the parallel one. This confirms the diagnosis stated above:

$$\Delta \text{Log } e^F = -0.33\, z(-1) - 0.05\Delta \text{Log } e^F(-1) + 0.36\,\Delta \text{Log } e^P(-1) + 0.02$$
$$\qquad\quad (4.67) \qquad\quad (0.54) \qquad\qquad\quad (1.95) \qquad\qquad\quad (1.58)$$

$$N = 87,\ \ R^2 = 0.31.$$

$$(4.1)$$

$$\Delta \text{Log } e^P = -0.04\, z(-1) + 0.03\Delta \text{Log } e^F(-1) + 0.29\Delta \text{Log } e^P(-1) + 0.02$$
$$\qquad\quad (0.91) \qquad\quad (0.45) \qquad\qquad\quad (2.77) \qquad\qquad\quad (1.73)$$

$$N = 87,\ \ R^2 = 0.11.$$

$$(4.2)$$

This opposition between the two sub-periods appears more clearly in figure 3.2 (p. 50), which shows the time profile of the premium on the US dollar in the parallel market. Before 1986, the premium is large and erratic, whereas it is smaller afterwards. Over the 1979:01–1993:11 period, its average value is close to 61%, with a standard error of 42.8%. However it is as high as 86.2% from

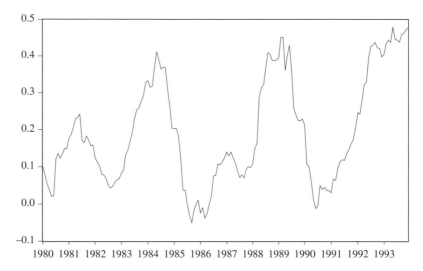

Figure 4.2. Inflation rate: Nigeria, 1979–1993, over twelve months

1979:01 to 1986:06, with a standard error of 43.2%, and this falls to 35.4% from 1986:07 to 1993:11, with a standard error of 22.6%. There is thus a sizable cut in the exchange rate premium, and in its standard error, starting at the time of the adoption of the SAP in July 1986. One may view this as a desire to increase the fiscal revenues that show up in the budgetary documents.

The time profile of the inflation rate goes in the opposite direction. As shown by figure 4.2, inflation has increased, and seems to accelerate during the second sub-period. We are looking at a moderate-inflation country, as defined by Dornbusch and Fischer (1993): the average annual inflation rate over this period is 19.5%, with a standard error of 14.7%. But it is smaller over the first sub-period, although the latter witnessed the second oil shock, causing hugely swollen foreign currency revenues for the Nigerian government, than over the second one. Until 1986:06, the average annual rate of inflation is 14.6%, with a standard error of 11.8%, while it rises to 23.8% after this date, with a standard error of 15.6%. Several peaks above 40 % per annum can be observed during the second sub-period, whereas such a peak occurs only during the first sub-period in 1984, a year of drought and collapse of agricultural production (Bevan, Collier, and Gunning, 1992). Moreover, the terms of trade of Nigeria were relatively low and stable

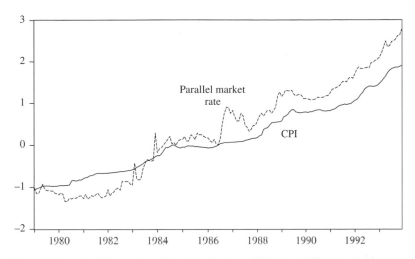

Figure 4.3. Parallel market exchange rate and CPI: Nigeria, 1979–1993, logarithmic scale

after 1986, while they were higher, with wider swings, during the previous decade (see, e.g., Faruqee, 1994).

Figure 4.3 shows that the parallel exchange rate and the consumer price index (CPI) are strongly linked to one another, as suggested by theory, when QRs trigger cross-border trade or when tariffs drive out official trade (Azam and Besley, 1989a, chapter 3 in this volume). This can be confirmed by econometric analysis: these two variables are cointegrated (in logarithms), with an augmented Dickey–Fuller (DF) test of −3.55, compared with a critical value of −3.37 (at 5%) (Banerjee *et al.*, 1993). The same test performed with the official exchange rate gives a value of −1.63, rejecting the cointegration hypothesis between these two variables during this period.

However, the dynamics of these two variables changed between the two sub-periods. Over the 1980:01–1986:06 period, the assumption that the premium does not Granger-cause the rate of inflation can be rejected, with a F-test of 2.62. The reverse assumption, that the rate of inflation does not Granger-cause the premium, passes the test easily, with a F-test of 0.46. Over the second sub-period, the two causality assumptions are rejected, with F-tests of 0.88 and 1.1, respectively.

To summarize, the brief quantitative analysis of the dynamics of the exchange rates and of the rate of inflation in Nigeria performed above leads to the following stylized facts: the parallel market

exchange rate is strongly linked with the CPI, whereas the official
exchange rate has a much looser relationship with it. Before the
adoption of the SAP, the official rate is fixed independently of the
parallel market rate, whereas after 1986, these two rates are strongly
linked to one another. In particular, there is a clear feedback from the
parallel rate into the official rate. Moreover, the inflation rate
increases, and becomes more volatile, after the SAP than before. The
premium clearly influences inflation during the first sub-period,
whereas these two variables seem to move independently during the
second sub-period. The very simple analytical model that follows
offers an interpretation of these stylized facts.

4.3 A glance at Kenya

Azam and Daubrée (1997) have performed a similar analysis for the
case of Kenya, using only yearly data. This does not allow as fine an
analysis as in the previous case; nevertheless, nothing in their data
suggests that Kenya had a very different experience, except for the
orders of magnitude. Figure 4.4 depicts the series of the parallel
market premium in Kenya over the period 1965–90. The first striking

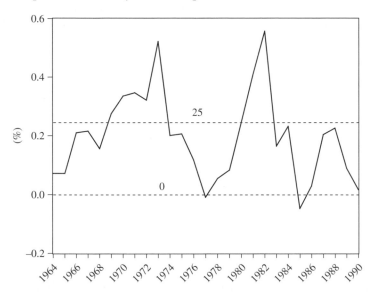

Figure 4.4. The parallel market premium: Kenya, 1964–1990
Source: World Currency Yearbook (various issues).

point is that it never reaches as high a level as in Nigeria, and goes above 25% on only two occasions: in 1969–73, when the government pushes the Asians to exit the country, without allowing them to take their capital with them, and in 1981–2, when there is political instability, with an attempted *coup* by some air force officers, as well as a food crisis. Otherwise, the premium has a more reasonable level in this case than in that of Nigeria.

Performing the same type of analysis as above yields a very comparable picture although the data are not as suitable, because of the smaller number of data points. Table 4.1 shows the results of a Granger non-causality test. Because of the small number of data points, the results corresponding to different lag length are presented, in order to suggest that the test seems quite robust.

Table 4.1 suggests quite strongly that backward indexation behavior is at work here, as well. This diagnosis is confirmed, and refined, by the following pair of error-correction equations, estimated by the maximum likelihood method over the whole sample, which reduces to 1967–90 because of differencing:

$$\Delta \log e^P = -0.25z\ (-1) + 0.15\Delta \log e^P(-1) + 0.12\Delta \log e^P(-2)$$
$$\quad (0.11) \qquad\quad (0.38) \qquad\qquad\quad (0.39)$$
$$\quad + 0.20\Delta \log e^F(-1) - 0.73\Delta \log e^F(-2) + 0.004 + 0.07D76$$
$$\quad\ (0.35) \qquad\qquad\quad (1.69) \qquad\qquad (1.00)\quad (0.86)$$
$$N = 24, \quad R^2 = 0.24.$$

$$(4.3)$$

$$\Delta \log e^F = 0.46\ z(-1) - 0.04\Delta \log e^P(-1) - 0.09\Delta \log e^P(-2)$$
$$\quad (3.06) \qquad\quad (0.29) \qquad\qquad\quad (0.74)$$
$$\quad + 0.25\Delta \log e^F(-1) - 0.18\Delta \log e^F(-2) - 0.01 + 0.10D76$$
$$\quad\ (1.15) \qquad\qquad\quad (1.11) \qquad\qquad (0.62)\ (3.13)$$
$$N = 24, \quad R^2 = 0.74.$$

$$(4.4)$$

Examination of this pair of equations suggests that causality runs from the parallel market exchange rate to the official one, and not vice versa. The official exchange rate is not significant in the parallel rate equation, neither directly nor through the error-correction term. By contrast, the error-correction term is strongly significant in the official

Table 4.1. Granger non-causality test between parallel and official rate (F-test)

Number of lags	1	2	3
Parallel does not cause official	12.65	5.34	5.38
Official does not cause parallel	0.02	1.14	1.00

Source: Azam and Daubrée (1997).

rate equation, suggesting that the parallel rate is an attractor for the latter. A dummy variable D76 has been included, to capture the change in behavior that seems to occur in 1976, from eyeballing the data. Its significance in (4.4) suggests that the behavior of the central bank concerning the pricing of foreign exchange on the official market did change that year. The same results are found, even more clearly, if one splits the sample after 1976. But then, of course, the number of data points is very small. One gets:

$$\Delta \log e^P = -0.10 \ z(-1) + 0.16\Delta \log e^P(-1) + 0.16\Delta \log e^P(-2)$$
$$(0.11) \qquad (0.21) \qquad\qquad (0.39)$$
$$- 0.05\Delta \log e^F(-1) - 0.69\Delta \log e^F(-2) + 0.69$$
$$(0.06) \qquad\qquad (1.24) \qquad\qquad (1.00)$$
$$N = 15, \quad R^2 = 0.22.$$

$$(4.5)$$

$$\Delta \log e^F = 0.99 \ z(-1) - 0.33\Delta \log e^P(-1) - 0.21\Delta \log e^P(-2)$$
$$(3.84) \qquad (1.14) \qquad\qquad (1.74)$$
$$- 0.15\Delta \log e^F(-1) - 0.24\Delta \log e^F(-2) + 0.11$$
$$(0.72) \qquad\qquad (1.49) \qquad\qquad (4.15)$$
$$N = 15, R^2 = 0.86.$$

$$(4.6)$$

The backward indexation rule seems stronger on this restricted sample. Unfortunately, given the series, it is impossible to test for the change by estimating a similar equation over 1967–75. Nevertheless, the feedback seems stronger on the restricted sample, suggesting that the central bank was probably obeying a different rule before that date.

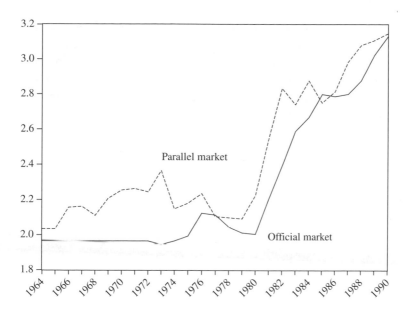

Figure 4.5. Official and parallel exchange rates: Kenya, 1964–1990
Source: Azam and Daubrée (1997).

Then, if one tentatively accepts this diagnosis, one would expect from the results of section 4.2 that much more instability should be observed after the adoption of the backward indexation rule in 1976. A glance at figure 4.5 suggests that this is indeed the case: while the official rate seems to close the gap with the parallel rate in 1978, a massive and sustained depreciation occurs throughout the 1980s.

The study by Nkurunziza (2002) suggests that a similar phenomenon has been going on in Burundi since the end of the 1980s. While the premium in this country was averaging 23% in the 1970s and 1980s, it grew to an average value of 45% in the 1990s. The annual rate of depreciation moved from an average value of 3.6% in the former period to an average rate of 14.9% in the latter one.

The model presented in section 4.4 offers an explanation for these facts.

4.4 The model

Denote M the quantity of money and p the price level. Real money balances are then defined as $m = M/p$. Let E be the official exchange rate and e be the parallel market exchange rate, and define (1 plus) the parallel market premium by $q = e/E \geqslant 1$. For the sake of simplicity, units are selected such that the international price of tradables in terms of foreign currency is equal to 1, and non-tradables are neglected. The price of goods is then determined by the marginal exchange rate – i.e. the parallel market rate: $p = e$. Government expenditures and revenues are split into two different budgets, depending on whether they are directly affected by the official exchange rate or not. I assume that the government has, on the one hand, more expenditures than revenues that are indexed on the price level p, and, on the other, more revenues (foreign aid included) than expenditures indexed on the official exchange rate. Let D and F be the excess of expenditures over revenues indexed on p and the excess of revenues over expenditures indexed on E, respectively. Hence, the monetary financing of the overall deficit implies:

$$dM/dt = pD - EF. \qquad (4.7)$$

Let $\pi = d \log p/dt = d \log e/dt$ denote the rate of inflation and the rate of depreciation of the domestic currency in the parallel market, respectively. Let $\delta = d \log E/dt$ denote the rate of devaluation of the national currency at the official exchange rate.

Using the notation m for real money balances presented earlier, (4.7) may be rewritten as:

$$dm/dt = D - F/q - \pi m. \qquad (4.8)$$

Assume that the demand for real money balances is determined *à la* Cagan (1946) as a function of the expected rate of inflation π^e by the following function:

$$m = \lambda(\pi^e), \lambda' < 0. \qquad (4.9)$$

The analysis is restricted to the case of rational expectations equilibria, where (4.9) holds with $\pi^e = \pi$ and $|\pi^e| \ll \infty$, $\forall \, t > 0$, where 0 is the present date. This entails in particular that no discontinuous "jump" in the price level is allowed at any future date. This requirement makes perfectly good sense in a rational expectations equilibrium model for the following reason. If at a future date T the agents were expecting an infinite rate of inflation to prevail, they would rationally get rid of their cash balances at date $T - dt$, in order to avoid seeing their monetary asset wiped out by inflation at the next date. However, if everybody tries at date $T - dt$ to get rid of their cash balances, then the price level jumps to infinity at that date. The agents would anticipate this rationally, and thus try to get rid of their cash balances at date $T - 2dt$ ... The argument can be repeated backwards like this until date 0. Hence, no price level jump can occur at any future date in a rational expectations equilibrium. The same reasoning cannot be repeated at date zero (the present) because the agents cannot go back in the past; thus, in this type of model, a jump can occur only at the initial date.

Using (4.8) and (4.9) yields:

$$d\pi/dt = (1/\lambda')(D - F/q - \pi\lambda(\pi)). \tag{4.10}$$

Inflation is therefore stabilized ($d\pi/dt = 0$) for all pairs $\{q, \pi\}$ such that:

$$D - F/q = \pi\lambda(\pi). \tag{4.11}$$

Real seigniorage, represented by the left-hand side of (4.11), is a concave increasing function of q. Notice that this would be reinforced if we assumed D and F to be functions of q, as the natural assumptions to make would be $D' > 0$ and $F' < 0$, as an increase in the premium would probably induce a diversion of exports to the parallel market, entailing a fall in tax revenues, both directly, as the proceeds of the taxes on official exports fall, and indirectly as more incomes go underground, evading income tax. The increase in the premium may also trigger some increases in wages and salaries, as the cost of living would go up, given the official exchange rate. Hence, our simplifying assumption ($D' = F' = 0$) does not entail any loss of generality. The proceeds of the inflation tax, represented by the right-hand side of (4.11) is a non-monotonic concave function of π, according to the inflation tax Laffer curve mechanism (Bruno and Fischer, 1990; Dornbusch and Fischer, 1993). (4.11) can therefore be represented as a non-monotonic concave curve, labeled *mm* in figures 4.6 and 4.7 (pp. 84 and 87). The inflation rate increases over time for the $\{q, \pi\}$ pairs located below this locus, according to (4.10), and it decreases over time above this locus. This captures the fact that, if the premium q increases, so does the deficit, and agents must absorb increasing real money balances. This is consistent with the rational expectations equilibrium only if inflation is slowing down, providing the incentive to hold higher money balances.

I shall compare the dynamics of inflation implied by this model under two different assumptions concerning the behavior of the government. I analyze the cases where the government pursues either:

(a) The policy of indexation of the official exchange rate on the parallel market one:

$$E = e/q^*, \tag{4.12}$$

where q^* is the constant target chosen by the government for the premium, or:

(b) The nominal anchor policy:

$$\delta = \delta^*, \tag{4.13}$$

where δ^* is the constant rate of devaluation chosen by the government.

In this case, the dynamics of the premium is governed by the following equation:

$$dq/dt = q(\pi - \delta^*). \tag{4.14}$$

The properties of the dynamic system comprising (4.8), (4.9), and either (4.12) or (4.13) and (4.14), can be analyzed using phase diagrams. Figure 4.6 represents the case where the government pursues the former policy, selecting $q = q^*$ such that two stationary points E and E' exist. Point E is unstable with respect to the dynamics illustrated by the arrows. In this model without predetermined variables, this corresponds to a saddle point, with a zero-dimensional convergent sub-space. Conversely, point E' is stable. Consequently, there exists a *continuum* of rational expectations equilibria: E, and all the points located to the right of E, which belong to some trajectory converging eventually to E'. The points to the left of E are not rational expectations equilibria, because they belong to trajectories where, eventually, $\pi^e \to -\infty$.

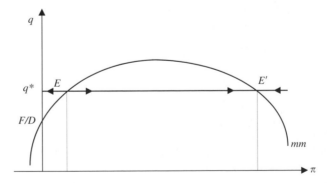

Figure 4.6. Indexation policy

Notice that the government could choose a too high target premium q^*, relative to the exogenous variable F/D, for a stationary point to exist. In this case, there exists no rational expectations equilibrium. Let us assume that this is not the case i.e. that D is small enough relative to $\max_\pi \pi\lambda(\pi)$, for this case to be ruled out.

If the government adopts the policy of indexing the official exchange rate on the parallel market rate, it thus loses control of the price level and of the inflation rate. The price level at the initial date, and its rate of growth, are then determined by the self-fulfilling expectations of the private agents. They could be based on sunspots or any other information whose only relevance is that it affects expectations. The level of the premium loses any link with the rate of inflation here, as we have found in the case of Nigeria after 1986.07.

The real-world translation of a continuum of rational expectations equilibria is the prediction of a high volatility of the variables involved. The system has no anchor, so that the variables can jump from one trajectory to the other as a response to any information whose only relevance is to affect the agents' expectations. In the theoretical literature, models of sunspot equilibria have been devised to capture this idea (see Blanchard and Fischer, 1989, for an introduction). There is no point in going into the mathematical developments of this theory here, as the main component of these equilibria is a continuum of rational expectations equilibria, like that which has been shown to exist in the neighborhood of point E' in figure 4.6. Then, Shigoka (1994) and Drugeon and Wigniolle (1996) have shown that Woodford's conjecture applies even in continuous-time models. This conjecture states that there exist stationary sunspot equilibria in the neighborhood of any stationary point of a deterministic model where there exists a continuum of perfect foresight equilibria converging to this stationary point. In this case, any information that affects the agents' expectations will be self-fulfilling, even if it has no other intrinsic relevance for the economy than that of affecting expectations. As the economy is not anchored to a unique equilibrium trajectory by the fundamentals, it can be buffeted away by any random shock affecting the agents' expectations.

Figure 4.7 represents the case where the government chooses the nominal anchor policy, assuming that the stationary point E lies to the left of the maximum point of the *mm* locus. According to the econometric results by Adam, Ndulu, and Sowa (1996), such an inflation

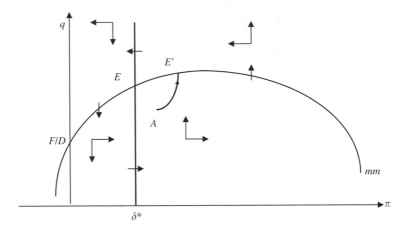

Figure 4.7. Nominal anchor policy

tax-maximizing point is usually found in Africa at a pretty low rate of inflation, between 15% and 20%. The arrows drawn in the four regions of the phase space show the dynamics of the model. One can observe that E is unstable; in other words, E is again a saddle point, with a zero-dimensional convergent sub-space. As π and q are "jump variables," the economy directly reaches point E at the initial date, and stays there, provided the chosen value of π^* is immutable and perfectly credible. If, on the contrary, agents believe that at a given future date the government is going to increase the rate of crawl up to the level of point E', say, then they will anticipate the move and will follow the path labeled AE'. Such a phenomenon probably occurred in Nigeria in the early 1980s, as can be seen in section 4.2. Notice also that this argument falls apart if the rate of crawl is chosen too high, so that E falls on the downward-sloping part of the *mm* locus. The stationary point becomes stable again, and the continuum of rational expectations equilibria occurs again.

The intuition for this result is as follows. Assume that we start at point E, and that agents expect inflation to increase. The price level goes up, so they try to reduce their money balances. This increases the nominal value of some public expenditures and, thus, the deficit. As real money balances are going down at the same time, this entails that the price level is pushed further up, and with it the parallel market exchange rate. If the official exchange rate does not accelerate, the deficit increases still further, and the dynamics become fully explosive.

This is ruled out by the rational expectations equilibrium. Rational agents will thus not embark on this path, and will thus stay at E in the first place. By contrast, if the official exchange rate is indexed, the value of tax revenues goes up as well, keeping the fiscal deficit constant. All the burden of adjustment therefore rests on the inflation tax. Because of the inflation tax Laffer curve, the economy can settle at a higher inflation rate, where this fixed level of real seigniorage is matched by an inflation tax of the same value.

The nominal anchor strategy, as defined here, thus removes the problem of multiple equilibria raised by the policy of indexation of the official rate on the parallel market one. Consequently, provided it is credible, the choice of a pre-determined path for the official exchange rate, which has come to be known as a *"tablita"* (Corbo and de Melo, 1987), is an effective means of controlling inflation. In other words, even if the official rate does not directly affect the price level, as argued above, it affects it indirectly by its impact on the fiscal deficit and the growth of the money supply. It can thus serve as a nominal anchor, as the quantity of money or the unified exchange rate can do in an economy without a parallel market (Bruno, 1991).

However, this policy raises a fundamental issue of credibility. Figure 4.7 illustrates how a nominal anchor policy that is deemed temporary by economic agents is unable to fix instantly the rate of inflation and the parallel market premium. On the contrary, an expected increase in the rate of devaluation is enough to trigger some anticipation, with the rate of inflation and the premium starting to grow even before the policy changes. It was suggested above that this explained why the premium kept increasing in the early 1980s in Nigeria, while the official exchange rate was kept more or less fixed against the US dollar. This credibility problem can be analyzed in a more structural way, as the government may have an incentive to create some surprise inflation (Persson and Tabellini, 1990); this is done in section 4.5.

4.5 The credibility issue

In order to analyze this point, one needs to complement the model, by answering the question why the government should decide to sell its hard currencies at a discount compared to the market price, as is the case in Nigeria. This seemingly paradoxical behavior is in fact rational: by keeping control of who has access to the sales of hard currencies by the central bank, the government selects who can benefit from import subsidies, or even lump-sum subsidies, if the buyer can resell the currencies straight away in the parallel market, by this mechanism. These implicit subsidies do not show up in the budgetary documents, and thus escape control by parliament or the Bretton Woods institutions. The government thus keeps for its own use a discretionary budget, which allows it to use some of the dollars from oil or from international aid as it likes. The theoretical effect of this observation is that the level of the premium must affect positively the government's utility function.

Let us therefore assume that the government has a strictly quasi-concave utility function of the following type:

$$U(q, \pi). \qquad\qquad (4.15)$$
$$(+)(-)$$

According to this specification, inflation is the price that the government accepts for getting a larger premium. The indifference curves corresponding to (4.15) are represented in figure 4.8 by the upward-sloping convex curves, the higher ones representing a higher level of utility. The optimum choice, represented by point A, is derived by maximizing (4.15) under constraint (4.10). However, this is not a credible choice, as the government has an incentive to cheat _ex post_ by creating some surprise inflation.

In fact, the true constraint that is faced by the government is not (4.11), but (4.11′), where due account is taken of the assumption that what determines the demand for real money balances is not the observed rate of inflation, but the expected one:

$$D - F/q = \pi\lambda(\pi^e). \qquad\qquad (4.11')$$

This constraint has a steeper slope than (4.11) in the neighborhood of point A. Hence, if the government were to announce that it was to choose the policy corresponding to this point, and if this was believed by private agents, it could in fact reach point B by creating a surprise increase in inflation equal to the difference between the abscissae of B and A. Rational agents will take this incentive into account when forming their expectations, so that the only credible equilibrium is point N, which belongs to (4.11) at a point where the indifference curve of the government is tangent to (4.11′). This is the Nash equilibrium of this

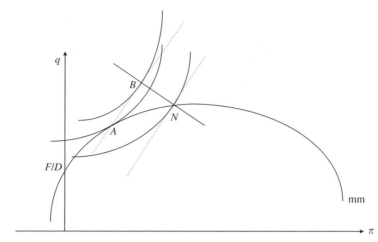

Figure 4.8. The credibility issue

game, where no incentive to cheat remains. The *BN* line connects all the points where the indifference curves of the government are tangent to the (4.11′) constraint, given the value of π^e corresponding to the intersection of the latter with *mm*. It can be interpreted as a representation of the government's reaction function.

This credibility constraint bearing on the conduct of macroeconomic policy by the government thus gives rise to a sub-optimal equilibrium, where the rate of inflation is higher than its optimal value. The parallel market premium is not necessarily higher than its optimal value, as the Nash equilibrium might be located on the downward-sloping part of the *mm* locus, lower than point *A*. But, then, a problem of uniqueness of the equilibrium or controllability of the inflation rate would occur, as discussed above. In most cases, however, provided the Nash equilibrium is not too far from the optimum point, one may also expect the premium to be larger than optimal. This model therefore sheds some light on the divergent behavior of the official and the parallel market exchange rates that we observed in section 4.2 in Nigeria before 1986:06 while the government was trying to peg the official rate, the private agents were probably expecting this behavior to be unsustainable. It also sheds some light on the events that took place at the end of our sample period. General Abacha took over by a *coup* in November 1993, and decided in January 1994 to revert to the pre-1986 monetary arrangements, by fixing the official exchange rate, by centralizing the legal sale of foreign currencies at the central bank, thus forbidding

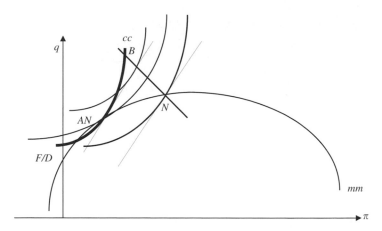

Figure 4.9. The conservative governor

the parallel market, and by suing the former governor of the central bank before a special court. One year later, in February 1995, he *de facto* abandoned this policy.

The credibility problem discussed above is similar to the type of problems discussed in the literature on the credibility of monetary policy. Similar solutions are available, such as the conservative banker approach (Rogoff, 1985), or the contractual approach (Persson and Tabellini, 1993; Walsh, 1995). Figure 4.9 illustrates the case of the conservative governor: the government can delegate the conduct of the foreign exchange pricing policy to an independent central banker whose preferences are more averse to inflation than those of the government, and are represented here by a steeper indifference curve labeled *cc*. Figure 4.9 shows that by choosing a governor with the right preferences, the government can make the Nash equilibrium point and the optimum one coincide, at the point labeled *AN*.

This theoretical discussion sheds some light on the experience of Guinea, where the official exchange rate has been used to stabilize the price level, resulting in a narrowing of the parallel market premium, as predicted by the model discussed above. This case stands in sharp contrast to the example of Nigeria discussed in section 4.2.

4.6 The case of Guinea, 1986–1996

During the transition period after the fall of the totalitarian Sékou Touré regime, the central bank of Guinea followed a pricing policy for the foreign exchange that the government gets from the mining sector (bauxite and gold), and from foreign aid, which was akin to that advocated above: it adopted a relatively low rate of crawl, independently of the evolution of the parallel market rate. The central bank had been independent since 1986, and the credibility of the pricing rule followed was attached to the personality of the rigorous governor Kerfalla Yansané, formerly professor of law and public finance at the University of Dakar (Senegal). He remained governor for ten years, up to July 1996, and built a strong reputation for resisting all pressures in favor of a more inflationary policy. This good reputation, together with a tight domestic credit policy, which enabled the central bank of Guinea to accumulate foreign reserves, was used to implement an exchange rate-based stabilization policy, described below (Azam and Diakité, 1997). This was done against a background of deteriorating terms of trade, due to a pretty depressed bauxite market. The resulting negative wealth effect probably generated some inflationary pressure, because of a liquidity effect "*à la* Neary" (1984), as the demand for real money balances went down, and also because of the negative fiscal impact of low export revenues.

This nominal anchor approach to the foreign exchange market, similar to that described in previous sections, as well as some conscious efforts by the central bank, resulted in a near- unification of the parallel and the official markets. Figure 4.10 represents the time profile of the parallel and the official exchange rates of the New Guinean Franc (NGF) against the US dollar, using monthly data. It is quite clear from figure 4.10 that these two series do not diverge dramatically from one another, so that the premium remains within a reasonable range (it is described in more detail below). There was a fairly high rate of depreciation of the official exchange rate between 1986 and 1992, at an annual average rate of 16.03%, followed by a relative stabilization, with a smaller rate of depreciation – namely, a 2.06% annual average rate (splitting the sample after 1992:04). The corresponding figures for the parallel rate are 15.49% and 1.59%, respectively (splitting after 1992:06). Hence, the two rates seem to move together, and this is confirmed by the following econometric exercises. First, table 4.2 shows that these two series are $I(1)$, according to the augmented DF-test.

Second, the close relationship between the two rates is clearly brought out by the application of the Johansen Cointegration Test. It

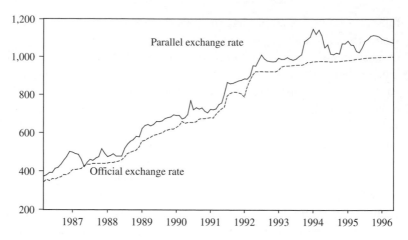

Figure 4.10. Official and parallel exchange rates: Guinea, 1986:03–1996:05, NGF/US$

Note: NGF = New Guinean Franc.

Source: Central bank of the Republic of Guinea.

Table 4.2. Augmented DF-tests, parallel/official rates: Guinea

	Level	*First difference*
Parallel rate	−1.18	−5.41
Official rate	−1.52	−5.11

Note: 5% *c.v.* = − 2.89

yields a likelihood-ratio statistic of 2.69, compared to a 5% critical value of 3.76. Moreover, the normalized cointegrating vector gives a coefficient for the official exchange rate of 1.041, with a standard error of 0.02: In other words, it is not significantly different from 1.

Third, table 4.3 presents the Granger non-causality test, which suggests that the official exchange rate is the driving force in the NGF market, where the parallel rate seems to play the part of the follower. The central bank thus seems to have kept control of the market rate, a policy quite different from that pursued by Nigeria between 1986 and 1993, and by Kenya after 1976, both described above (see also Ndung'u, 1996; Azam and Daubrée, 1997; Azam, 1999), where

Table 4.3. Granger non-causality test, parallel/official rates: Guinea (111 observations)

(log 12 lags)	F-test	Probability
Official does not Granger-cause parallel	2.81	0.003
Parallel does not Granger-cause official	0.89	0.56

the official rate was also more or less tracking the parallel market one, with a lag, through a similar kind of backward-looking indexation formula. By contrast, in Guinea, over this period of analysis, the central bank remained the dominant seller of foreign exchange in the market.

This diagnosis is confirmed by the following pair of dynamic equations (4.15) and (4.16), including the cointegration restriction, as an error-correction mechanism. This is more satisfactory than the unrestricted Granger non-causality test performed above, which nevertheless yields the same result. In these equations e^P is the parallel market exchange rate and e^F is the official one, while $z(-1)$ is the error-correction term, the residuals from the cointegrating equation lagged once. The negative numbers in parentheses after the estimated coefficients represent the number of lags, while those presented below the coefficients are the usual t-ratios. N is the number of active data points, after taking into account the different lags and differencing operations. While (4.16) shows that the official exchange rate significantly affects the parallel one, via the error-correction term, (4.17) shows no feedback effect from the parallel exchange rate to the official one:

$$\Delta \text{Log } e^P = -0.35\, z(-1) + 0.20\ \Delta \text{Log } e^P(-1) + 0.17 \Delta \text{Log } e^P(-2)$$
$$\quad (4.84) \qquad (2.11) \qquad\qquad (1.82)$$
$$+\, 0.18 \Delta \text{Log } e^P(-3) + 0.17 \Delta \text{Log } e^F(-1) - 0.06 \Delta \text{Log } e^F(-2)$$
$$(1.91) \qquad\qquad (0.89) \qquad\qquad (0.31)$$
$$+\, 0.03 \Delta \text{Log } e^F(-3) + 0.002$$
$$(0.14) \qquad\qquad (0.75)$$
$$N = 119, \quad R^2 = 0.23.$$

$$(4.16)$$

$$\Delta \mathrm{Log}\, e^F = -0.003\, z(-1) + 0.06\Delta \mathrm{Log}\, e^P(-1) + 0.001\Delta \mathrm{Log} e^P(-2)$$
$$\qquad (0.09) \qquad\qquad (1.24) \qquad\qquad\qquad (0.01)$$
$$\qquad + 0.06\Delta \mathrm{Log}\, e^P(-3) + 0.24\Delta \mathrm{Log}\, e^F(-1) + 0.10\Delta \mathrm{Log}\, e^F(-2)$$
$$\qquad\quad (1.26) \qquad\qquad\qquad (2.48) \qquad\qquad\qquad (1.06)$$
$$\qquad - 0.11\Delta \mathrm{log} e^F(-3) + 0.01$$
$$\qquad\quad (1.15) \qquad\qquad (3.22)$$
$$\qquad N = 119, \;\; R^2 = 0.13.$$

$$(4.17)$$

Figure 4.11 represents the parallel market premium, defined as the log-difference between the parallel and the official exchange rates. Its mean value over the sample is 8.64%, which is very small by African standards, and one can notice a slightly downward trend in this series. It is stationary, with an ADF test of – 4.90, to be compared to the 5% critical value of –3.44, as could be expected from the results presented above. It remains below 15% most of the time, except for a peak at about 25% at the end of 1986, and the odd peaks just above 15% at the end of 1987, in mid-1990, and in late 1993–early 1994. The latter peak might be explained by the anticipation of the devaluation of the CFA Franc, the common currency of the neighboring WAEMU, which is held as an inflation-proof asset in the region. A temporary scarcity of US dollars, driven by the speculation against the CFA Franc, might then explain the spike in the series at these dates. The parallel market premium has been small and declining over most of

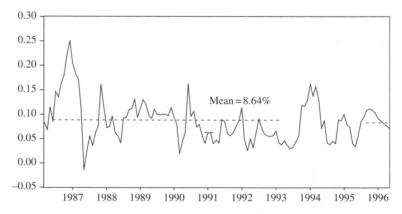

Figure 4.11. Parallel market premium (%): Guinea, 1986:03–1996:05

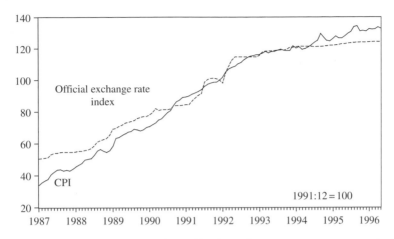

Figure 4.12. The CPI and the official exchange rate: Guinea, 1986: 03–1996:05, 1991:12 = 100

Table 4.4. Augmented DF-tests, inflation/official rate: Guinea

	Level	First difference
Inflation rate	−0.86	−4.69
Log official rate	−2.38	−4.09

Note: 5% c.v. = − 2.89

the period under study, so that we can focus on the official exchange rate below, as a meaningful indicator of the stance of exchange rate policy, since it has been actively used for controlling the price level during this period.

The official exchange rate reaches a kind of plateau in 1992, followed by a period of relative stability, with a small upward trend, as seen above. Figure 4.12 shows that the CPI follows roughly the same pattern, but with a slightly larger upward slope, and with a lag. This simply reflects the upward trend of the world price level, as the real exchange rate in Guinea shows a depreciation over this period (see Azam and Diakité, 1997).

Table 4.4 shows that both the inflation rate and the log of the official exchange rate can be regarded as $I(1)$. Equations (4.18) and (4.19) provide an error-correction representation of their dynamic relationships. They show that the official exchange rate actually

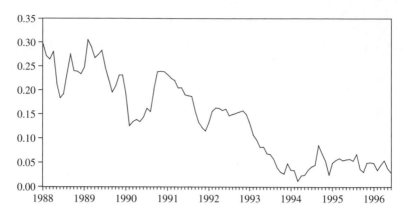

Figure 4.13. Rate of inflation: Guinea, 1986:03–1996:05

affects the rate of inflation positively, while there is no significant feedback from the latter onto the former. It thus seems that the official exchange rate behaves over this period of analysis like a fairly autonomous variable, directly targeted by the central bank. The post-1992 plateau in both the official exchange rate and the CPI that we have observed in figure 4.12 can be interpreted as an example of exchange rate-based stabilization policy, which seems to have succeeded in stabilizing the price level to a large extent. This comes out clearly from figure 4.13, where we can see that the rate of inflation fell steadily from a high value about 30% in 1998–9, to a stable rate about 5% in 1993–6. Azam and Diakité (1997) show that this stabilization came at a low cost, as the growth rate of the economy, relatively high since 1986, showed only a small slowdown:

$$\Delta \text{Infl} = -0.15 \ z(-1) + 0.22 \ \Delta\text{Infl}(-1) + 0.40 \ \Delta\text{Log } e^F(-1) - 0.005$$
$$\quad\quad (3.65) \quad\quad\quad (2.31) \quad\quad\quad\quad (2.90) \quad\quad\quad\quad\quad (2.31)$$
$$N = 99, \quad R^2 = 0.17.$$

$$(4.18)$$

$$\Delta\log e^F = 0.05 \ z(-1) - 0.08\Delta\text{Infl}(-1) + 0.29\Delta\log e^F(-1) + 0.006$$
$$\quad\quad\quad (1.75) \quad\quad\quad (1.20) \quad\quad\quad\quad (2.92) \quad\quad\quad\quad (3.45)$$
$$N = 99, \quad R^2 = 0.17.$$

$$(4.19)$$

4.7 Conclusion

A simple analytical model has been used in this chapter to discuss the appropriate pricing policy that should be adopted when the government is the main provider of foreign exchange to the economy. This case is typical of most African countries, where the government owns a large share of the mining sector that supplies the bulk of the exports revenues, or even taxes largely export crops through a marketing board or a stabilization fund. Foreign aid, which typically amounts to more than 10% of GDP in many of these countries, reinforces the relevance of this case. This model, analyzed under the assumption of a rational expectations equilibrium, supports the view that the government should select a low and constant rate of crawl, rather than attempt to catch up on the changes in the parallel market rate. If credible, such a policy would result in a low inflation rate and a low parallel market premium.

This theory sheds some light on two interesting case studies presented in this chapter, dealing with Nigeria and Guinea, respectively, with a glance at the case of Kenya. It could probably also be applied *mutatis mutandis* to many other developing countries where there is a parallel market, and where the fiscal deficit is an increasing function of the parallel market premium. It allows us to bring out the different effects of two commonly adopted methods of pricing the foreign exchange sold by the government. If the latter adopts a policy of indexation of the official rate on the parallel market rate, it loses a nominal anchor, and the price level and the rate of inflation are both indeterminate. These two variables are then determined by the expectations of private agents, and their path can be changed at any time by any kind of information that agents regard as relevant for forming their expectations. The real-world translation of this theoretical prediction is the observation of an erratic rate of inflation, without any link with the parallel market premium. This fits quite well with the situation that we have observed in Nigeria for the post-1986:06 period, as well as with the Kenyan experience.

If the government chooses a credible *tablita*, with a low enough rate of devaluation, the problem raised by multiple equilibria disappears, and inflation can be controlled. In this case, the model predicts that the rate of inflation should be less erratic, with a significant relationship with the parallel market premium. This is what we have found for the period before the SAP was adopted. However, the premium in the Nigerian parallel market reached some extremely high levels – the government was giving away several percent of GDP via the sale of foreign exchange by the central bank to "authorized dealers." The inflation tax was used indirectly as a means to finance the covert subsidies given to the happy few who had access to the sales of hard currencies at the official exchange rate. The observed divergence of the two rates that occurred in Nigeria prior to 1986 has been interpreted as a signal that the policy of pegging the official exchange rate then gradually lost its credibility.

A theoretical analysis was then offered of the credibility problem in this setting, showing how the standard "conservative governor" approach *à la* Rogoff (1985) could solve it. The case of Guinea then illustrated that the policy advocated in this chapter could realistically be applied in a small African country. The central bank kept the price level under control and managed to achieve an exchange rate-based stabilization policy. As a result, the parallel market premium remained very low, decreasing slightly over time, and inflation went down drastically.

The scope of this chapter has been limited by examining only the effects of two decision rules regarding the pricing of foreign exchange on the official market. Other policies can be conceived for controlling inflation. One obvious solution is to make public expenditures, say D in the model, some function of the inflation rate. The problem of the multiple equilibria might then be avoided by the appropriate choice of the $D(\pi)$ function, even with a fixed parallel-market premium (say, zero). As the aim of this exercise is to remove the effect of the inflation tax Laffer curve, one can check easily that a policy of reducing local public expenditures as inflation increases, with a steeper slope as inflation goes up, could do the trick. This is left as an exercise. However, the problem would be to make such a rule of behavior credible in the eyes of the general public.

Appendix 4.1 The case of $F < 0$

I deal here with the case where, although it is a net seller of foreign currencies to the private sector, so that it keeps the control of the official exchange rate, the government has a deficit on its budget indexed on the official exchange rate, as noted in section 4.1. The

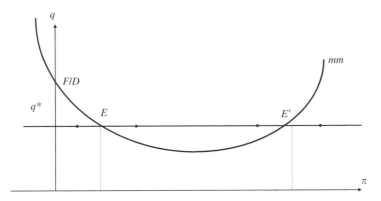

Figure 4A.1. Indexation policy

analytical model can be kept nearly as in section 4.3, but changing the signs of D and F. As will become clear below, it is more convenient to change both signs than just the sign of F. The main difference with the analysis done in section 4.3 is that the *mm* locus is now convex, instead of being concave.

The indexation policy can be analyzed with the help of the phase diagram in figure 4A.1. We find, as in figure 4.6, that there may be two stationary points in the case where the government pursues an indexation policy. The same conclusion follows, namely that there is a continuum of rational expectations equilibria, so that the government has lost control of the rate of inflation. The impact of the nominal anchor policy is quite different from the analysis performed in figure 4.7, in that the convergent sub-space is now one-dimensional. Therefore, we still get a continuum of rational expectations equilibria, unless we exogenously get an initial value for one or other of the variables. This underlines the crucial importance of the assumptions made in the model of section 4.3.

Appendix 4.2 Microfoundations

Many readers might object to assumption (4.5), which posits a reduced-form demand for money function directly instead of deriving it from an explicit optimization exercise. The aim of this appendix is to reassure them that the model used is consistent with the standard assumptions of economic theory. Such a behavioral assumption can be derived from many different models. A classic approach originates

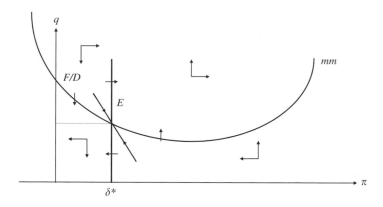

Figure 4A.2. Nominal anchor policy

in Sidrauski (1967), and it is still widely used nowadays, with minor modification – as done, for example, by Benhabib, Schmitt-Grohé, and Uribe (2002). The short presentation that follows is a simplified version of the latter, aiming at deriving a demand for money function akin to (4.5) from first principles.

Assume that the representative individual chooses her saving and portfolio behavior with a view to maximizing the present value of her welfare over an infinite horizon. This infinitely-lived individual may be interpreted as a dynastic family, with successive generations linked by some altruism. She can allocate her wealth a freely between the holding of some productive asset k, with a known exogenous real rate of return r, and interest-free cash balances m. The latter are assumed to yield a flow of liquidity services, which affects positively the individual's utility function. She then seeks to solve the following problem:

$$\max \int_0^\infty u(c,m)e^{-rt}dt, \tag{4A.1}$$

where $u(c, m)$ is strictly increasing and concave, subject to a wealth constraint

$$a = k + m, \tag{4A.2}$$

where a is the state variable, while k and m are control variables. She is also subject to an initial condition on wealth

$$a(0) = a_0, \tag{4A.3}$$

and a budget constraint

$$da/dt = [rk - \pi m] - c. \tag{4A.4}$$

The term between square brackets is the real income of the individual, net of the inflation tax πm, where π is the inflation rate, assumed fixed exogenously. This can be rewritten as $ra-(r+\pi)m$, the difference between the full asset income, evaluated at the ruling real interest rate, and the value of the consumption of liquidity services, whose price is evaluated as the sum of their opportunity cost and the inflation tax rate.

Applying the standard technique of control theory, namely Pontryagin's Maximum Principle, one gets the following four optimality conditions, in addition to the constraints presented above. The variable q denotes the Lagrange multiplier attached to the dynamic constraint (4A.4), and partial derivatives are denoted by a subscript:

$$u_c(c,m) = q, \tag{4A.5}$$

$$u_m(c,m) = (r + \pi)q, \tag{4A.6}$$

$$dq/dt = 0, \tag{4A.7}$$

$$\lim_{t \to \infty} qae^{-rt} = 0. \tag{4A.8}$$

Condition (4A.8) is the transversality condition, which ensures that the individual does not leave at the end of time an asset having a strictly positive present value. Otherwise, she could improve her consumption trajectory by spreading this value over her lifetime to increase her consumption slightly. Leaving a negative present value asset at the end of time is also precluded by this condition.

Using (4A.5), (4A.6), and (4A.7), one can derive the following expressions for m and c, which are valid whatever the future path of π

$$m = m(r + \pi, q), \tag{4A.9}$$

$$c = c(r + \pi, q). \tag{4A.10}$$

In these expressions, time-invariant q encapsulates all the relevant information about the future path of π and a. One observes that, given this information, we have in (4A.9) the demand for money function, which is decreasing in the rate of inflation, as assumed in (4.5). Its derivative is

$$\frac{\partial m}{\partial \pi} = \frac{qu_{cc}}{\Delta} < 0. \tag{4A.11}$$

where $\Delta = u_{cc}u_{mm} - u^2_{cm} > 0$, by concavity. Notice also that (4A.10) entails that consumption, and therefore saving, is predicted to be a function of the rate of interest. In Africa, many researchers have failed to confirm the existence of such a relation econometrically, in part because of the problem inherent in finding the right interest rate. For the case of Kenya, undoubtedly one of the most financially developed countries in Sub-Saharan Africa, Azam (1996) has found a significant impact.

The other important assumption made about the demand for money function in this chapter is that it produces an inflation Laffer curve in the steady state. This is a well-documented phenomenon, at least for African economies, illustrated in particular by the econometric analyses presented by Adam, Ndulu, and Sowa (1996) and Randa (1999). This requires us to impose some restrictions on the utility function. Let us first analyze the steady state, assuming that the rate of inflation is fixed for the whole future. Then, again using (4A.5), (4A.6), and (4A.7), or equivalently (4A.9) and (4A.10), one can easily find that c and m are also time-invariant, and can thus be treated parametrically in the dynamic analysis. The motion of the system is governed by the asset accumulation equation (4A.4) which may be written as

$$da/dt = ra - (r + \pi)m - c. \qquad (4A.12)$$

Equation (4A.12) shows that da/dt is an increasing function of a, for any value of c and m, treated parametrically, as explained above. This implies an explosive dynamics. It follows that this dynamic system has a unique steady state, which is a saddle point with a zero-dimensional convergent sub-space. We thus find $a = a_0$, $\forall t$, as any departure from this point would lead the system on a divergent path. It can readily be checked that all the trajectories where a is on a divergent path do not fulfill the transversality condition (4A.8), and can thus be ruled out.

Define $v(c, m)$ as the marginal rate of substitution between consumption and money, which measures the subjective value of liquidity services, as follows:

$$v(c, m) = \frac{u_m}{u_c}. \qquad (4A.13)$$

The steady-state values of the endogenous variables can then be calculated as the solutions to the following pair of equations:

$$ra_0 = (r + \pi)m + c, \tag{4A.14}$$

and

$$v(c, m) = r + \pi. \tag{4A.15}$$

The resulting demand for money function may be written as

$$m = m(r + \pi, ra_0). \tag{4A.16}$$

Interpreting ra_0 as the real income of the representative individual, we see that (4A.16) can be interpreted as a standard Keynesian liquidity preference function, with the demand for money being an increasing function of real income and a decreasing function of the nominal rate of interest.

Now, the crucial variable that determines the inflation Laffer curve effect is the elasticity of m with respect to the inflation rate. Recall that the proceeds of the inflation tax are governed by the function $\pi\lambda(\pi)$, whose derivative is here:

$$\frac{\partial \pi m}{\partial \pi} = (1 - \eta)m, \tag{4A.17}$$

where

$$\eta = \left| \frac{\partial \log m}{\partial \log \pi} \right| > 0, \tag{4A.18}$$

is the elasticity of the demand for money function with respect to the inflation rate. Its slope thus depends on the elasticity η just defined. The latter can be calculated by taking the total differential of (4A.14) and (4A.15), eliminating c, and rearranging the terms. It can be written as:

$$\eta = \frac{\pi(1 + v_c m)}{m(v_c(r + \pi) - v_m)}. \tag{4A.19}$$

Notice that $\eta > 0$ means that the denominator is also positive. In order to derive an inflation Laffer curve, we want this elasticity to be increasing in π, being at first below 1, and then becoming larger than 1 at some point as π becomes quite large. Examination of (4A.19) shows that $\eta = 0$ when $\pi = 0$, provided $\lim_{\pi \to 0} v_c > 0$, and that $\eta = 1$ if $\pi = m(v_c r - v_m)$. The latter is not an innocuous condition, and may be impossible to get with a finite and positive rate of inflation in some cases. The crucial condition for getting an inflation Laffer curve is:

$$\lim_{\pi \to \infty} \eta > 1. \qquad (4A.20)$$

If we assume that:

$$\lim_{\pi \to \infty} v_c \ll \infty \text{ and } \lim_{\pi \to \infty} |v_m| \ll \infty, \qquad (4A.21)$$

then we get:

$$\lim_{\pi \to \infty} \eta = \frac{1 + v_c m}{v_c m} > 1. \qquad (4A.22)$$

However, these conditions are not innocuous. For example, one may easily check that if the utility function is of the constant elasticity of substitution (CES) type, the condition for getting an inflation Laffer curve is that the elasticity of substitution between consumption and money be larger than 1. This is left as an exercise.

5 | *The public debt constraint in the CFA Zone*

5.1 Introduction

The exchange rate between the CFA Franc and the French Franc remained fixed from 1948 to January 1994. This was a credible commitment to prevent inflation. Exchange rate stability, obtained without exchange controls, had been made possible by two basic rules: (i) the ability of the governments of the member countries of the CFA Franc Zone to finance their deficits by printing money is drastically restricted, and (ii) the French treasury provides a virtually unlimited credit line (the "*compte d'opérations*") to the two central banks (the BCEAO in the UEMOA (West Africa), and the BEAC in the CEMAC (Central Africa)). Moreover, all member countries were required to pool a large share of their foreign reserves (generally 65%). Allechi and Niamkey (1994) argue that this is a net cost to participants. These two rules provide the CFA Franc with a guarantee of convertibility that makes it a "hard currency." As a result, it is an international currency in West and Central Africa, held as an inflation-proof asset by many people in Nigeria, the former Zaïre, etc. The governments of the CFA countries are thus able to extract some seigniorage from asset holders of neighboring countries.

The aim of the present chapter is to analyze the macroeconomic policies that were tried to restore macroeconomic stability after the commodity booms of the late 1970s, and the post-1986 crash of export revenues. Its focus is on the real exchange rate, seigniorage, and the

This chapter owes much to discussions with Patrick and Sylviane Guillaumont, and to written comments by Shanta Devarajan on Azam (2001b), on which the current chapter to some extent draws. Vittorio Corbo and Ibrahim Elbadawi also offered useful comments, which are gratefully acknowledged, with the usual disclaimer. Financial support by the AERC is gratefully acknowledged, without implicating. Some of these ideas were discussed at the 11th World Congress of the International Economic Association (Tunis), at the T2M Conference (Paris), and at seminars in Clermont-Ferrand, LSE, Ouagadougou, and Oxford. I wish to thank the participants for their comments, with the usual disclaimer. This chapter is an adapted version of Azam (1997).

public debt. As shown by Fischer (1983), the main opportunity cost of fixing the exchange rate might be a sub-optimal level of seigniorage. Here, I emphasize how the accumulation of public debt might result from the commitment not to use the inflation tax. I describe mainly the cases of the three large countries of the CFA Zone – Cameroon, Côte d'Ivoire, and Senegal – which have already attracted some attention (Devarajan and de Melo, 1987a). I add Burkina Faso to the list in order to represent the smaller and poorer economies of the Zone. A lot of background information on this country can be found in Zagré (1994).

I present a brief historical overview of the macroeconomic performance of these countries in section 5.2. Section 5.3 is devoted to a theoretical framework that helps us to understand the adjustment policies pursued in the 1980s and the first half of the 1990s. Its focus is on how the rules of the CFA Zone affect the determination of the debt/GNP ratio. I then discuss in section 5.4 the real-side adjustment strategy which was adopted until the end of 1993, aimed at stabilizing the economies without devaluing the CFA Franc. Section 5.5 reports on the reforms adopted during the summer of 1993, which contributed to making the January 1994 devaluation of the CFA franc unavoidable. Some provisional comments on the effectiveness of this historical policy move are also offered; a more thorough analysis is presented in chapter 8.

5.2 Historical overview

Most of the literature on the CFA Zone focuses on Cameroon, Côte d'Ivoire, and Senegal (e.g. Devarajan and de Melo, 1987a). Beside Gabon, which is a special case because of its oil wealth, they are the largest countries of the Zone in GDP terms. I also devote most of my attention to these countries in this chapter. However, the smaller countries of the Zone are also of interest, and I devote some attention to the case of Burkina Faso. This country is quite representative of the smaller countries of the Zone in terms of GDP, but it is a remarkable special case: unlike the other member countries, Burkina Faso did not sign an agreement for a SAP with the Bretton Woods institutions until 1991. This was partly due to a local tradition of conservative macroeconomic policy (Zagré, 1994), and partly to gold mining, which started in 1984 and provided a substantial flow of foreign exchange in 1987–90 (EAOIC, 1993).

Like most developing countries, the members of the CFA Zone are highly dependent on the export of a small number of primary

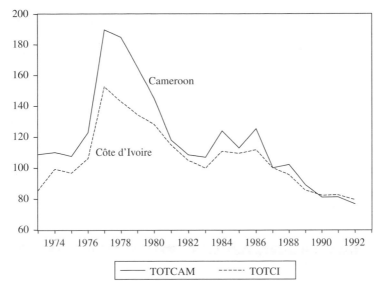

Figure 5.1. TOT: Cameroon and Côte d'Ivoire, 1974–1992, 1987=100
Source: World Tables 1995 (World Bank, 1995b).

commodities. They are thus subject to large external shocks, as international markets for primary commodities are especially volatile (Bevan, Collier, and Gunning, 1993). Figures 5.1 and 5.2 present the terms of trade series for the four countries under study. Cameroon and Côte d'Ivoire had an impressive export boom between 1975 and 1981. The latter benefited only from the international price increases for cocoa and coffee, while Cameroon benefited in addition from the oil shock, as it became an oil exporter in 1978. Benjamin, Devarajan, and Weiner(1989) analyze this shock, as does Devarajan (1999). The Cameroonian government is often praised for having bought foreign assets with the proceeds of the oil shock, in order to stretch out the resulting investment flow over time and avoid the "Dutch Disease." This view is challenged by Fielding (1995), who argues that a better rate of return could have been achieved by investing domestically. Ghanem (1999) and Azam and Morrisson (1994) analyze the commodity boom in Côte d'Ivoire, while Devarajan and de Melo (1987a) discuss the shocks and the subsequent adjustment policies in these three countries. The groundnuts and phosphates boom that hit Senegal started earlier, in 1974, and ended earlier as well, in 1978. Azam and Chambas (1999) describe this episode, and analyze the way

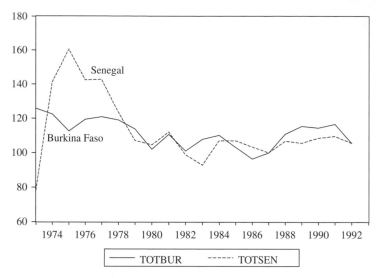

Figure 5.2. TOT: Burkina Faso and Senegal, 1974–1992
Source: World Tables 1995 (World Bank, 1995b).

in which the Senegalese government handled the shock. Burkina Faso
(previously called Upper Volta) did not benefit from any noticeable
trade shock during this period; its main export is cotton, which did
not enjoy a comparable boom. However, Burkina Faso benefited from
a large spillover from the Ivorian boom, because its labor market is
largely integrated with that of Côte d'Ivoire. Migrant workers from
Burkina Faso have gone to work on Ivorian plantations since colonial
days, and still provide a large share of the workforce in Côte d'Ivoire
(see, e.g., Azam, 1993; Azam and Morrisson, 1994; Zagré, 1994). A
large return flow of remittances thus follows: In 1981, workers'
remittances were worth US$ 109.8 million, representing 52.5% of
exports, and 19.9% of imports of goods and services. Côte d'Ivoire is
also a very significant outlet for Burkina Faso exports, and this trade
flow is one of the largest intra-ECOWAS trade flows (Ariyo and
Raheem, 1991). Some spillover effect thus also came through
increased demand by Côte d'Ivoire for goods from Burkina Faso.

Low inflation

The basic goal of the monetary unions is to provide a credible nominal
anchor to these economies, and this was achieved very successfully.

Table 5.1. Growth rates in the CFA Franc Zone, 1970–1993 (% per annum)

	Population 1980–93 (1)	GNP per capita 1980–93 (2)	GDP deflator 1970–80 (3)	GDP deflator 1980–93 (4)
(a) UEMOA				
Côte d'Ivoire	3.7	−4.6	13.0	1.5
Mali	3.0	−1.0	9.9	4.4
Burkina Faso	2.6	0.8	8.6	3.3
Niger	3.3	−4.1	10.9	1.3
Senegal	2.7	0.0	8.5	4.9
Benin	3.0	−0.4	10.3	1.4
Togo	3.0	2.1	8.9	3.7
(b) CEMAC				
Cameroon	2.8	2.2	9.0	4.0
Chad	2.3	3.2	7.7	0.7
Central Africa	2.4	−1.6	12.1	4.2
Congo	2.9	−0.3	8.4	−0.6
Gabon	1.7	−1.6	17.5	1.5
Equator. Guinea	n.a.	1.2	n.a.	−0.6

Source: World Tables 1995 (World Bank 1995b).

Columns (3) and (4) of table 5.1 show the growth rate of the implicit GDP deflator for the 1970–80 and 1980–93 periods, respectively. The first period witnessed a few inflation rates above 10%, whereas all the rates fall below 5% during the adjustment era. Figures 5.3 and 5.4 show the rates of inflation of the CPI. Most of the time, inflation remains below the 15% per annum threshold that Dornbusch and Fischer (1993) use for defining the range of moderate inflation. The only exceptions are associated with the commodity booms of the 1970s. The first oil shock in 1974 left its mark on most of these countries. The groundnuts and phosphates boom results in Senegal in the only peak above 15%, in 1975. The beverage boom led the inflation rate over 15% in Burkina Faso and Côte d'Ivoire in 1977. One also finds in figures 5.3 and 5.4 several examples of negative inflation, mainly during the commodity crashes of 1987 or 1988, for all the countries except Côte d'Ivoire.

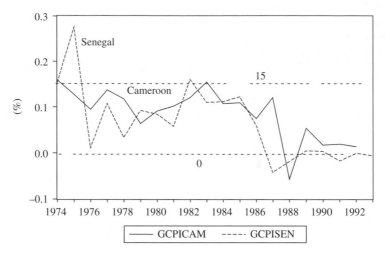

Figure 5.3. Inflation rates (%): Cameroon and Senegal, 1974–1992
Source: World Tables 1995 (World Bank, 1995b).

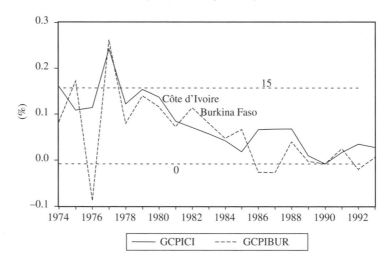

Figure 5.4. Inflation rates (%): Burkina Faso and Côte d'Ivoire, 1974–1992
Source: World Tables 1995 (World Bank, 1995b).

Notice that this good inflation performance was achieved despite the very rapid depreciation of the nominal exchange rate against the US dollar during the period 1980–5. The price of the dollar in CFA Francs increased at an average rate of 15.1% during these five years. Figure 5.5 represents the nominal exchange rate between the CFA Franc and the US

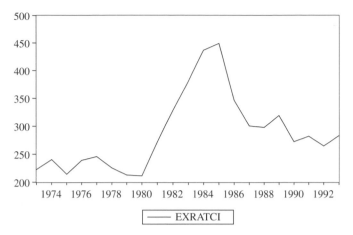

Figure 5.5. Nominal exchange rate: Côte d'Ivoire, 1974–1992, CFA Franc/US$; annual average: Côte d'Ivoire
Source: World Tables 1995 (World Bank, 1995b).

dollar. There was on average some depreciation of the CFA Franc, but one can see its gradual appreciation over the period 1986–93, which probably made adjustment to the post-1986 commodity price crash quite difficult. The *"franc fort"* strategy pursued by France over this period (Blanchard and Muet, 1993) was instrumental in bringing about this appreciation. It aimed at both stabilizing the French economy after the untimely expansionary policy adopted by the socialist government in 1981–3, and at giving France some kind of monetary leadership in Europe, on a par with Germany, in the process of groping towards the European monetary union (EMU).

Low growth

Without attempting to disentangle what is due to the negative terms of trade shock or to the inadequate policy responses adopted by the different countries, on the one hand, from what is due to the single fact of participating in the CFA Zone, as Devarajan and de Melo (1991) would have it, on the other, one can observe that the growth performance of the CFA countries was very poor throughout the 1980s and early 1990s. This is shown in column (2) of table 5.1, which presents the average growth rate of GNP *per capita* over the period 1980–93. With the exception of Chad and Equatorial Guinea, which are special cases, most countries have either a negative growth

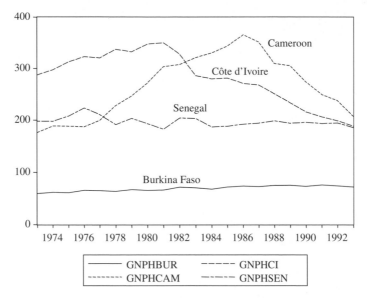

Figure 5.6. GNP *per capita*: Cameroon, Côte d'Ivoire, Senegal, and Burkina
Faso, 1974–1992, 000 1987 CFA Francs
Source: World Tables 1995 (**World Bank, 1995b**).

rate, or – like Burkina Faso – just above zero. The performance of
Côte d'Ivoire and Niger is especially dismal. The population growth
rates, presented in column (1), provide part of the answer: demographic growth is extremely high in these countries, especially in Côte
d'Ivoire (to a large extent because of immigration) and Niger. Hence,
except for the latter two countries, the growth rate of GNP is positive
on average for the CFA countries over this period.

Figure 5.6 represents GNP *per capita* for the four countries highlighted in this study. The three large countries show an interesting
example of convergence towards a common value of GNP *per capita*
at the end of the period, after fairly divergent trajectories. Senegal has
a stagnant series, with a nearly flat profile just wrinkled by the
groundnuts and phosphates boom of 1974–7, and the drought years
of 1978, 1981, and 1984. Côte d'Ivoire and Cameroon experienced
much wider swings. The former was regarded as an "economic
miracle" up to the end of the beverage boom of the late 1970s (Azam
and Morrisson, 1994). Thereafter, there was an uninterrupted
downward slide until 1994. Growth in Cameroon lasted much longer,
after the impulse of the 1978 oil bonanza. However, the downturn

came in 1988, after an unsustainable public investment boom in 1984–5. Notice that in both Côte d'Ivoire and Cameroon, the downturn arrived precisely when the SAPs with the Bretton Woods institutions began: 1981 in Côte d'Ivoire and 1988 in Cameroon. Similarly, the downturn came in Burkina Faso in 1992 after the first agreement with the Bretton Woods institutions was signed. The various governments probably called the Bretton Woods institutions when they correctly forecast the downturn. These economies are exposed to enough exogenous shocks to explain the downturn without blaming the Bretton Woods institutions.

This is shown clearly by comparing the growth rates of the two Sahelian countries, as is done in figure 5.7. Senegal, which had an SAP from 1979 to 1980, and Burkina Faso, which had one only in 1991, have highly correlated growth rates of GNP *per capita*. Except for the phosphates boom of 1974–7, figure 5.2 also shows that the terms of trade of these two countries are also highly correlated. The correlation between the growth rates of Cameroon and Côte d'Ivoire is not so close, as shown by figure 5.8. Nevertheless, one can contrast a positive growth period during the commodity booms, and a negative growth period after the 1987 crash, for the two countries. The main difference between these two series is that Cameroon went unscathed over

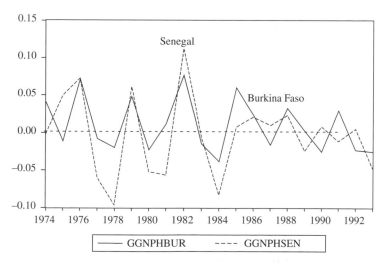

Figure 5.7. GNP *per capita* growth rates: Burkina Faso and Senegal, 1974–1992, % per annum
Source: Computed from World Tables 1995 (World Bank, 1995).

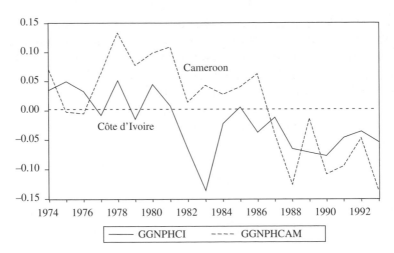

Figure 5.8. GNP *per capita* growth rates: Cameroon and Côte d'Ivoire, 1974–1992, % per annum
Source: Computed from World Tables 1995 (World Bank, 1995b).

the 1982–6 period, while Côte d'Ivoire fell into a deep recession. Part of the answer is probably the fact that Côte d'Ivoire was already heavily indebted during that period, while Cameroon had little debt to service at that time. Over that period, Côte d'Ivoire and Nigeria were the only problem debtor countries in Africa (Greene, 1989; World Bank, 1987a). Côte d'Ivoire had to go to the Paris Club and the London Club for important debt restructurings every year during the 1984–7 period. The burden of the ensuing debt service probably crowded out investment, according to the mechanisms emphasized by either Cohen (1993) or Eaton (1993). Demery (1994) shows that high debt service and low investment simultaneously plagued the Ivorian economy in the late 1980s and early 1990s.

The following analytical model provides a framework for understanding the adjustment strategies pursued in the CFA Zone. It focuses on the real exchange rate and the public debt, which are the two major macroeconomic variables to be analyzed in a fixed exchange rate system.

5.3 A theoretical framework

Denote by Y the level of income, p the price level, and e the nominal exchange rate. Define $q = e/p$ as the real exchange rate, and $\delta = d\log e/dt$

the rate of depreciation, which is exogenously given, $\pi = d \log p/dt$ the rate of inflation, and $g = d \log Y/dt$ the growth rate of the economy, also regarded as exogenous in what follows.

Denote by B the government deficit before debt service, net of grants, measured in terms of local currency. In the following, I assume that $b = B/pY$ is constant. It can be financed either by printing money, or by increasing debt D. Denote C the central bank credit to the government. For the sake of simplicity, assume that the whole public debt is owed to foreign lenders, and bears a unique interest rate equal to r^*. The government budget constraint can then be written:

$$d\,C/dt + e\,d\,D/dt = B + e\,r^*D. \tag{5.1}$$

The rules of the monetary unions

Beside the fact that δ is exogenous, the policy rules of the CFA Zone impose a ceiling on total credit by the central bank to the government, as a fraction of the fiscal revenues of the previous year. Denote T the real value of the taxes indexed on p (payroll taxes, excise taxes on non-traded goods, etc.), and $T^\$$ the dollar value of the taxes indexed on e (trade taxes, etc.). The government credit constraint (also called statutory allowance) may then be written:

$$C \leq \beta(p\,T + e\,T^\$). \tag{5.2}$$

Normally, β is equal to 20% in the UMOA and the BEAC. Up to the 1970s, few CFA countries had borrowed up to their statutory allowance, and the governments were not generally constrained by (5.2). Since then, this has changed drastically, and (5.2) can nowadays be regarded as holding with equality. Define $\theta'(q) = (p\,T + e\,T^\$)/pY$, and $\theta' > 0$ as the ratio of tax revenues to GDP. It is an increasing function of the real exchange rate, as a real depreciation of the currency increases the real value of the trade-related fiscal revenues. This results from the combination of various effects, including an "invoice effect," as the real depreciation increases the real value of a given level of trade flows, an increase in exports, and a fall in imports, both of which affect the level of trade-related tax revenues. I assume that the former two dominate the latter, which is negative. Then, denoting $\beta^* = \beta(\pi + g)$, the increase in government credit may be written, in the neighborhood of the steady state $(dq/dt = 0)$:

$$dC/dt = \beta^* \theta(q)\, pY. \qquad (5.3)$$

Hence, $\beta^*\theta(q)$ measures the authorized seigniorage as a percentage of income.

Notice that in the CFA Zone, the fiscal revenues indexed on the exchange rate are a highly significant share of total fiscal revenues. This was presented in table 2.1 using the data from Tanzi (1987, 1992).

The debt and real exchange rate dynamics

The main dynamic mechanism at work in this model concerns debt. Define $R = e\, D\, /pY$ as the debt/income ratio. Using the government budget constraint (5.1) and the government credit constraint (5.3), one can write:

$$dR/dt = b - \beta^* \theta\,(q) + (r^* - g + d \log q/dt)\, R. \qquad (5.4)$$

In the neighborhood of the steady state $(dq/dt = 0)$, this is a decreasing function of q. The mechanism at work here is very simple: a real depreciation allows the government to extract more seigniorage, by increasing the value of trade-related taxes, so that it can reduce its external borrowing.

The debt/income ratio becomes (locally) sustainable when $dR/dt = 0$. This occurs when:

$$R = (\beta^* \theta\,(q) - b)/(r^* - g + d \log q/dt). \qquad (5.5)$$

Let us call this the *sustainable debt locus*. One can find the steady-state value of R by putting $d \log q/dt = 0$ in (5.5). One thus finds:

$$R^* = \frac{\beta^* \theta\,(q) - b}{r^* - g}. \qquad (5.6)$$

It has a nice interpretation, as the present value of the excess of seigniorage over the fiscal deficit, using $(r^* - g)$ as the "natural" discount rate. The steady-state level of the public debt is thus equal to the present value of the future debt service flows. As I am interested only in the post-1982 era, I assume $r^* > g$ in the following. The steady-state debt/income ratio is then positive only if $\beta^* \theta(q) > b$. Moreover, the sustainable debt locus (5.5) is upward-sloping in the neighborhood of the steady state, as can be checked by differentiating (5.6) with respect to q.

The determination of the real exchange rate in the CFA Zone is not the main focus of this chapter, so I follow an extremely simplified approach. It is useful to assume that the real exchange rate q does not adjust instantaneously, but is instead groping sluggishly towards its equilibrium value q^*:

$$d \, q/dt \, = \, \alpha(q^* - q), \, \alpha \, > \, 0. \tag{5.7}$$

In the CFA Zone countries, as in many other Sub-Saharan countries, the usual dichotomy between traded and non-traded goods needs to be refined (Azam, 1991b; Delgado, 1992). Beside the goods that are traded on the international market, which Azam (1991b) calls "European goods," there are goods that are not traded with industrialized countries, but are involved in cross-border trade. They are called "African goods" by Azam (1991b). Some other goods are simply turned into imperfectly tradable goods at the margin by QRs that are made "softer" by smuggling. The price of these goods is more loosely linked to foreign prices than those of "European goods."

Among the motives for cross-border trade between CFA Zone countries and their neighbors, which may involve both "African goods" and restricted "European goods" (Azam, 1991a), there is the desire by many agents in the region to accumulate CFA Francs, either as an inflation-proof asset or as a vehicle for exporting capital to foreign banks in Switzerland or in London. This is due to the role of the CFA Franc as an international currency. Insofar as this external demand for CFA Francs grows, this mechanism results in a flow of international seigniorage, such that CFA countries are able to acquire goods from the neighboring countries at no real cost, as they are able to pay with fiat money rather than goods. This is an important element to be taken into account even in a very simplified framework. In order to do so, let us assume that:

$$\xi(q) \, p \, Y \, = \, d \, N/dt \tag{5.8}$$

where $\xi(q)$, $\xi'(q) > 0$ is the excess of CFA countries' demand for imperfectly tradable goods over the local supply (quotas included), as a percentage of income, while N is the quantity of CFA Francs held abroad. Assume that the latter grows at a constant rate n. Let $p^N Y^N$ be the relevant foreign income level, and define the equilibrium real

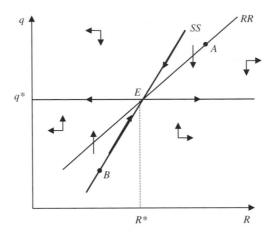

Figure 5.9 Determination of the solvency frontier *SS*

exchange rate as:

$$q = q^* \mid \xi(q^*) = n(N/p^N Y^N/pY). \tag{5.9}$$

In the following, I consider $(N /p^N Y^N)^*$, the foreign demand for CFA Francs, and $p^N Y^N/pY$, as exogenous. This captures in a simple way the impact of foreign seigniorage on the real exchange rate in CFA Zone countries: the more CFA Francs foreigners are willing to hold, the more imperfectly tradable goods are available in the markets of CFA countries, and the more depreciated is the real exchange rate.[1] However, this simplified model cannot be regarded as a satisfactory analysis of the determination of the real exchange rate in CFA Zone countries, as too many important determinants – such as the TOT, government expenditures, etc. – are neglected. But this extreme simplification enables us to focus on the most original features of the macroeconomics of CFA Zone countries.

One can analyze the properties of this system of two differential equations ((5.4) and (5.7)) using the phase diagram in figure 5.9. The locus $dq/dt = 0$, corresponding to (5.9), is labeled q^*. The real exchange rate q moves downwards whenever it is located above this locus, according to the mechanism sketched above. The upward-sloping locus labeled RR is the sustainable debt locus. The debt stock goes down (i.e. leftwards), as a

[1] An interesting extension of this model would take into account a wealth effect in the excess demand function for imperfectly tradable goods. Then, depending on whether or not the Ricardian equivalence is taken into account, R could appear as an argument of the $D(-)$ function.

ratio to the level of income, whenever q is located above this locus because, as seen above, real depreciation increases the authorized seigniorage, thus reducing the borrowing requirement of the government.

The joint dynamics of q and R result in the steady state E being a saddle point. There exists a unique pair of trajectories converging to E, that I label SS. Call this convergent sub-space the *solvency frontier*, because all the points on or to the left-hand side of SS belong to dynamic trajectories that converge either to a finite value of R or to a negative value of it. On the other hand, all points to the right-hand side of SS lead to a Ponzi game, as they are all heading towards an infinite positive value of R. Let us call R^* the equilibrium debt/income ratio.

Policy analysis and shocks

Figure 5.9 can be used to show a few of the pitfalls that can be met when using some standard arguments for assessing the macroeconomic situation of CFA countries. For example, take point A on the RR locus. At this point, debt is sustainable by construction, and the real exchange rate is under-valued, as q is above q^*. Nevertheless, the economy is not solvent, as this point is located on a Ponzi-game trajectory. This implies that there is a stable debt/income ratio associated with an appreciating currency. By contrast, point B is located to the right of RR, showing a non-sustainable debt level, and below q^*, showing an over-valued exchange rate; but this economy is perfectly solvent, as B is located on the solvency frontier SS. This entails an increasing debt/income ratio, associated with a depreciating currency.

Now let us use figure 5.9 to simulate the impact of the shocks that hit the CFA economies in the 1980s, and in particular the commodity crash of 1987. A downward shift in $\theta(q)$ – i.e. a fall in the ratio of tax revenues/GDP – makes the RR locus shift leftwards, as the cut in seigniorage leaves less room for servicing the debt. A monetary contraction is thus automatically added to a fiscal one, by the rules of the CFA Zone. The solvency frontier thus shifts to the left, as does R^*. If the economy was initially at E, and if q does not jump by an appropriate amount, then a solvent economy can be turned into a Ponzi-game one by such a shock. This is unsustainable, and calls for an adjustment policy. This is probably what happened to most CFA countries to some extent after the end of the commodity booms, and particularly after the 1987 commodities crash.

A public expenditure spree of the type experienced in Cameroon in the mid-1980s or in Côte d'Ivoire at the turn of the 1980s, captured here by an increase in b, also affects R^* and the location of the SS locus. We can see from (5.6) that the RR locus, and thus R^*, shifts leftwards. This is intuitive, as an increase in public expenditures, given the level of seigniorage, leaves less room for servicing the debt. Roughly speaking, the outcome is not fundamentally different from that of the negative external shock analyzed above. An economy that is initially solvent can be sent on a Ponzi-game trajectory by a public expenditure spree.

Another important shock that can result in the same outcome is the slowdown of growth. As seen above, this is especially relevant for Cameroon and Côte d'Ivoire, after 1988 and 1981, respectively. A glance at (5.6) shows that a fall in g entails a leftward shift of both RR and R^*. The solvency frontier SS shifts inwards as a result. Hence, the slowdown of growth is also likely to send the economy on an explosive debt path, even if it was initially perfectly solvent.

These shocks are the main types of problems faced by these economies during our period of analysis; they all met with external financing problems that forced them to change their policies. The rest of this chapter is devoted to a brief characterization of the adjustment policies adopted for solving this problem.

5.4 The real-side adjustment strategy

Côte d'Ivoire and Senegal started to adjust very early, with the help of the Bretton Woods institutions, while Cameroon and Burkina Faso, as seen above, started much later. This does not mean that the latter came out of the commodity booms without stabilizing their economies; but they did it without external support. Burkina Faso launched a process of *"auto-ajustement"* in the 1980s (Zagré, 1994). Although the details of the policies pursued in these countries can differ quite widely, some common elements can be singled out. Until the 1994 devaluation, the basic philosophy was that of real-side adjustment: All these countries had to cut public expenditures in order to stabilize their economies without changing the nominal exchange rate. The model presented above helps us to understand the basics of this strategy.

Ponzi-game trajectories cannot go on for a long period; the lenders soon realize that an economy embarked on such a course of action

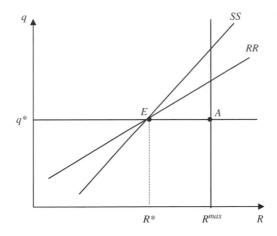

Figure 5.10. Imposing a ceiling on R

will face a crisis, and they will thus try to stop the process. In order to take into account in a simple way this type of external constraint on borrowing, assume that the international financial community is able to impose a ceiling on R:

$$R \leq R^{\text{max}}. \tag{5.10}$$

Assume that the lenders have enough insight not to impose $R^{\text{max}} < R^*$. It is natural to measure the debt overhang by $R^{\text{max}} - R^* > 0$, when (5.10) is binding. Figure 5.10 represents the case of an economy that is constrained by such a debt ceiling. For the sake of simplicity, assume that it is initially at point A. This is a simple way of taking into account the fact that, in this model, a debt problem is as likely to be met from a position of under- or over-valuation of the currency. Hence, assuming that the real exchange rate is initially in equilibrium is a natural starting point for this analysis.

The real-side adjustment strategy is simply aimed at shifting the solvency frontier to the right of A. Once this is achieved, then the RR locus can be allowed progressively to shift back to its initial position, following the gradual decrease in R. Hence, ideally, a successful real-side adjustment policy needs only a temporary and sharp austerity package to trigger a reflux of the debt/income ratio. However, the larger the debt overhang, the more severe it needs to be.

This move can be based on a cut in public expenditure. As can be seen by looking at (5.6), if b is cut without affecting $\theta(q)$, the RR locus shifts out. If the cut in the fiscal deficit is obtained by increasing taxes, the analysis becomes slightly more complicated, as an increase in seigniorage follows. The outward shift in *RR* is larger than above, which makes adjustment easier.

Côte d'Ivoire quite successfully pursued such a course of action for its first adjustment, after the beverage boom of the late 1970s was over (Azam and Morrisson, 1994; Demery, 1994). Its primary deficit was in surplus between 1984 and 1986 (Demery, 1994). In 1987, the country was regarded as a good pupil of the adjustment school, as most performance indicators had been met (World Bank, 1987a; Duruflé, 1988). This had been achieved mainly by cutting public investment. Kouassy and Bohoun (1994) argue that this lies at the heart of the Ivorian problem, as public investment crowds in private investment. This strategy reached its limit when it came to adjusting to the commodity crash of 1987. The problem was compounded because the president decided not to sell the cocoa crop in 1988, probably speculating on a price recovery, with the assurance that France would eventually bail him out if he turned out to be wrong (Azam and Morrisson, 1994). This episode destroyed any cred-itworthiness that Côte d'Ivoire had retained. The real and financial costs of the move were very high; the financial situation of the country became unviable, and new talks had to be opened with the Bretton Woods institutions in 1989. At that time, there was very little public expenditure remaining to be cut besides the wage bill. After the difficult electoral year of 1990, when Côte d'Ivoire discovered multiparty politics for the first time, the adjustment effort resumed only in 1991. However, very little effort was made to cut the government wage bill, which increased from 8% of GDP in 1985 to 12% in 1991 (Demery, 1994). Given the liquidity constraint faced by the government, the main way out of its payments problems was the accumulation of arrears, both internally (on its bills for the delivery of goods, subsidies or tax credits, etc.) and externally (relative to lenders other than the World Bank and the IMF). This progressively suffocated many firms that faced severe cash flow problems, and the whole economy.

Senegal similarly relied to some extent on public investment cuts for stabilizing its economy (Duruflé, 1988; Rouis, 1994). However, this country had two assets that the other CFA countries did not have. First, Senegal traditionally received a much higher level of aid *per capita* than any other African country (Rouis, 1994; Azam and Chambas, 1999). In 1991, net aid flow to Senegal amounted to US$ 84 *per capita*, or 12% of GDP *per capita* (Rouis, 1994). The reason for this privileged treatment is that Senegal was long regarded as a unique example of African democracy, with free competitive elections and a free press, and many donors wanted to show their support for democracy. The second asset that the Senegalese government possessed at the time of adjustment was a large portfolio of nationalized enterprises. The country had used the proceeds of the groundnuts and phosphates boom of 1974–7 to acquire several foreign firms, within a vast program of "Senegalization" of the economy (Azam and Chambas, 1999). A relatively large wave of privatization, mainly after 1989, helped to ease the need for adjustment. Moreover, as seen above, Senegal faced a less abrupt fall in its terms of trade than Cameroon and Côte d'Ivoire. Nevertheless, after a slow start to the adjustment process, Senegal got seriously involved in the late 1980s. A particularly spectacular and controversial move was the so-called "New Industrial Policy," which involved some trade liberalization. The tariff and non-tariff protection that many import-substitution firms were enjoying up to that point was lifted quite quickly (Chambas and Geourjon, 1992; Rouis, 1994). The controversy arose because most of the measures for liberalizing the labor market promised by the government during negotiations with the firms were never implemented, leaving labor costs quite high when firms faced increased competition (Chambas and Geourjon, 1992).

A common failure of the early programs of adjustment in both Côte d'Ivoire and Senegal was the attempt to mimic devaluation through a budget-neutral combination of an import tax and an export subsidy (Plane, 1994). In Côte d'Ivoire, the export subsidies were almost never actually disbursed to the firms (Azam and Morrisson, 1994), while the additional import tax triggered a large flow of smuggling, to the point that import-tax revenues decreased. A similar outcome, *mutatis mutandis*, resulted in Senegal (Plane, 1994). In short this textbook case turned out to be inapplicable in an African setting.

The real-side adjustment strategy had mixed results, depending on the countries and on the indicators used. We have seen above that inflation rates were very low during the period and that growth of GNP *per capita* was negative or near zero. Figure 5.11 focuses on the performance indicator emphasized in this chapter, the debt/income

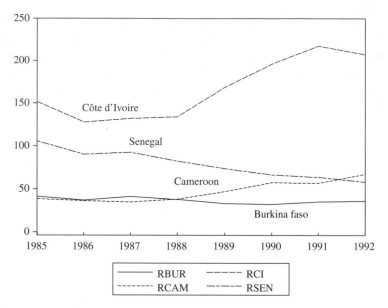

Figure 5.11. Debt/GNP ratio: Côte d'Ivoire, Senegal, Cameroon, and Burkina Faso, 1985–1992, %
Source: World Debt Tables 1993–94 (World Bank, 1995a).

ratio. One finds two groups of countries, with Burkina Faso and Senegal showing a falling debt/income ratio, while Cameroon and above all, Côte d'Ivoire have a growing ratio over the second half of the period. This is partly due to the low or negative growth of GNP. Notice, however, that this ratio also started to fall in Côte d'Ivoire in 1992. The next two years were to witness so many shocks that history will never tell us whether this was the beginning of a recovery, or a mere incidental event.

5.5 The historical devaluation

In 1993, Côte d'Ivoire was put under severe sanctions by the World Bank, which suspended all disbursements, adopting this radical position in order to obtain the decision that they felt was necessary for the resumption of growth: the devaluation of the CFA Franc. France managed to ease the pressure for a while by funding the Ivorian debt service to the Bretton Woods institutions. The IFIs were trying to undermine the resistance of President Houphouët-Boigny of Côte d'Ivoire, who had resolutely opposed this action before his death in December 1993. The decision to devalue had in fact been made in Paris early in the year. Only a few African governments accepted this idea at the time, and most remained to be convinced. However, what was regarded by some as a purely technical decision in the summer of 1993 turned out to make the devaluation unavoidable, by triggering an attack on the currency in August. The latter could be described as self-inflicted punishment, the predictable result of a thoughtless decision by the French treasury. The latter was in charge of the credit line opened in favor of the CFA Zone member countries, called the *"compte d'opérations,"* and had thereby acquired substantial bargaining power over the conduct of monetary policy. Unfortunately, the French civil servants had no understanding of the basics of monetary economics, as they had been trained to oversee the routine day-to-day management of the French government budget.

In June and July, the French treasury officials observed that CFA bank notes were being repatriated from Zurich and London. The rules governing the relationships between central banks were such that the BCEAO and the BEAC, the central banks of the two CFA monetary unions, had to pay the airfares for repatriating these bank notes. It then occurred to the French civil servants that this was a waste of money, and they convinced the African top officials of the central banks that costs could be saved. N'Guessan (1995) has shown convincingly that the central banks of the CFA Zone tended to react to any overheads, by displaying "bureaucratic behavior."

The flows of bank notes were mistakenly interpreted as the result of capital flight from within the CFA Zone, and the French and African officials involved were tacitly shocked by the capitalists' lack of civic spirit that these flows reflected, and were in favor of punishing them. Of course, this was based on a superficial analysis, as the resident investors were free to use other financial instruments to take their money out of the Zone because of the full convertibility of the CFA Franc that prevailed at the time. In fact, there was no massive capital flight from within the Zone. On the contrary, investors from neighboring countries with inconvertible currencies, especially from Nigeria, were facing serious problems in transferring their assets abroad. Many investors from south-west Nigeria used the banks in Cotonou (Benin) for their international financial operations, but people from other parts of Nigeria found it more convenient to transfer suitcases full of CFA bank notes directly: The "Alhaji" from Kano flying to London with a suitcase full of CFA Francs and a couple of bodyguards is a classic character in Nigerian stories. CFA Francs were thus kept by many savers outside of the CFA Zone as an inflation-proof asset, as good as the DM. By this mechanism, known locally as the "CFA pump," the countries of the CFA Zone were able to extract some seigniorage from their neighbors, with a favorable impact on the price level (see Azam, 1997a).

At the beginning of August 1993, the central bank of the WAMU, the BCEAO, gave in to French pressure and suspended the external convertibility of the CFA bank notes – its own notes as well as those from the neighboring Central African monetary union. The BEAC responded swiftly by suspending the external convertibility of the CFA Francs, i.e. refusing to buy CFA Franc bank notes, including West African ones and its own bank notes, if they came from outside its own monetary union. This was done obviously as a move to avoid being trapped with a large quantity of bank notes from its sister monetary union, but it was presented more aggressively as a gesture aiming at marking its dissatisfaction at having been kept out of the decision process, and at punishing the BCEAO for its unfriendly behavior. Although the idea was to stop capital flight, as they observed large numbers of bank notes being sold back to them by Swiss and English banks, the result was that the two monetary unions shot themselves in the foot.

Quite predictably, the outcome turned out to be worse than the initial problem, as the CFA immediately lost its international currency character. As we have seen, people in many neighboring countries had been using the CFA Franc as an inflation-proof asset, particularly in Northern Nigeria, where the Hausa traders had always had strong commercial ties with the Hausa traders from Niger, across the border (Azam, 1991a, 1991b). This was also true in Zaïre, stricken by hyperinflation, and in some other smaller countries of West Africa. Even in Ghana, CFA bank notes used to be accepted with a smile by traders in Accra markets. In fact, CFA bank notes were probably used as a vehicle for capital flight more by non-residents than by residents of the CFA countries, as the latter normally faced no controls on their movement of funds with the rest of the world.

Panic sales of CFA Francs resulted, as people desperately tried to reshuffle their portfolios in favor of other hard currencies, or even in favor of naira (the Nigerian currency) (Herrera, 1994; Grégoire, 1995). Within three days of these measures being taken, the naira went up from 10 (BEAC) CFA Francs/naira to 20 CFA Francs/naira on the Garoua parallel market in Cameroon, after an uninterrupted downward slide for more than ten years (Herrera, 1994). In Kano (Nigeria), it went from 8.2 (BCEAO) CFA Francs/naira to 11.8 on August 8, 1993 – i.e. an instant depreciation of 43.9% (Grégoire, 1995). A temporary shortage of hard currency bank notes occurred in many capital cities of the CFA Zone, and many Nigerians desperately bought goods in CFA countries in order to dump them at any price back in their own country.[2] These two effects probably had an inflationary impact in the CFA countries. The relative price of the two CFA Francs diverged on the parallel market, with the BEAC one falling 30% in terms of BCEAO CFA Francs (Herrera, 1994). For the first time, a parallel market developed for the CFA Franc.

Predictably also, the two central banks suffered very large losses of reserves after this thoughtless move. This can be seen graphically from figures 5.12 and 5.13, which represent the quarterly series of total reserves minus gold for the four countries under study, between 1992:1 and 1994:3. All these countries saw their reserves fall quite drastically after the policy change. This was not so pronounced for Côte d'Ivoire, which already had very few reserves to lose, but Cameroon's reserves were cut to a third, while those of Senegal, which were quite small initially, were halved. In Burkina Faso, which held quite substantial reserves, they fell by 50% within two quarters. It has been known for a long time that reserve losses of this size are a fairly certain lead indicator of a devaluation (see, e.g., Edwards, 1983).

In the end, the cost to the two monetary unions was enormous: estimates for the loss of reserves range from US$ 400 to US$ 610 million. Researchers present in the field at the time vividly described the panic triggered among Nigerian holders of CFA Francs by the decision (Herrera, 1994; Grégoire 1995). The attack started within three days, as CFA holders crossed the border in a rush to the banks to cash in their CFA notes for hard currencies. Within days, banks ran short of hard currencies, and the desperate Nigerians turned to the cattle market and to the consumer durable market. The price of cattle on the Adoumri market, near Garoua in north Cameroon, saw a price

---

[2] I owe this anecdote to Melvin Ayogu, then at Jos University (Nigeria).

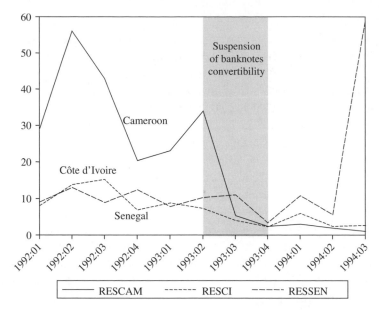

Figure 5.12. Total reserves minus gold: Cameroon, Côte d'Ivoire, and Senegal, 1992:01–1994:03, million US$
Source: International Financial Statistics (Washington, DC: IMF).

rise of more than 40% (Herrera, 1994). The capitalized value of all the international seigniorage accumulated over the years by the residents of the CFA Zone was rapidly recovered by foreign investors, within days of the decision. The currency crisis that affected the CFA Franc in August 1993 could thus hardly be called a "speculative attack"; it was rather the result of the *fait accompli* of the currency suddenly losing its international convertibility, making it worthless for foreign investors.

The massive loss of reserves inflicted on the CFA Zone member countries, at a time when they were receiving very little external support because of the waiting game being played between France and the IFIs over the devaluation of the CFA Franc, made a devaluation unavoidable, leading to the historic 50% devaluation that took place in January 1994, the first since 1948. This case illustrates that the building of a strong, credible institution such as the CFA system, supposed to be a strong agency of restraint, is no fool-proof protection against a currency attack. A large part of its credibility comes from its bureaucratization: as time passes, the institution becomes

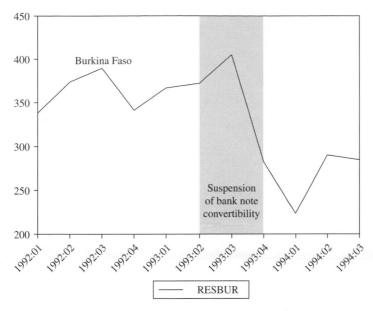

Figure 5.13. Total reserves minus gold: Burkina Faso, 1992:01–1994:03, million US$
Source: International Financial Statistics (Washington, DC: IMF).

more and more autonomous, shielded from outside shocks, and its routine behavior strengthens its commitment capacity. However, the price to pay is that the officials in charge progressively lose track of the role of their institution, as the rules governing promotions inside the system reward the ability mechanically to apply the fossilized rules of behavior, while any innovative action is regarded as a potentially dangerous deviation. This is very similar to the type of problems described by Stiglitz (2002), about the IMF under Michel Camdessus, including the fact that some French senior civil servants were also the core players in this game.

In terms of the theoretical framework presented above, such a move can be accommodated as a negative shock affecting the demand for CFA Francs by foreigners. It follows, by looking at (5.9) again, that q^* shifts downwards as a response to such a shock. Therefore, R^* shifts to the left, and this can create a debt overhang, as defined above. Hence, even if the country was perfectly solvent initially, the shock can send it on an explosive Ponzi-game path. This theoretical analysis clarifies how the decisions made in the summer of 1993 by the two central banks were the

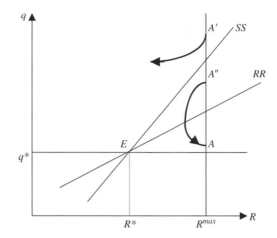

Figure 5.14. Impact of devaluation

final blows that jeopardized the real-side adjustment process, even for the countries for which it was already bearing some fruit.

On January 12, 1994, the CFA Franc was devalued against the French Franc by 50%. Many accompanying measures were hastily negotiated in the following weeks, including some debt relief and new agreements with the Bretton Woods institutions, involving new policy-based lending.

In terms of the model presented above, the aim of devaluation can be shown easily with the help of figure 5.14. Assume that the economy is initially in A, with a positive debt overhang. Then, if the price level is sluggish enough to allow for some effectiveness of a nominal devaluation, it is possible to move vertically upwards by increasing q. The aim of this exercise is to cross the solvency frontier SS, in order to escape from the attraction zone of the Ponzi-game trajectories, and reach a point such as A'. Then, the economy starts a movement towards the south-west, with a falling debt/income ratio, which can lead it to $R*$ (if A' lies on SS) or to eventually negative values of this ratio.

There are two risks involved in such an approach. First, the upward movement may be too small, so that the economy reaches only A'' instead of going across SS. This may occur if the price level reacts quickly to the increase in the price of foreign currencies, keeping the effectiveness of the devaluation rather low. If this point is located above RR, the economy responds initially by a south-westward movement, which looks like the trajectory starting in A'. However, the trajectory soon hits the RR locus, and then turns south-eastwards, heading again towards the debt ceiling R^{max}. The economy will go back to a debt overhang, again facing the prospect of devaluation. This analysis could then lead to a devaluation cycle, if the initial parity change were not large enough. Notice that an early debt relief enhances the chances of crossing the SS frontier, given the rate of devaluation.

The second risk of a devaluation strategy, especially for an international currency such as the CFA Franc which had never been devalued before, is to create a "Peso effect," whereby the newly revealed possibility of devaluation permanently reduces the rate of return on holding this currency, even when there is no precise expectation of a new devaluation. In terms of figure 5.14, this would shift q^* downwards. However, in the case of the 1994 devaluation of the CFA Franc, this risk had already been borne when the central banks shot themselves in the foot during the summer of 1993.

It is too early to offer a complete assessment of the effects of this devaluation; chapter 7 provides a more detailed analysis. It seems that it has succeeded in changing the real exchange rate, as the resulting increase in the price level was limited to about 47–50% in the UEMOA and 51–54% in the CEMAC two years after the 100% increase in the price of foreign currencies. This was quite effective, by the usual standards, with a real rate of depreciation in the range of 45–53% after two years. In particular, wages in the formal sector were extremely moderate, with no attempt made by the unions to catch-up on prices. As a Malian official said: "wages have not changed, but now they are actually paid!" The main difference was thus that public sector wages were paid on time, as arrears were progressively reduced. This wage and price moderation even resisted the elections in Côte d'Ivoire during the fall of 1995. The main worry that could be heard from officials was that fiscal revenues did not pick up as fast as had been expected, partly because of the fall in official imports.

The chances of success of the devaluation were also enhanced by the events simultaneously occuring in neighboring Nigeria. General Abacha took over the presidency after a *coup*, and decided to go back to the pre-1986 type of monetary arrangements, centralizing the sale of foreign currencies at the central bank, forbidding the parallel foreign exchange market which had been *de facto* legalized by the previous regime, and taking the previous governor of the central bank to a special court. All these measures undermined the confidence of the asset holders in the naira, restoring some attraction to the CFA Franc. The naira thus resumed its previous downward slide on the parallel market, providing some independent support to the CFA Franc (Grégoire, 1995). By September 12, 1994, the naira had recovered its CFA price of January 11, the day of the devaluation, in the parallel market in Maradi (Niger) (Dan Maradi, 1994). According to anecdotal and survey evidence, it seems that a strong diversion of intra-African trade has taken place, with the landlocked CFA Zone member countries becoming strongly competitive relative to the neighboring non-CFA countries. Official GDP growth series are discussed in chapter 7. Some member countries have evidently benefited tremendously from the devaluation, such as Côte d'Ivoire, which reached a GDP growth rate over 6% in 1995, with less than 10% inflation. Other countries, such as Cameroon, remained in a fairly difficult position for a while. However, the impact on poverty was unexpected, and is discussed at length in chapter 7.

5.6 Conclusion

This chapter has analyzed the macroeconomic policy reforms that were enacted in the CFA Zone in the 1980s and 1990s within a theoretical framework that emphasizes the trade-off between seigniorage and external debt as alternative ways of financing the fiscal deficit. We have seen that some of the usual tools for diagnosing macroeconomic problems can turn out to be 'quite misleading in the case of CFA countries. I have shown how a solvent economy could have both an unsustainable debt level and an over-valued currency, whereas another economy with a sustainable debt and an under-valued currency could just happen to be at the beginning of an explosive Ponzi-game path.

I used this framework to analyze how the CFA countries got into trouble after the shocks of the early and mid-1980s, because of external shocks or a public expenditure spree, or both. The post-1987 commodity crash seems to have been especially harmful. We saw that two main adjustment strategies have been applied. The real-side adjustment strategy was aimed at restoring solvency by cutting public expenditures and raising taxes. It did not provide quick results for

Cameroon and Côte d'Ivoire; the central banks then decided to suspend the external convertibility of bank notes, which caused a wave of flight against the CFA Franc, resulting in massive reserve losses. Devaluation then became unavoidable, and was enacted in January 1994. Its effectiveness seems to have been quite high after the first few years, with real growth picking up quite rapidly in some countries, as we shall see in chapter 7.

6 | Currency crises, food, and the "Cola nut" effect

6.1 Introduction

After the Mexican crisis of December 1994, the Asian crisis of 1997 attracted a lot of attention related to the fragility of the international financial system, as did the Russian and Brazilian ones that followed. Stiglitz has used these events as the basis from which to launch a stinging attack against the IMF (Stiglitz, 2002). Although his argument has more nuance, many readers have understood his book as either an outright criticism of globalization, or as a case against capital account liberalization. I had the privilege of being the discussant of his presentation at a plenary session of the AERC in Nairobi in December 1998, where he discussed many of the ideas developed in his later book. He presented a very detailed discussion for analyzing the relatively rare and spectacular events that are currency crises, taking the case of the Asian crisis as his main source of examples. The most important message of his presentation was no doubt that financial markets are in fact dealing in information, so that financial and currency crises can provide a lot of information on the underlying trends in the economy. He blamed the occurrence of the Asian crisis, at least to a large extent, on the real estate speculation that was going on, with too much production of empty office space. A lot of non-performing loans were thus piling up on the banks' accounts. However, other researchers tend to conclude that currency crises are to a large extent self-fulfilling, and thus provide very little information on the fundamentals of the affected economy. In particular, Eichengreen, Rose, and Wyplosz (1995) have argued that the empirical evidence leans in favor of diagnosing most currency crises as

A preliminary version of a part of this chapter was given as discussant to Joe Stiglitz's plenary presentation at the AERC Biannual Meeting of December 1998 in Nairobi. Comments on my oral presentation by Chris Adam, Jan Gunning, and Chris Udry are gratefully acknowledged, without implicating. The chapter also draws on Azam and Bonjean (1995), and on Azam and Samba-Mamadou (1997).

of the self-fulfilling kind. In this case, the information content of the crisis is pretty weak.

In my comments, I wanted to point out that African currency crises are unduly neglected, as they provide very interesting examples that can shed some valuable light on the theoretical debate, although they rarely hit the newspaper headlines. The first part of the present chapter is an extended version of these comments. The main message of the following analysis is that you do not need to liberalize the capital account to trigger a currency crisis. What matters is either that the government has, one way or another, reduced the desirability of holding its own currency for many agents, or that some external events have had the same effect. Even a deficient financial sector cannot prevent a crisis from occurring in such circumstances, as the goods market can provide the alternative assets that speculators need – they can import consumer durables, such as cars or livestock. In poor countries, in particular, the food market is, unfortunately for the poorest, also an asset market, and I proceed inductively to show this point. This is discussed in section 6.2, based on the case of Madagascar, which had a currency crisis in May 1994, involving a nominal depreciation of 56.5%. There is clear evidence that paddy was, for most of that year, the main asset that households held, because of their lost confidence in the local currency: in the course of a yearly production cycle, paddy is clearly an inflation-proof asset to hold.

In chapter 6, I have extensively discussed the attack against the CFA Franc which took place in August 1993. The CFA episode is especially interesting, as it illustrates the following proposition in favor of a liberalized capital account: restricting capital mobility is also a dangerous route that can trigger a currency crisis. In this case, under the influence of the French treasury, the central banks of the CFA Zone suspended the external convertibility of the CFA Franc bank notes, which were held as inflation-proof assets in many countries of the region. For many people from these neighboring countries, they also served as a vehicle to get their capital out. The punishment came very swiftly, without involving any sophisticated financial instruments, as CFA Franc holders from neighboring countries simply crossed the border to get rid of their CFA Franc holdings. They bought first whatever hard currency was available in the local banks, and then purchased any type of assets that were on offer, including a lot of livestock, in the Sahelian area. No capital flight was really involved, and so the currency crisis could not have been avoided by restricting capital mobility further. The Malagasy experience took place in an institutional framework where capital movements are limited by the external inconvertibility of the currency. Other avenues were open to vent the flight against the currency, and in this case it was the paddy market that provided the alternative asset. This analysis is developed in section 6.3, which discusses the special role of food as an asset in poor countries. The Guinean failed speculative attack of July–November 1996 illustrates that, when the attractiveness of a currency comes from the good reputation of the governor of the central bank that issues it, as described in chapter 4, then changing the governor involves a serious risk. In this case, disaster was avoided thanks to the huge reserves that had been accumulated beforehand. The failure of the attack provided significant information about the new governor, who was ready to invest substantial reserves to defend the exchange rate.

Another interesting speculative attack took place in Kenya in 1991. I have already shown in chapter 4 that some instability had prevailed in this country in the 1980s, probably because of the inappropriate rule of behavior chosen by the central bank for pricing foreign exchange. In 1991, the IFIs imposed on Kenya a financial sector liberalization which sent the nominal magnitudes astray, and the banking sector went through a crisis. This is a very good example of an African speculative attack which conforms to the Stiglitz case sketched above. Kenya undoubtedly has one of the most developed financial sectors in Africa (see, e.g., Azam and Daubrée, 1997). The government responded to the attack, and to the downward slide taken by the Kenyan shilling, in a very interesting way, which is probably inaccessible to many other, less developed, African countries. It issued some interest-bearing government bonds with a very high interest rate. In modern parlance, this might be viewed as a way of mimicking the so-called "Taylor rule," with a very "active" reaction function, as described by Benhabib, Schmitt-Grohé, and Uribe (2002). It worked beautifully, as the footloose capital immediately returned, leading in fact to some temporary over-valuation. I shall provide an analysis of the collapse of the Nigerian naira which occurred in September 1994 in section 6.4. My claim is that this was a "contagion" effect from the CFA devaluation, which illustrates a case of an "African Tequila" effect. I would rather call it the "Cola nut" effect, out of respect for the local cultural setting. This suggests that, like the Latin American or East Asian crises, African currency crises can get transmitted to a neighbor across the border, as the present value of future trade flows is reduced, with a negative impact on wealth.

Before that, in section 6.3, I present briefly the three generations of currency crises models, in a synthetic way. This literature may become quite technical at times, using models involving some kind of Phillips curve, whose relevance for Africa remains to be proved. My presentation focuses on the bare essentials, using a model of seigniorage based on Dornbusch (1987), which permits sufficient extensions to grasp the main points.

6.2 Food as an asset, and the Malagasy currency crisis of May 1994

One of the most damaging effects of currency crises in Africa is that they usually involve speculation on some food items. Most foods are storable, at least for a while, but this is most obvious for grain and livestock. We have already seen when discussing the CFA crisis of August 1993 that the price of cattle reacted very briskly to the speculation, with some evidence from the Adoumri market in northern Cameroon. However, this is arguably a particular type of attack, concerning an international currency, widely held abroad, and responding to an obvious blunder by the monetary authority in restricting the international role of the CFA Franc.

The unsuccessful speculative attack against the NGF that lasted from July to November 1996 was also a response to a visible policy change. It seems to correspond to the type of "probing attacks" analyzed by Krugman (1997). The event that triggered this attack was the removal of governor Yansané from the central bank, after ten years of rigorous resistance against the politicians' demands for increased central bank credit for the government. The president succumbed to "rigor fatigue," and decided to put a new governor in charge. While governor Yansané had invested for ten years in building a strong reputation of "conservative central banking" (see Azam, 1999a, and chapter 4 in this volume), the newcomer had no reputation. The market could not know that the newcomer was basically coming from Yansané's school; an unsuccessful "probing attack" took place immediately after the news of Yansané's departure became known, and lasted until November. However, the reserves of the central bank were very high, and the bank won the battle, despite pressure from the IMF to give in. The attack subsided in November, after the new governor had paid the price for a strong reputation as a rigorous central banker. According to the accounts that I got from interviews in Conakry, the speculators were accumulating either paddy or consumer durable goods such as Mercedes cars and other luxuries. Storage capacity was full at the time when the attack ended.

The Malagasy case

The currency crisis that affected the Malagasy Franc in May 1994 is a much more representative one, in that it seems to have been devised to illustrate the seminal analysis contained in Krugman (1979), or at least some of its later developments. The analysis of the Mexican crisis presented by Edwards (1997), in particular, looks like a road map for analyzing the Malagasy one. However, it involves many institutional features that are clearly irrelevant in the latter case, which took place in a much simpler setting. Azam (2001a) analyzes the Malagasy experience in a broader historical perspective, focusing on the causes of inflation and macroeconomic instability.

The attack against the currency occurred after a prolonged period of real appreciation (over 1992–4), as illustrated by figure 6.1. The central bank responded to the attack by a temporary move to floating. As in Krugman's classic analysis, this currency crisis occurred against a background of falling central bank reserves, as a ratio to domestic credit, over 1992–4, and of a massive increase in central bank credit to the government over the same period. This lax monetary policy was the mark of the government elected in 1991, after a short period of political turmoil. As a result, the May 1994 attack entailed a 56.5% depreciation of the Malagasy Franc. Figure 6.1 shows that, as far as the impact on the real exchange rate was concerned, this depreciation was effective for about two years, before the real exchange rate returned to its initial level.

The discussion of the behavior of the paddy market presented below highlights the fact that the financial markets did not play a crucial part in this attack against the currency. What was really important was the loss of confidence in the local money, due to the unrestrained expansion of credit from the central bank to the

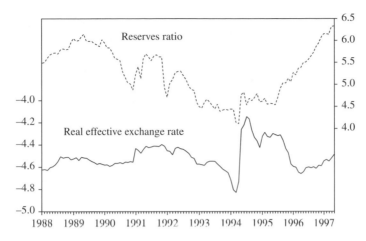

Figure 6.1. Reserves ratio and real effective exchange rate: Madagascar, 1988:01–1997:05
Note: Log scales.

treasury. This comes out very clearly from figure 6.2, which shows that the new government elected in 1991 was increasing the level of credit to the treasury at a rapid rate. The latter had been reduced drastically by the previous government, with a view to stabilizing the economy, in the wake of the 1987 devaluation. The price level was going up sharply, with accelerating inflation, and the increase in the inflation rate before the currency crisis is shown in figure 6.2. A crucial difference between currency attacks in poor countries, relative to richer ones, is the role played by the markets for some staple foodstuffs. Most staples can be stored, at least between two harvests. For rural people, granaries and herds play a major role for accumulating savings. Food, as we have seen, is often used as the main inflation-proof asset by the majority of poor people, as they have little access to hard foreign currencies (with the notable exception of the CFA Franc in neighboring countries). Nevertheless, we have seen that the cattle market in northern Cameroon responded very rapidly to the August 1993 speculative attack against the CFA Franc. A similar effect has been observed in Madagascar involving the rice market.

Other agricultural goods also serve as a store of value, even if they deteriorate rapidly. The data presented by Azam, Collier, and Cravinho (1994) show how peasants in Angola were keeping their crops in store while the currency had been almost demonetized. This

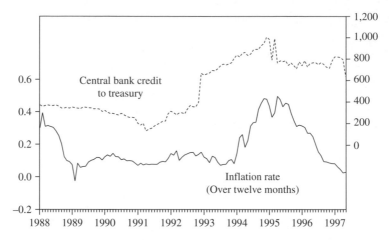

Figure 6.2. Central bank credit to the treasury and inflation rate: Madagascar, 1988:01–1997:05

was a response to the shortage of goods on the official market, where prices were controlled, and high inflation on the parallel market. By the mid-1980s, prices on the parallel market were around fifty times those on the official market. This flight against the currency was due to heavy deficit financing of military expenditures and support to loss-making public enterprises. The Angolan Coffee Board estimated that by the mid-1980s eight years' production were stored at the household level. A minor liberalization occurred in 1986, and prices on the parallel market for consumer goods began to fall consistently. The rate of return on holding money suddenly became positive, while that on holding agricultural goods remained negative, because of deterioration, pests, risk of theft, etc. Crop sales in 1988 were three times larger than in 1986, in real terms; this strongly suggests that the peasants' portfolio behavior was an integral part of the theory of agricultural supply response.

A simple model of food price determination

The simple model presented by Azam and Bonjean (1995) to explain the formation of the price of rice in a closed economy can help us to understand this phenomenon. It belongs to the line of analysis which analyses food markets as asset markets, following Working (1949), Samuelson (1957), and Ravallion (1985). It differs from these models in that it does not assume that some agents derive some utility from the simple fact of holding inventories, as Working and Ravallion do and, unlike Samuelson, it allows for expectations errors. The latter uses "back-to-back" diagrams, which are less convenient that that used by Azam and Bonjean, and reproduced in figure 6.3 (p. 143), which depicts the joint determination of the present and future prices.

Let us call "rice" the food item analyzed here. In order to focus on the seasonality of the marketing of rice, assume that there are only two seasons: harvest time and the lean season. Decomposing the seasons into a larger number of periods would not raise any conceptual problem; in the case of paddy in Madagascar, the harvest takes place between June and September, with a peak in July. Rice cannot be stored for more than two months without deteriorating, but unhusked paddy can be stored for about eighteen months. In Madagascar, there is no shortage of husking capacity, with a fairly homogeneous transformation rate of 67%. People thus store bags of paddy, and get it husked whenever they need it. The price of rice has a very typical seasonal profile, with a steady rise from June to May, interrupted by a fall in May, or just before, when the new harvest begins, and storage capacity has to be cleared for housing the new crop. Azam and Bonjean (1995) show that the real price of rice in the central market of Antananarivo, the capital city of Madagascar, is stationary at the seasonal frequency. This means that the real price of rice in each given month of the year is generated by a stationary stochastic process.

In Madagascar, most households store bags of paddy: I knew of a judge, related to the fellow economist who was working with us in our fieldwork, whose house was filled with bags of paddy. For the sake of clarity, it is nevertheless convenient conceptually to distinguish the traders from the other households, peasants, or consumers. If some rice is held by the traders between the harvest and the lean season, then the following arbitrage equation must hold:

$$\frac{1-\gamma}{1+r}p^e = p^H \qquad (6.1)$$

where p^H is the current price of rice, at harvest time, and p^e is the price expected to prevail in the lean season. The relevant rate of interest is r, and the cost of storage is γ, expressed as a percentage loss, and assumed constant. In most developing countries, the relevant rate of interest must be evaluated as the opportunity cost of capital, because of credit market imperfections that prevent most traders from approaching formal banks. This arbitrage equation (6.1) says that the trader holds an inventory of rice if the expected increase in price, between the harvest and the lean season, pays for the storage cost and the opportunity cost of capital. If the expected price were higher than this, then storage would go up, pushing the current price upwards, and if it were lower, then storage would go down, leading to a reduction in the current price.

Let H denote the size of the harvest, and assume that consumption demand at harvest time is given by $D^H(p^H)$, with a negative slope. The quantity purchased at harvest time for storage must then be, in equilibrium:

$$S(p^H, H) = H - D^H(p^H). \tag{6.2}$$

Obviously, the assumption that H is given is a simplification, which is acceptable in the island of Madagascar, which may be regarded as a closed economy as far as rice is concerned. Paddy or rice is a low-value ponderous good, which is worth importing only by a cargo of at least 10,000 tons, which implied in 1992 a financing worth about US\$ 2.5 million. It happens occasionally, but does not respond in a precise way to the day-to-day fluctuations of the market. Nevertheless, it would be easy to make H an increasing function of the market price, by adding some imports, at each season. This would better fit the case of other African countries with inland borders. Assume that the consumption demand at the lean season is $D^L(p^L)$, also with a negative slope. Then, the lean-season market equilibrium requires:

$$D^L(p^L) = (1 - \gamma)S(p^H, H). \tag{6.3}$$

The model is determined by defining expectation error as:

$$p^L = p^e + \varepsilon. \tag{6.4}$$

Azam and Bonjean (1995) discuss various possibilities of generating ε, including also the case of adaptive expectations, but it is more natural to assume that it is drawn at random, as in the standard rational expectations hypothesis. The model can then be solved for $\{p, p^e, p^L\}$, treating $\{H, \varepsilon\}$ as parameters. This is done graphically in figure 6.3, for the perfect foresight equilibrium, assuming $\varepsilon = 0$. The

upward-sloping curve represents the stock of rice left after the consumers have purchased their share of the harvest, as a function of the
price prevailing at that time, as described by (6.2). This can also be
regarded as the inverse supply curve of rice for storage at harvest time,
giving the market price as a function of the stock left. The dotted
curve drawn above it scales up the harvest-time price by the inverse of
the discount factor used in (6.1). The resulting curve thus represents
the price expected by the traders to prevail at the lean season. The
downward-sloping curve is simply the demand by consumers at the
lean season, scaled up to account for the storage loss.

The perfect foresight equilibrium is found as depicted in figure 6.3,
where the lean-season price is equal to the expected price. The harvest
time price can then be derived immediately from the graph. The prices
prevailing at the two seasons are derived at once, given the value of
the expectations error. In figure 6.3, the latter is assumed nil. One
simply finds that the equilibrium price pair will be found along a
vertical line located more to the left, if the expectations error is
positive, driving a wedge between the two curves. If the error com-
mitted is very large, then a famine can result, with the price of rice
becoming out of reach of the poorest consumers during the lean
season, while it is depressed at harvest time. The traders will not have
stored enough, because they did not expect the price to go up so
much. Sen (1981) and Ravallion (1987) have documented the role of

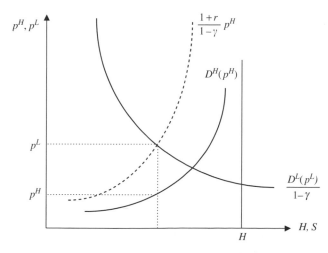

Figure 6.3. Joint determination of harvest-time and lean-season rice price

speculation and high food prices in triggering several famines, and this simple model sheds some light on these events. Conversely, if the expectation error is negative, traders have over-stored, and the equilibrium is found to the right of the perfect foresight one. The prices are too high at harvest time, and peasants get richer, while urbanites face some hardship. This is what happened in 1992, when we did our survey of the rice market in Madagascar with Catherine Bonjean, Laurence Kent, Emilienne Raparson, and others: prices were too high for the first part of the year, and eventually fell before May, in part because some unexpected food aid arrived during the spring.

This model can be slightly extended by making the expectation error about the lean-season price a function of the expectation error about the size of the crop – or, more generally, about the quantity of paddy available in the country. Assume that the traders form their expectations about the lean-season price on the basis of their knowledge of the functions $D^L(.)$ and $D^H(.)$, of r and γ, and p^H, which they observe at harvest time. But they do not know H at this point. Let H^e be their expectation about H, formed at harvest time. Then, under the rational expectation hypothesis, it must be true that:

$$D^L(p^e) = (1 - \gamma)[H^e - D^H(p^H)]. \qquad (6.5)$$

Let $H = H^e + \xi$, where ξ is the expectation error about the size of the crop. Then, subtracting (6.5) from (6.3), and substituting from (6.2), we get:

$$D^L(p^L) - D^L(p^e) = (1 - \gamma)\xi. \qquad (6.6)$$

Using a Taylor expansion $D^L(p^L)$ of about $p^L = p^e$, we find:

$$D^L(p^L) = D^L(p^e) + \varepsilon D^{L'}(p^e), \qquad (6.7)$$

and thus:

$$\varepsilon = \frac{1 - \gamma}{D^{L'}(p^e)}\xi. \qquad (6.8)$$

There is therefore a negative relationship between the expectation error about the lean-season price and the expectation error about the crop size, or the available quantity of paddy in the country, allowing for imports.

To sum up, this very simple model shows how the market for a storable staple such as rice in Madagascar can be analyzed like an

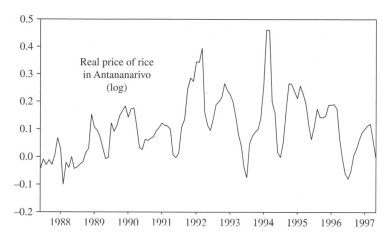

Figure 6.4. The real price of rice: Madagascar, 1987:06–1997:05

asset market, as storage is required to bridge the gap between the harvest and the lean season. The seasonal increase in price is required to compensate the traders for the cost of storage and the opportunity cost of capital. It follows that rice, or more precisely paddy, is the most commonly held asset among Malagasy households for most of the year. This does not work in May, or just before, as the price then usually collapses. Figure 6.4 shows the seasonal pattern of the price of rice in Madagascar, after the 1987 reforms had been completed (see Azam and Bonjean, 1987; Berg, 1989).

The price of rice in Antananarivo in 1993–1994

During the year preceding the 1994 currency crisis, paddy has been the star performing asset in Madagascar: those who bought paddy in June 1993 and sold it in March 1994 made a record real return of 49.8%. Figure 6.4 represents the time profile of the real price of rice in the central market of Antananarivo, the capital city of Madagascar, over roughly a decade. It clearly shows that the trough-to-peak increase in the real price of rice that occurred over the 1993–4 season was impressive by historical standards. Comparing figure 6.4 to figure 6.1 shows that the currency crisis of May 1994 occurred at the end of a highly profitable speculation on paddy. Its price was low in real terms at harvest time, but eventually reached a historical high by the end of the lean season. According to the theoretical analysis performed in figure 6.3, this might reflect either a positive expectation error about the lean-season price, or a large opportunity cost of capital. The latter was probably enlarged by the expected devaluation: while the fall in reserves seen in figure 6.1 fueled a flight from the domestic currency, the exchange rate was probably protected from the speculative attack as long as the paddy market offered a highly performing asset.

However, seasonality implies that rice necessarily has a negative own rate of return in May, when the new harvesting season starts. Then, over a month or two, speculators need to find an alternative asset to hold, and the attraction of foreign currency then becomes high, despite the fixed costs involved because of the highly imperfect banking sector. I was unable to find a parallel market for foreign currency in Antananarivo, during my visits in 1992 and 1997. My experience in other African countries is that, as a European visitor, if you cannot find the parallel market, the latter usually can find you. This happened to me even in Mozambique in 1987, where the *"candongeiros"* (illegal traders) faced severe penalties if caught. It also happened to me in Addis Abeba in February 1992, just after the fall of the Derg regime, when Tigrayan boys were controlling the capital city. It thus seems that the local currency is nearly convertible in Madagascar, at least over the period under study. The *World Currency Yearbook* gives a premium of 7.1% in 1990, 12.4% in 1994, and 5.4% in 1995. By African standards, these premiums are very low, which suggests that people are generally able to run on the central bank's reserves in Madagascar, as well as those of the formal commercial banks, directly or using some intermediary. It would probably have been profitable to import rice at some point during 1994–5, but this did not happen because of financing problems. The ability to access foreign exchange, or credit, was thus probably restricted for the rice importers, and one may guess that reserves were pretty low in May 1994, relative to the demand for foreign exchange. The central bank was thus unable to resist when some of the gainers from the ending speculation on rice came to acquire foreign exchange.

In fact, the previous speculative attack against the Malagasy Franc (FMG) also took place in May and June in 1987, and ended up with a 48.5% depreciation. The story is less clear cut then than in 1994, because it came at the end of a reform process, initiated by a SAP with the Bretton Woods institutions. Not surprisingly, however, the liberalization of the rice market was the mainstay of the reform program in 1985–7 (Berg, 1989). Several currency problems also occurred in Madagascar, such as the devaluation of June 1986 (by 22.4 %), after a rapid increase in the price of rice documented in Berg (1989) and Azam and Bonjean (1995), and then two smaller ones, not obviously connected with this seasonal pattern, in March 1984 (15.2%) and in January 1991 (12.2%) (see Azam, 2001c). The latter was probably related to the political turmoil going on at that time; a glance at figure 6.4 shows that the rice market reacted strongly to these political events, which entailed a change in government, but there was no second devaluation in the course of the year. This analysis suggests that the real price of paddy, deflated by the CPI, should be used by the central bank as part of a potential early warning device for speculative attacks against the FMG. Moreover, this link between the price of foreign currency and the real price of food demonstrates that speculative attacks are liable to create significant hardship for the poor, through their impact on the real price of food. In this case, an early devaluation might be a progressive measure, by relieving some of the speculation on rice.

This section has shown that speculative attacks, or other forms of currency crises, can occur even with a very under-developed financial market. Humans have been storing food at least since the end of the ice age, 13,000 years ago (Diamond, 1997), and this provides an asset that can compete with money. The crucial fact to understand therefore is why the demand for money may sometimes abruptly fall, forcing the central bank to run out of foreign reserves, and to give up its preferred exchange rate. Many models have been offered to explain this fact, since Krugman's seminal analysis (Krugman, 1979). It is customary to classify these models by "generation," depending on the factor that triggers the attack, and on its type. I present the main point of the three generations that I know of, using the simplest setting of all, derived from Dornbusch (1987).

6.3 The three generations of currency crisis models

The seminal model of currency crisis is due to Krugman (1979), but I use here a simpler setting, due to Dornbusch (1987). Let the balance sheet of the central bank be given by:

$$M = R + B \qquad (6.9)$$

where M is the quantity of money, R the stock of reserves, and B the outstanding credit to the government. Commercial banks are neglected, and the central bank is the only issuer of money. The government is assumed to raise no taxes, and its expenditures g are financed by the "printing press":

$$dB/dt = pg. \qquad (6.10)$$

As in chapter 4, the analysis is restricted to rational expectations equilibria, and the demand for money is again given by $\lambda(\pi)$.

Initially, the government maintains the exchange rate fixed which, again neglecting non-traded goods, means that $\pi = 0$. On the one hand the price level is fixed by this exchange rate, and on the other the real quantity of money is fixed at $m = \lambda(0)$. It follows that:

$$dM/dt = dp/dt = 0. \qquad (6.11)$$

Differentiating (6.9) with respect to time, and using (6.10) and (6.11) yields:

$$dR/dt = -dB/dt = -pg. \qquad (6.12)$$

As the initial stock of reserves is necessarily finite, (6.12) shows that this policy package, involving a fiscal deficit and a fixed exchange rate is not sustainable. Reserves are gradually going down, and the moment will come when the government will have to change its policy. The beauty of Krugman's analysis is to show that the gradual process of reserves depletion will not go on smoothly until the stock runs out, but will instead involve a sudden speculative attack where the speculators will capture all the remaining reserves at once. This is done by assuming that after the attack the government, which is deprived of all reserves at that time, lets the exchange rate float freely.

The aim of the following exercises is to show that the main results of the so-called "three generations" of currency crisis models can be got in this simple setting, by slightly changing either one of two assumptions. Let us start by presenting the first-generation version of the model.

First generation

The crucial point to grasp to understand the following is that the price level cannot jump discontinuously at a future date in this type of perfect-foresight continuous-time model. This is easily understood by reasoning *ad absurdum*. Assume that the price level was to jump discontinuously upwards at a future date t. Because we are assuming perfect foresight, the representative agent would then have an incentive to give up any cash balances that she holds just before this discontinuity, at date $t - dt$, and buy any other real asset instead. Otherwise, she would make a loss on her cash holding *at an infinite rate*, computed as the ratio of the finite jump, divided by the infinitesimal time period dt. Then, at time $t - dt$, all the agents get rid of their cash, and buy the alternative asset; this creates a discontinuous jump in the price level, as the real quantity of money goes abruptly to zero, since nobody wants to hold it. We can then repeat the previous argument: as we are in a perfect-foresight framework, the agents realize that the jump is going to happen at date $t - dt$, and thus want to get rid of their cash at date $t - 2dt$. This would trigger the jump in price, providing the incentive for the agents to get rid of the cash at $t - 3dt$. The argument can be repeated over and again until we reach the present date, normalized to 0. If a jump in price occurs at date zero, the agents cannot anticipate it and get rid of the cash at date $0 - dt$: they are trapped by the irreversibility of time. In other words, in this setting, the future trajectory of the price level has to be continuous, and any jump can occur only at date 0.

Let us now work backward to identify the trajectory of the different variables. After the attack, the economy is in a flexible exchange rate regime. There are no reserves left on the central bank's balance sheet, and the quantity of money is equal to the stock of credit to the treasury $M = B$. It follows that the real quantity of money grows according to the following equation:

$$dm/dt = g - \pi m. \qquad (6.13)$$

A crucial assumption for determining the properties of the equilibrium path concerns how public expenditures are determined. Following Krugman (1979), assume that the government follows a Friedman rule, aiming at letting the quantity of money grow at a constant rate μ in the post-attack regime. This implies that the level of public expenditures is specified as:

$$g = \mu m. \tag{6.14}$$

The dynamics of the inflation rate is then governed by the following equation:

$$\frac{d\pi}{dt} = \left(\frac{-1}{\lambda'}\right)(\pi - \mu)\lambda(\pi). \tag{6.15}$$

Figure 6.5 helps us to analyze the determination of the equilibrium inflation rate in the flexible exchange rate regime. First, the flexible-rate steady state is located at E, where $\pi = \mu$. Second, it is clear from (6.15) that the rate of depreciation and inflation increases over time when it is located above this value, as shown by the arrow pointing upwards, and that it decreases over time when it is located below that line. E is therefore a saddle point with a zero-dimensional convergent sub-space. This determines the target for the rate of inflation and the level of money balances. The question is now: how does the economy get there, starting from a regime of fixed exchange rate?

Initially, we are at $\pi = 0$ and $m = \lambda(0)$. Denote b the real value of the stock of credit to the treasury, and assume that it has a low value at the initial date. It then grows over time, according to (6.10). Krugman's point is to show that the attack will occur exactly when $b = \lambda(\mu)$. Assume that it occurred earlier, for example at the point where $b = \tilde{b}$. All the reserves are then grabbed by the speculators, and

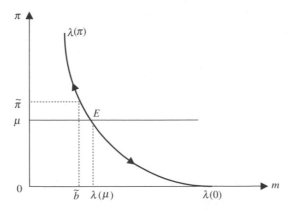

Figure 6.5. The first-generation currency crisis model

the quantity of money falls to the level of the credit to the treasury alone. We know that the price level cannot jump at this point, so that the quantity of money after the attack is $m = \tilde{b}$. We can now read off from figure 6.5 that such a level of real cash balances corresponds to a level of inflation $\tilde{\pi} > \mu$. If the attack occurred in such a way, the economy would therefore embark on an explosive path, and this is ruled out in a rational expectations equilibrium. So, the attack cannot occur before we reach the value $b = \lambda(\mu)$. It cannot occur beyond this point, either, because the economy would then embark on a divergent path aiming in the other direction, which is ruled out as well. The attack thus occurs exactly at this point. What happens then is that the speculators pocket all the remaining central bank's reserves, whose real value is $\lambda(0) - \lambda(\mu)$, and thus acquire an asset which is protected from the subsequent inflation. This way, the real cash balances jump to their new equilibrium value without the price level making any jump.

Second generation

This simple model, with its neat prediction that the attack occurs at a precise point in time, can be made fuzzier in its predictions by changing either of two assumptions. First, I have implicitly assumed above that $\lim_{\pi \to \infty} \lambda(\pi) > 0$. This is clear from figure 6.5. What happens if we remove this "no de-monetization" assumption? Figure 6.6 helps to give us the answer. The demand for money function is drawn with a finite intercept; in other words, we now assume that there exists a rate of inflation high enough that agents give up the use of the currency at this point. This is a kind of "Weimar republic" point, where the currency is worthless while the agents return to barter. Examination of (6.14) shows that this is a perfectly acceptable steady-state equilibrium point, labeled E_2 on figure 6.6.

This creates a completely new situation, well characterized by looking at point $\tilde{b}$ again. Looking vertically above this point, we find a flexible rate equilibrium characterized by an arrow pointing to the north-west. Now that the implicit "no-demonetization" assumption has been dropped, this equilibrium is perfectly acceptable, as it does not diverge towards an unacceptable infinite inflation rate, but is moving instead in the direction of a demonetized equilibrium of the E_2 type. Hence, this point cannot be ruled out, as it is on a trajectory

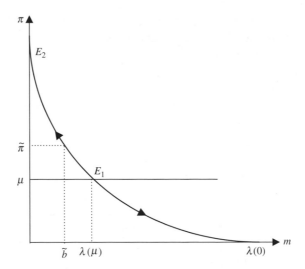

Figure 6.6. A continuum of rational expectations equilibria

that converges to an acceptable steady state. The same reasoning can be repeated for any point to the left of $\lambda(\mu)$. We therefore have here a continuum of rational expectations equilibria. We have met this type of phenomenon already in chapter 4, and we know that this introduces the possibility of sunspot equilibria, according to the so-called "Woodford conjecture." In this case, random shocks can occur, called sunspots in the theoretical literature, which push the economy to move from one of these trajectories to another, displaying significant instability. These equilibria are such that expectations are self-fulfilling. What drives the dynamics of the nominal variables is the expectations that the agents are forming about them.

This is the hallmark of the second-generation models of currency crises: the attacks can be due to self-fulfilling predictions. This was first brought out by Obstfeld (1994). It follows that in these cases a currency crisis does not reveal any useful information about the fundamentals of an economy, except that there is a fiscal deficit. However, given this deficit, the Krugman-type trajectory analyzed above remains valid, as just one of an infinite number of acceptable trajectories. It starts at the last possible date for the occurrence of the currency crisis. Such an economy can therefore either behave like a first-generation model, or instead display significant instability, with a self-fulfilling speculative attack liable to occur at almost any level of credit to the treasury. In this case, there is no economic policy that can prevent the crisis, even putting the deficit to zero. It is straightforward to check that in figure 6.6 the currency crisis can occur even if $\mu = 0$.

The same phenomenon can occur in this model without lifting the "no-demonetization" assumption, but by changing the assumption governing the behavior of public expenditures. In the Krugman model, we have specified that $g = \mu \lambda(\pi)$. This assumption has a nice pedigree, as it is reminiscent of Friedman's rule of a constant rate of growth of the quantity of money. However, it implies that the government has in fact an active anti-inflation fiscal policy, reducing its deficit as inflation grows larger. At the other extreme, we can assume that the government values public expenditures for their own sake, and will not adjust them for fighting inflation. For example, the government might seek to minimize a loss function $\kappa(\hat{g}-g)^2$, with a large κ, where $\hat{g}$ is the preferred level of expenditures. The simplest assumption of this kind is to assume that g is constant. In this case, the steady-state equilibrium point is to be found on the hyperbola

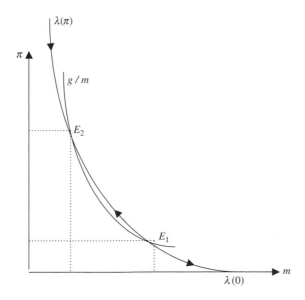

Figure 6.7. A second-generation currency crisis model

$\pi = g/m$. We can again have two steady-state equilibrium points, if the conditions for an inflation Laffer curve hold.

Figure 6.7 depicts the resulting dynamics. The lower steady-state equilibrium is again a saddle point with a zero-dimensional convergent sub-space. But the higher one is stable, with all the trajectories starting to the left of $\lambda(\mu)$ converging to it. We therefore again have a continuum of rational expectation equilibria, and currency crises are again of the self-fulfilling type, occurring possibly at any time.

Third generation

A new generation of currency crisis models has now appeared in the literature, initiated by Burnside, Eichenbaum, and Rebelo (2001). Their paper aims at explaining the Asian crisis without having recourse to a self-fulfilling type of analysis, which many people find unsatisfactory. For example, Tirole (2002) expresses skepticism about it, suggesting that there exist solutions for preventing self-fulfilling attacks that are too easy for assuming that governments would not adopt them. The stylized facts that Burnside, Eichenbaum, and Rebelo want to take on board are that these economies had some problems with their banking sectors, tainted by non-performing loans, as mentioned in section 6.1. However, the fiscal situation looked satisfactory in all these countries at the time of the shock. Moreover, Burnside, Eichenbaum, and Rebelo produce a model which is capable of explaining why econometricians fail to pick up any convincing correlates with currency crises. Besides Eichengreen, Rose, and Wyplosz (1995), already cited, Berg and Pattillo (1999) have documented how difficult it is to find good econometric models which can help to predict such events. From a methodological point of view, it is interesting to take such a constraint into account in the modeling strategy. The self-fulfilling attack approach accommodates this observation beautifully, but creates some tension with the fact that detailed case studies usually allow us to identify quite clearly the causes of each crisis, admittedly with the benefit of hindsight. The model by Burnside, Eichenbaum, and Rebelo (2001) reconciles these two observations to a large extent. The idea is to take due account of future events that the general public was to some extent able to forecast. Just before the start of the Asian crisis of summer 1997, reports were being published showing that (i) many banks in the area were running into trouble, and (ii) the governments would have to run relatively important deficits to bail them out. The attacks occurred before these deficits were observed, but after they became predictable.

To understand their point, let us go back to the first-generation model presented above, and simply change the specification of the fiscal deficit (6.14). Let us change it into:

$$g = 0 \text{ for } t < T, \tag{6.16}$$

and

$$g = \mu^T m, \text{ for } t \geqslant T, \tag{6.17}$$

In words, this assumes that the government is not running any deficit at the present date, but will start running one at a future date T.

The resulting dynamics can be analyzed with the help of the phase diagram in figure 6.8. Before date T, the horizontal line labeled μ^T does not exist, and all the movements along the demand for money function above the m axis are characterized by arrows pointing upwards. After date T, the motion below the μ^T horizontal line changes direction, now pointing downwards. Therefore, after date T, point E is again a saddle point with a zero-dimensional convergent sub-space, as in the original Dornbusch–Krugman model. The new phenomenon introduced in this variant of the model is that before that date, a transitional dynamics is possible, that gropes gradually towards E, reaching this point exactly at date T, when it is locked in

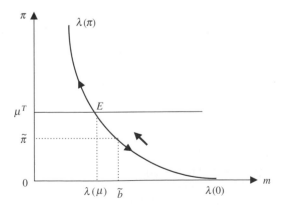

Figure 6.8. A third-generation currency crisis model

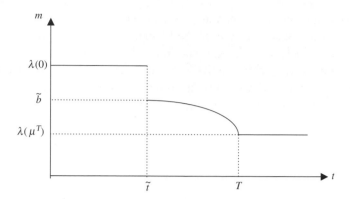

Figure 6.9. The dynamics of money balances in the third-generation model

there. Then, given an initial stock of credit to the treasury out-standing, say $\tilde{b} \geqslant \lambda(\mu^T)$, the attack will occur at a date $\tilde{t}$ such that it takes precisely $T-\tilde{t}$ units of time to go from $\tilde{b}$ to $\lambda(\mu^T)$, according to the dynamics governed by (6.15), with $\mu = 0$.

Hence, instead of splitting the time line into two fractions, before and after the attack, as in all the previous currency-crisis models, we now have three time spans: (i) before the attack, (ii) between the attack and the occurrence of the fiscal deficit, and (iii) after the fiscal deficit is observed. Figure 6.9 helps visualize this dynamics.

This third generation of currency crisis models I have just sketched, using the simplest possible setting, thus seems quite powerful in that it provides a useful analysis that helps to pinpoint the cause of the attack in a perfect-foresight framework, while it shows that this cause is not necessarily to be found in an event that takes place at the same time as the attack does. In their paper, Burnside, Eichenbaum, and Rebelo (2001) show how this framework illuminates the analysis of the Asian crisis. This has a very important methodological implication – namely, that case studies supported with an analytical model, also called "analytic narratives" (Bates *et al.*, 1998), are an indispensable component of macroeconomic research, beside pure theory and econometric analysis. I combine all three in section 6.4.

6.4 African Tequila? The "Cola nut" effect

A characteristic feature of recent currency attacks has been the "contagion" effect, as the weakness of one national currency affected the currencies of the neighboring countries. This contagion effect has been called the "Tequila" effect, after the Mexican crisis had been followed by various attacks against other Latin American economies. It seems that Guinea and Madagascar are too small economies to affect their neighbors in such a way. However, it is probable that the CFA Zone is a large enough player to affect its neighbors. An interesting test is thus to look at the possible impact of the CFA Franc devaluation on the value of the naira. We know from chapter 5 that the interesting exchange rate to look at, from a market point of view is the parallel one, as far as the naira is concerned (especially before February 1995). The official market is just a device for diverting some export revenues and redistributing the proceeds to some selected players.

Nigeria is the largest demographic and economic power in West and Central Africa, located roughly at the geographical center of the CFA Zone, which surrounds it on three sides. With the exception of Senegal, which is located further away, all the countries of the UEMOA and the CEMAC are located almost entirely within 1,500 km of its borders. With 124 million people in 1999, at least, its population is larger than that of the whole CFA Zone, which amounted to only 99 million at the same date. In terms of GDP, the difference is in the other direction, with US$ 43.8 billion for the CFA Zone, and US$ 37.9 billion for Nigeria. Nigeria and the whole CFA Zone are therefore two players of similar strength, from an economic as well as a demographic point of view, and they are neighbors. Almost all of the preceding chapters have illustrated how important their cross-border trading relations are, mostly through informal channels, as well as their financial interdependence. Nigeria is a federal state, whose internal political and economic integration is not much more pronounced than that of the CFA Zone. Although the naira is supposed to be the unique currency of this country, the parallel currency markets are very active. The CFA Franc is in wide currency in the border zones, while the US dollar is commonly used in the Lagos area, as well as in other cities. Hashim and Meagher (1999) have produced some fascinating fieldwork from Nigeria, and in particular a monographic analysis of the Wapa market in Kano, illustrating vividly how foreign currencies are present in Nigerians' everyday life. The monetary integration of Nigeria may thus be less deep than that of the CFA Zone, but the main difference is really that the CFA Franc had a fixed exchange rate with the French Franc, and now with the euro, whereas the exchange rate of the naira is market-determined, by the parallel market. As described in chapter 4, accumulating some CFA Francs is thus a way to acquire some hard currency for many Nigerians, and they figure prominently in their portfolios. Because of the inconvertibility of the naira, many Nigerians thus use Cotonou in Benin as the "off-shore" financial center of Lagos. Both trade and financial transactions are thus going on between the CFA Zone and Nigeria. The 1994 devaluation therefore had some impact on the naira market, as comes out quite clearly from an examination of figure 6.10.

Figure 6.10 represents the nominal exchange rate of the naira on the parallel market in terms of US dollars and of CFA Francs, respectively, in logarithms, over the period 1991:01–1995:02. The downward slope of both series before 1994:01 shows that the naira was depreciating quite steadily, and that the relative price of the US dollar and of the CFA Franc was relatively stable. This steady depreciation is just the continuation of the trend depicted in figure 3.1 (p. 49). The impact of the devaluation of the CFA Franc of January

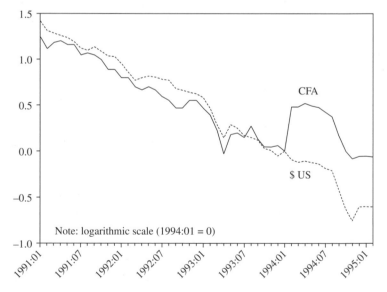

Figure 6.10. Parallel exchange rate of the naira in US dollars and in CFA Francs, 1991:01–1995:02
Source: Azam and Samba-Mamadou (1997).

1994 can be seen very clearly in figure 6.10. At first, the effect on the naira/CFA exchange rate is almost one-to-one, without any impact on the naira/US dollar exchange rate. This gives rise to a visible "hump," lasting about nine months. However, as Nigerian traders and producers realize that this devaluation has resulted in a sizable fall in their outlets in neighboring countries, as well as in the value of their remaining CFA balances, then a negative wealth effect occurs. Their demand for naira suddenly falls, and the value of the CFA Franc falls as well, relative to the US dollar, as occurred in September 1994. In that month, the naira/CFA exchange rate fell back almost to its previous trend value, while the naira/US dollar rate collapsed. It fell by 20.8% in September, by 20.4% in October, and by another 13.3% in November. It then picked up somewhat by 15.2% in December, but its dollar value remained below the trend until February 1995, the year of the *de facto* unification of the naira market. After that date, only the military were allowed to buy foreign currencies on the official market, making its actual role more transparent. Komolafe (1998) describes the reforms which took place in 1995 and in 1997, significantly liberalizing the foreign exchange market.

In fact, similar effects occurred in other neighboring countries. For example, in 1994, the Ghanaian cedi, the currency of another important neighbor of the CFA Zone, also lost about 25% of its value in US dollars, and another 25% in the course of the following year.

The aim of the present exercise is to determine whether this fall in the naira exchange rate resulted from the CFA Franc devaluation. The most commonly offered explanation blames this fall of the naira on the strikes that blocked the oil sector and the harbors during the summer of 1994, in July and August, which automatically reduced Nigeria's exports (LARES, 1995). This is not convincing, for two reasons: (i) the timing is not congruent, as the fall occured mainly in September and October, while the strikes were in July and August, and (ii) if this temporary fall in export revenues was the only cause, we would expect a return to the trend value, while in fact we observe a lasting fall below trend. Oil production resumed in September, increasing by more than 25%, as well as agricultural exports; the world price of cocoa was 120% above its 1993 level. According to the Ministry of Agriculture, it was "the best crop of the decade" (cited in LARES, 1995). These explanations based on export flows do not fit the facts, and Azam and Samba-Mamadou (1997) offer another

explanation, based on the indirect impact of the CFA Franc devaluation.

A regional equilibrium model

The analytical model is a two-country variant of Neary (1984),
extended to include the following three modifications: (i) it is turned
into a two-country model open to the rest of the world, (ii) there
are transactions costs in the trade between the two countries, and
(iii) rational expectations affect the demand for money. It is thus a
small general equilibrium model aiming at capturing the relationships
between Nigeria and the CFA Zone which dominate the regional
macroeconomy. As explained in almost all the previous chapters, I do
not use the usual distinction between "tradable" and "non-tradable"
goods. I use instead the more relevant distinction between "African"
and "European" goods, justified by Azam (1991b) and Delgado
(1992). The former are involved in cross-border trade, but not in the
trade with the rest of the world. Their price is thus determined by the
regional market equilibrium. The CFA Zone and Nigeria are the big
players on this market. By contrast, the European goods are traded
with the rest of the world, and both African entities are price-takers
on this market.

Let D and D^F denote the excess demands for African goods in
Nigeria and the CFA Zone, respectively, assuming for the sake of
simplicity that no other country is involved in this market. In what
follows, the superscript F identifies the variables pertaining to the
CFA Zone. Denote e and E the price of the US dollar in naira and in
CFA Francs, respectively. Hence, unlike in figure 6.10, a depreciation
of the naira is here described by an increase in e, and the devaluation
of the CFA Franc is captured by an exogenous increase in E. The price
of European goods on the world market is normalized to 1, so that
these exchange rates are also the prices in local currency of these
goods. Let p^A and p^{AF} represent the prices in terms of national currencies of the African good in Nigeria and the CFA Zone, respectively.
Lastly, let W and W^F be the household wealth in the two economic
entities, to be defined more precisely below. I assume that, in both
countries, the excess demand for African goods is an increasing
function of the real exchange rate, defined here as the relative price of

the European and African goods, and also an increasing function of the households' wealth. Then, equilibrium on the regional market for the African good requires:

$$D\left(\frac{e}{p^A}, W\right) + D^F\left(\frac{E}{p^{AF}}, W^F\right) = 0. \tag{6.18}$$

I assume that there exists a trading margin driving a wedge between the prices of the same African good in the two countries. This is meant to capture an empirical fact which has been widely observed, and which is akin to the "pricing-to-market" phenomenon described by Krugman (1989). The observations reported by LARES (1995) clearly show that the prices of Nigerian goods exported to the CFA Zone did not follow one-to-one the changes in the prices in Lagos, translated into CFA Francs using the parallel market exchange rate, in the wake of the devaluation. In fact, because of the ensuing decrease in parallel trade, the trading margins fell significantly, suggesting that the supply of smuggling services had a positive slope – i.e. an increasing marginal cost. This is the standard assumption made in partial equilibrium models of parallel markets, as presented in part I of this volume. Here, in the general equilibrium framework, one needs to be more careful in specifying this response, because this trading margin on cross-border trade affects prices at both ends.

I assume that the following arbitrage condition holds:

$$p^{AF} = (1+x)p^A\frac{E}{e}, \tag{6.19}$$

where the trading margin x is assumed increasing with the trade flow, here written directly as an import into the CFA Zone from Nigeria, which is the normal state of affairs:

$$x = x(D^F), \ x(0) = 0, \ x'(.) > 0. \tag{6.20}$$

As is well known, this type of sectoral supply curve with increasing marginal cost may be interpreted as capturing the fact that the new entrants in the trade as the quantity traded expands are less efficient than the incumbents. Maybe their relationship with the customs officers does not benefit from reputation effects, their knowledge of the terrain is not as good, and their trucks are less appropriate for this exercise.

Combining (6.19) and (6.20), as well as the $D^F(.)$ function used at (6.18) allows us to write:

$$D^F = D^F\left(\frac{e}{p^A}, W^F\right). \tag{6.21}$$

Figure 6.11 us helps to understand how the triplet $\{p^A, x, p^{AF}\}$ is determined in equilibrium. The situation depicted is one where there is a positive excess demand for African goods in the CFA Zone, matched by a negative excess demand from Nigeria. As the goods are transported through the border, some transactions cost is incurred, captured here by the increasing trading margin. The upward-sloping curve, drawn here as a straight line for simplicity, is the supply curve from Nigeria, which can be interpreted as an inverse supply curve representing the price of the African goods in Nigeria in terms of US dollars, or, equivalently, of European goods. The trading margin must be added to this price to find the supply price on the other side of the border. The downward-sloping curve is the demand by the CFA Zone for these goods, to be imported from Nigeria. It can also be interpreted as an inverse demand curve, representing the price of these goods at the other end, also in terms of US dollar. Equilibrium is

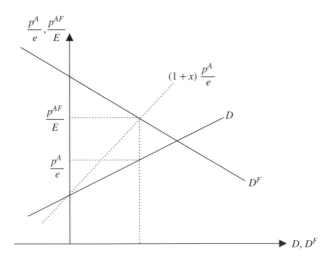

Figure 6.11. Equilibrium in the African goods market

found where the wedge between these two prices precisely covers the trading margin corresponding to the equilibrium flow of trade.

It is easy to understand from figure 6.11 how the two prices for African goods, once expressed in the same currency, are jointly determined, and how they would move were any of the excess demand curves to shift. Correlatively, it can immediately be seen from figure 6.11 why the imports of African goods in the CFA Zone can be expressed directly as a function of the price prevailing inside Nigeria, as written in (6.21).

Let us now turn our attention to the assets held by the households in the two countries. Assume that the households hold three different currencies: N and N^F of naira, F and F^F of CFA Francs, and R and R^F of the currency of the rest of the world. Then, neglecting other assets, their wealth can be written in real terms as:

$$W = \frac{N + e(R + F/E)}{p} \text{ and } W^F = \frac{F^F + E(R^F + N^F/e)}{p^F}, \quad (6.22)$$

where the price levels in the two countries are given by the following indices, duly assumed to be homogeneous of degree one:

$$p = p(e, p^A) \text{ and } p^F = p^F(E, p^{AF}). \quad (6.23)$$

General equilibrium and dynamics

It is convenient to re-write the African goods market equilibrium condition (6.18) as:

$$D\left(\frac{e}{p^A}, E, e, \ldots\right) + D^F\left(\frac{e}{p^A}, E, e, \ldots\right) = 0. \quad (6.24)$$

This allows us to distinguish two types of effects. First, there is the relative price effect, involving mainly the substitution effect. It affects the demand for African goods positively, as European goods become dearer. It also involves a partly offsetting wealth effect due to its impact on price levels, assumed of secondary importance. Second, there is the wealth effects of the exchange rates, which work negatively, reducing the purchasing power of the different currency balances held. This equilibrium condition can be represented in figure 6.12 as the upward-sloping locus labeled AA. Its upward slope reflects the fact that as e increases, the demand for African goods increases, as

European goods become dearer. But the resulting price increase is not proportional, as the various currency balances lose some purchasing power. Hence, the wealth effect provides a dampening influence, and *AA* is less steep than a ray through the origin. Above it, the price of African goods is too high, entailing excess supply. A downward adjustment will thus take place, described by the arrows pointing downwards. By a symmetrical argument, the points located below this locus involve excess demand, and an upward adjustment of the price, as shown by the arrows pointing upwards. This locus shifts downwards if the real value of the assets held by the households in any of the two economic entities falls. This occurs in particular when E increases, as implied by the devaluation of the CFA Franc.

In order to close the model, I follow Neary (1984) in focusing on the asset market – more precisely, on the market for the naira, where e is determined. Assume that the total quantity of naira $N + N^F$ is fixed, and that there is perfect capital mobility between the two neighboring economic entities. Let $\delta = d\log e/dt$ be the expected rate of depreciation of the naira in terms of US dollars, identical in the two countries, and r^* the world rate of interest. Assume that the real demands for naira in the two countries have the usual specification, being decreasing in $r^* + \delta$, the real return on holding foreign assets, and increasing in wealth:

$$n(r^* + \delta, W) \text{ and } n^F(r^* + \delta, W^F). \qquad (6.25)$$

This formulation implicitly assumes that the CFA Franc is perfectly substitutable with the currency of the rest of the world. The naira market is in equilibrium if the following condition holds:

$$p(e, p^A)n(r^* + \delta, W) + p^F(E, p^{AF})n^F(r^* + \delta, W^F) = N + N^F. \qquad (6.26)$$

This simply says that the sum of the nominal demands for naira in the two countries, computed as the real demands multiplied by the relevant price levels, must add up to the total nominal supply.

The $\delta = 0$ locus, derived from (6.26) by substitution, can be represented by the downward-sloping *NN* curve in figure 6.11, for a given value of E. Given e and E, an increase p^A would increase the nominal demands for naira by increasing the price level in both countries, while creating some offsetting wealth effects which are unlikely to dominate the former one. To restore equilibrium along the

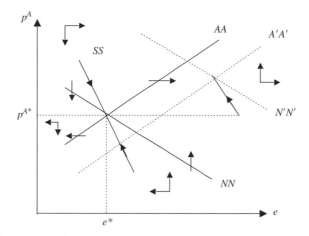

Figure 6.12. Regional equilibrium and dynamics

NN locus, a fall in *e* is required to reduce the price level in Nigeria, with some offsetting wealth effects. The downward slope assumes in both cases that the wealth effects are relatively weak. Any point located above *NN* entails a higher price level, which is consistent with equilibrium on the naira market only if the real demand for nairas is lower. This occurs if the agents are expecting depreciation – i.e. a movement of *e* to the right, as represented by the horizontal arrows. Below this locus, the naira holders are expecting an appreciation, with a negative effect on the price level. This is described by the horizontal arrows pointing to the left.

In order to complete the dynamics of the model I assume, like Dornbusch (1976), that p^A is predetermined, and cannot jump in response to the increase in *E*, whereas *e* can adjust instantly. This is a standard way of capturing the idea that the foreign exchange market adjusts more quickly than the African goods market. The steady state of this dynamic system is found where the two loci *AA* and *NN* intersect, and it is easily derived from figure 6.12 that it is a saddle point with a one-dimensional convergent sub-space. We can rule out the divergent trajectories as usual.

Now, we can use figure 6.12 to simulate the impact of the CFA Franc devaluation. The *AA* locus shifts downwards, because the devaluation has a negative wealth effect in Nigeria, and also in the CFA Zone, unless the share of foreign assets in household wealth there is implausibly large. This entails an excess supply of African goods at the original price, which is corrected by lowering it. The negative wealth effect shifts the NN locus upwards, subject to the same caveat. The new steady state will be found at the intersection of the two loci in their new positions, labeled $A'A'$ and $N'N'$. The case represented in figure 6.11 assumes that the impact on the naira market is larger than the impact on the African goods market. In this case, both e and p^A increase to their new steady-state position. If the impact on the goods market was dominant, then only the increase in e would be retained, while the other effect would change sign. In the case of figure 6.12, where the monetary effect dominates, the model predicts that the naira should respond by depreciating relative to the US dollar, with an overshooting trajectory. The latter is identified in two steps. First, we know that the new steady state will be reached along the saddle path. Second, as the price of African goods is supposed not to adjust instantly, while the exchange rate does, then the impact point resulting from the devaluation must be found on the same horizontal line as the initial price. Hence, the transitional dynamics will look like those in figure 6.12, with a large jump in e at first, followed by some gradual correction in the opposite direction. In the other case, not represented here, we would predict a more gradual depreciation of the naira, together with a gradual fall in the naira price of African goods. Notice that, in both cases, the model predicts some depreciation of the naira. The difference concerns the dynamics, which has no overshooting in the second case, and the impact on the price of African goods in terms of naira, which goes up in the former case, and down in the latter. Of course, this should be understood as changes relative to trend, for an empirical application. The model also predicts that the relative price of African goods falls, in both countries. This implies in particular that we are predicting that the price level will go up in the CFA Zone by less than the full percentage of the devaluation. This is precisely what happened in fact, as briefly mentioned in chapter 5 and discussed in more detail in chapter 7. The model also implies that the real exchange rate will also depreciate in Nigeria. The exchange rate of the CFA Franc relative to the hard currencies of Europe and the USA is thus in fact a regional exchange rate, affecting both CFA Zone member countries and their neighbors.

An empirical test

Some testing can be done with the series used to generate figure 6.10. Two predictions come out clearly from the modeling exercise, namely that (i) the exchange rate of the CFA Franc in terms of US dollars should have a positive impact on the naira exchange rate in US dollar terms, and (ii) the transitional dynamics may be complex, possibly involving some overshooting. The following dynamic equation has been estimated after deleting the insignificant variables, for the sake of parsimony. It involves an implicit error-correction mechanism *à la* Banerjee *et al.* (1993), as it includes both the growth rates and the levels of the two variables:

$$\Delta \log e = 0.55 + 0.018 \, trend - 0.47 \log e(-2) + 0.20 \Delta \log E$$
$$(1.69) \ (4.37) \qquad\qquad (4.73) \qquad\qquad (2.27)$$
$$- 0.19 \Delta \log E(-6) + 0.10 \log E(-4)$$
$$(2.03) \qquad\qquad (1.92)$$

$$(6.27)$$

$$N = 43, \quad R^2 = 0.44, \quad F = 5.72, \quad LM(3 \text{ lags}) = 0.05,$$
$$\text{Chow} (1994:02) - F = 2.14.$$

The numbers in parentheses below the coefficients are the hetero-skedasticity-consistent *t*-ratios. All the coefficients are significant. The overshooting assumption receives some support from the negative sign of the CFA Franc depreciation rate lagged six months, while the other two coefficients concerning this variable are positive. The *LM*-test shows that there is no residual autocorrelation, up to the third order, while the Chow-breakpoint test shows that the assumption that the estimated coefficients are the same before and after 1994:02 is not rejected by the data. This suggests that the devaluation of the CFA Franc did not change the structure of the relationship between the two exchange rates. Equation (6.27) supports the two main predictions of the analytical model, namely that the CFA/US dollar exchange rate has a positive impact on the naira/US dollar exchange rate, and that the dynamics is not monotone. The estimated dynamics is obviously more complex than that of the analytical model; however, the latter could be enriched by assuming that wealth effects work with some delay, as in Eastwood and Venables (1982), to make it more complicated, without changing the basic insights provided by the version presented here.

6.5 Concluding comments

This chapter has discussed several themes relative to African currency crises. These crises do not hit the headlines of the main international newspapers, but do provide a lot of material that is liable to have some bearing on the debates about speculative attacks that are going on in the literature. The various cases mentioned provide nice examples of different types of currency attacks discussed in the theoretical literature: the misguided decision-driven attack, the excessive seigniorage-driven attack, and the probing attack. Each is of a different kind, while the comparison of the CFA episode to the Guinean one suggests that there are limits to how much strong institutions can substitute for good policy-makers. Both the Malagasy and the CFA case suggest that simple monetary theory provides very useful insights into the conduct of exchange rate policy: the strength of the local currency depends on its attractiveness to money-demanders, which in turn depends on its ability to be used in foreign transactions, or as an inflation-proof reserve of value. The central bank plays a crucial part in determining its attractiveness, in particular by keeping a high enough level of reserves relative to domestic credit. When the issue of reserves does not arise, because of a credible credit line, as in the CFA Zone, then only an institutional failure such as the misguided decision made by the French treasury in August 1993, or the cost of borrowing foreign exchange, can undermine the parity.

The three generations of currency crisis models have been discussed in the simplest setting, where the government is simply seeking to extract some seigniorage from the public. More complex models can be found in the theoretical literature which fall outside the scope of this presentation. The important methodological point brought out in this literature is that detailed case studies are required to understand these rare events that elude a general econometric analysis. The main reason behind this relative failure of econometric analysis is that the expectations of future deficits, rather than any contemporaneous event, may trigger the crisis; this could be taken on board using some survey data on investors' subjective views about the future, something that is not commonly available. However, the Malagasy crisis described here involved only a contemporaneous fiscal deficit.

I have also illustrated how the impact of the speculative behavior on the food market may provide a specific African link that may permit a deeper analysis of the distributional consequences of monetary instability. Lastly, the issue of cross-border contagion of currency crises, the so-called African "Tequila" – or, rather "Cola nut" – effect is most probably present when the currency of a big continental player collapses, as illustrated by the CFA Franc devaluation. The model discussed suggests that the devaluation of the CFA Franc entailed a real depreciation at the regional level – i.e. a change in the relative price of African and European goods. My hope is that many economists in Africa or abroad will take up this lead, and provide a more systematic analysis of African currency crises.

PART III

Longer-term growth in African countries

7 | *Exchange rate, growth, and poverty*

7.1 Introduction

The decision to devalue the CFA Franc in January 1994 was probably one of the longest awaited decisions in the modern history of adjustment policies. The exchange rate with the French Franc had not changed since 1948. While the performance of the CFA Zone economies had been much better than those of the other African economies until the collapse of most commodity prices in 1986–8, the latter had been undoubtedly much better at adjusting to these shocks (Devarajan and Rodrik, 1992). It was probably in 1989 that the need to devalue was the most acute, after the collapse of the TOT in most of the Zone at the end of 1987, and the decision by President Houphouët-Boigny of Côte d'Ivoire to withdraw the whole cocoa crop from the market in 1988; he tried single-handedly to support the world cocoa market, and ruined his country's creditworthiness (Azam and Morrisson, 1994). The impact of this worsening of the macro-economic situation on poverty can be analyzed only in the case of Côte d'Ivoire, among the CFA Zone countries, as none of the others has two household surveys performed at the relevant dates, allowing us to compare the outcomes before and after this shock. Figure 7.1, derived from Demery and Squire (1996), shows that Côte d'Ivoire saw its poverty level increase as macroeconomic policy deteriorated over the 1985–8 period, relative to the comparator countries. Not everybody suffered equally in this country from the downturn, which had a positive distributional effect on some groups (Grootaert and Kanbur, 1995).

This chapter draws partly on Azam and Wane (2001) and Azam (2004). It has benefited from comments by Lionel Demery and participants at an IDS/World Bank meeting in Brighton (UK) in April 1999, as well as by David Fielding and participants at a WIDER meeting in Helsinki in June 2003. The views expressed are those of the author, and do not necessarily represent those of the World Bank. Special thanks are due to Idrissa Ouattara, without implicating.

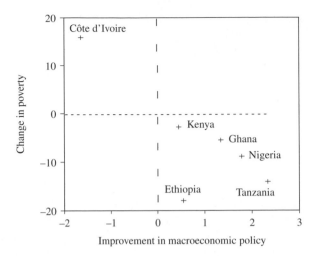

Figure 7.1. Poverty and macroeconomic policy
Source: Derived from Demery and Squire (1996).

It would probably be a mistake to take Côte d'Ivoire as representative of the whole CFA Zone, although it is the leading economy of this area. It fared especially badly after 1986, as its TOT deteriorated catastrophically, while some unhelpful policy decisions were taken. Nevertheless, the analyses of the evolution of poverty over a period of deteriorating macroeconomic policies provides some clues about the phenomena to look at when observing the general impact of policy changes on poverty (Grootaert and Kanbur, 1995; Grootaert, 1996). They show the diversity of the impact on different groups of households, depending on the regions where they lived, their occupation, and their socio-economic status. Grootaert and Kanbur (1995), for example, show that households from the east forest area had a 20.4% probability of improving their poverty status despite the worsening macroeconomic situation in 1987–8, while the food crop farmers had a 39.1% probability of doing so over the same period. One might expect to meet similarly diverse effects in response to the improved macroeconomic situation that resulted from the devaluation and the accompanying policy measures. In fact, a much simpler picture emerges from the results presented below.

Despite the general increase in poverty in 1987–8, in the wake of the TOT crash, it was not until the president's death in January 1994 that the decision to devalue was obtained by Michel Camdessus, on behalf of the IMF. The theory of postponed policy reforms, developed in particular by Alesina and Drazen (1991), Fernandez and Rodrik (1991), and Casella and Eichengreen (1996), points to uncertainty about the distributional impacts of the reforms as the main cause of delay. The results presented below, which are rather unexpected, may provide some support to this view (see also Azam, 1994). It turns out that the observed growth recovery left many people aside, as poverty increased.

In the case of the CFA Zone economies, the fixed exchange rate with the French Franc, which has been *de facto* linked to the DM since 1983, together with the swings in the US dollar and in the prices of their main export commodities, had resulted in excessively high wages in the formal sector (see Van de Walle, 1991). The fixed exchange rate was thus protecting "The lucky few amidst economic decline" (Grootaert and Kanbur, 1995). Many felt that the only remaining uncertainty was about the ability of the wage earners from the formal sector to pass on any devaluation to wage increases, thus triggering an inflationary wage–price spiral mediated by repeated devaluation. The French were wary about this, and until the Fall of 1993 supported the resolve of most CFA countries rulers not to devalue, probably fearing a contagion effect onto the French franc. This did not happen, although the 1994 devaluation took place in an electoral context. Wages in the formal sector did not respond significantly, as shown below, and from a macroeconomic point of view this explains the success of this policy reform.

Section 7.2 briefly presents the main impact of the devaluation on growth and inflation, focusing on the WAEMU countries. The oil-rich CEMAC countries probably require a different analysis. Growth resumed, while inflation fell short of catching-up on the devaluation, creating a high degree of effectiveness. A simple model is presented in section 7.3 to provide a theoretical framework for thinking about the way in which a cut in real formal sector wages can work through the various segments of the labor market to affect the incomes of the workers in the informal sector, where most of the poor earn their living. This model is a simple dynamic analysis which takes on board the widely observed fact that formal sector workers are generally running businesses in the informal sector, where they often hire workers from their social network (kin group, village of origin, extended family, etc.). Section 7.4 looks at the net effect of the devaluation package on poverty in the cases of Côte d'Ivoire and Niger, where the availability of two household surveys, before and after the devaluation, permits some tracking of the change in poverty. The focus is put on the changes affecting the different occupational categories, which are likely accurately to represent the different segments of the labor market.

7.2 The macroeconomic impact of the devaluation

The over-valuation of the CFA Franc was taking its toll on the CFA Zone economies before the 1994 devaluation, as can be seen by looking at their growth performance. Panels (a)–(c) of figure 7.2 show that the most affected economy was Côte d'Ivoire, which experienced negative growth after 1987, when its TOT began a steep downward slide until 1992. Almost all these economies experienced some negative growth in the early 1990s, most of them in 1993, and sometimes earlier, such as Niger and Togo. Benin seems to have been unaffected by this phenomenon. Two main events explain the bad performance experienced in 1993 in the WAEMU. First, Côte d'Ivoire was put under sanctions by the IFIs, who wanted to induce the president to accept a devaluation, and the resulting lack of any external funding to support effective demand decimated the industrial sector; second, in August 1993, under the pressure of the French treasury, the BCEAO (the central bank of the WAEMU), suspended the external convertibility of the CFA bank notes (see Azam, 1997a, and chapter 5 in this volume). The cost of the resulting speculative attack, which could easily have been predicted from elementary open-economy macroeconomics, was estimated at US\$ 610 million of foreign exchange reserves. A further credit squeeze followed and made the slump even more damaging. Part of the benefit of the devaluation resulted from the lifting of sanctions and from the massive external loans that the countries received. The IMF and the World Bank began new SAPs with these governments, which relieved the self-inflicted foreign exchange shortage. With the exception of Benin, which survived 1993 without apparent trouble, growth recovered in all these countries after the devaluation, and became smoother.

The WAEMU countries have traditionally had very low rates of inflation, for two reasons. First, the fixed exchange rate with France, translated into a fixed exchange rate with low-inflation Germany after

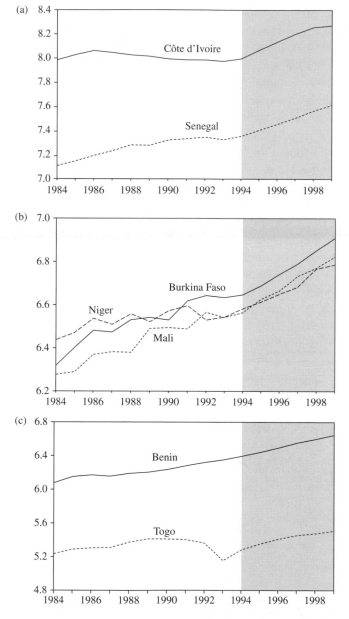

Figure 7.2. Real GDP: Côte d'Ivoire, Senegal, Burkina Faso, Mali, Benin and Togo, 1984–1998. (a) Côte d'Ivoire and Senegal, log scale (b) Burkina Faso, Mali, and Niger, log scale (c) Benin and Togo, log scale

1983. Second, for some of these countries, consumer goods markets are largely integrated with Nigeria, through unrecorded cross-border trade, so that the rapid depreciation of the naira on the parallel market entailed some price deflation in some of its CFA neighbors (see Azam, 1991b, and chapter 3 in this volume). Although some of the 100% devaluation was passed on to consumer prices in 1994 and subsequent years, its effectiveness was quite high. Between 1994 and 1996, the cumulative rate of inflation ranged between 35.6% in Burkina Faso and 48.5% in Benin. By 1999, this range was between 36.3% in Burkina Faso and 52.6% in Benin. Despite this high degree of effectiveness, the 1994 devaluation did not greatly affect relative consumer prices, as shown econometrically by Azam and Wane (2001). Using some disaggregated CPIs for Côte d'Ivoire, Niger, and Senegal, they have tested for a significant change in the structure of relative prices by running some regressions on monthly prices. They conclude that this cannot be the main effect of the devaluation as, for most goods, no significant impact is found.

Figure 7.3 illustrates the main problem that faced the CFA Zone before the devaluation: the excessive wages in the public sector (see Van de Walle, 1991; Rama, 2000). In figure 7.3, the ratio of the wage

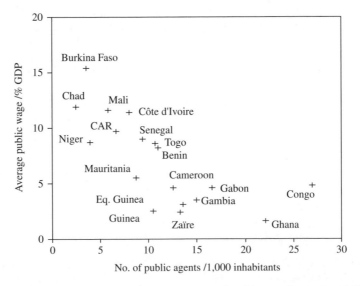

Figure 7.3. Relation between public wages and public employment, 1987
Source: Azam (1995a).

rate in the public sector to *per capita* GDP is on the *y*-axis, while the number of public agents per 1,000 inhabitants is on the *x*-axis. Figure 7.3 shows that the WAEMU countries are massively located in the north-western quarter of this space, where the average public sector wage is more than eight times larger than *per capita* GDP – more than ten times so for Burkina Faso, Mali, and Côte d'Ivoire. By contrast, the supply of public services, as measured by the number of public agents, is below standard. Chad and the Central African Republic, the non-oil exporting members of the CEMAC, are also located in the same part of figure 7.3. Figure 7.3 also suggests that wage rigidity lies at the heart of the problem, because in the lower half of this space one finds either oil economies, where the denominator is inflated by oil revenues, or countries with a flexible exchange rate and a history of more or less rapid depreciation, that kept a check on the real wage cost of public sector employees. The non-oil fixed-rate countries all suffer from excessive public sector wages, relative to the rest.

Rama (2000) has analyzed wage misalignment in the CFA countries, and concludes that real wage rigidity is involved in the long run, and not the type of nominal wage rigidity that makes devaluation work. However, the post-devaluation record shows that the catching-up of public sector wages on the price level was very slow. This might be due to a structural break in the real-wage series, as public sector workers had for a long time relied on France to prevent the devaluation of the CFA Franc and a fall in their real wages. In this interpretation, the 1994 decision came as a revelation that the former colonial power would no longer stand ready automatically to finance any level of public sector deficit, and therefore would not support the purchasing power of the civil servants forever. However, wages and salaries had been cut already in some countries, such as Cameroon, and frozen in others, so that civil servants and formal sector wage earners were probably expecting a downward adjustment of their earnings, one way or another in any case.

Wage moderation in the public sector was in fact remarkable after the devaluation, when several electoral episodes had led some to fear a wage explosion. In particular, the 1995 elections in Côte d'Ivoire gave rise to no wage increases, and this stability remained in place until the military *coup* of December 24, 1999, which triggered a significant increase in the wages of military personnel. The level of public sector wages does not matter only from a budgetary point of view; Rama (2000) has shown that it in fact affects the level of wages in the whole formal sector of the economy, by contagion. As productivity is much higher there than in other sectors, the real cost of labor in this sector has important macroeconomic effects because it affects employment and output in this sector.

In Côte d'Ivoire, the hourly minimum wage rate had been CFA Franc 191.4 between January 1982 and February 1994, when it was increased to 212.0, its value until the turn of the century (IMF, 2000a). In Senegal, it was 174.9 between April 1983 and January 1985, when it became 183.8, until July 1989, when it reached 201.1. It increased to 209.0 in December 1996, and to 209.1 in December 1997 (IMF, 2000b). However, Rama's (2000) results suggest that we should not pay too much attention to this minimum wage, which does not seem to affect the wages actually paid in any sector. More significant is the annual rate of change of the average wage in the central government, presented in table 7.1, for the two leading economies of the WAEMU – Côte d'Ivoire and Senegal. Table 7.1 shows that wage increases had been extremely moderate in the civil service, at an annual rate below 4.6% on average in Côte d'Ivoire, and below 0.8% on average in Senegal, mainly because of the fall preceding the devaluation. This provides the basic stylized fact of the impact of the 1994 devaluation on the WAEMU economies: it engineered a sizable cut in the real wages in the civil service, and most probably also in the whole public sector and, by contagion, in the whole formal sector. At the same time, some downsizing of the staff of the central government, by 5.1% in 1994 and 1.9% in 1995 occurred in Côte d'Ivoire, while this was negligible in Senegal.

This fall in real wages in the formal sector certainly contributed to the resumption of GDP growth, by restoring the fiscal balance, allowing public investment to recover, and restoring the profits of the

Table 7.1. Annual rate of change of the average wage in central government, 1993–1999, %

Year	1993	1994	1995	1996	1997	1998	1999
Côte d'Ivoire	n/a	7.4	3.7	0.0	1.5	10.2	4.5
Senegal	−7.2	12	−5.3	3.2	−1.8	0.7	3.6

Source: IMF (2000a, 2000b).
Note: n/a = Not available.

modern sector firms, boosting their incentive to invest and expand their activity. This explains the recovery seen above, but leaves unexplained the increase in poverty that took place at the same time.

Section 7.3 presents a simple model that can help us to think about the way in which this type of real wage cut should work through the various segments of the labor market, to impact the earnings of the workers in the informal sector.

7.3 A model of informal sector wage dynamics in the shadow of devaluation

In order to go further in the analysis, we need to take into account the type of labor market rigidity that can be observed in many developing countries: wages in the formal sector are higher than in other sectors, and do not respond flexibly to the fluctuations of the demand for, and supply of, labor. The first authors to have drawn some consequences from this observation were Harris and Todaro (1970). In their model, workers are facing a trade-off between working in the rural sector (where full employment prevails) or in the urban sector (where there is some unemployment), on the one hand, and a formal sector with a rigid wage, on the other. The migration equilibrium is found where the mathematical expectation of the urban wage, which is equal to the formal sector wage multiplied by the probability of finding a job there, is equal to the rural wage. This model has been criticized by Jamal and Weeks (1993) as giving a distorted picture of the working of the typical African labor market, putting too much emphasis on the rural–urban wage gap, related to the so-called "urban bias" (Lipton, 1977), while wage inequalities within the urban sector are probably more significant. The model presented here does not fall under this criticism, and it takes on board the typical stratification of African labor markets. It is widely said that formal sector workers support the livelihood of more than forty people with their earnings; the relatively well-off formal sector workers provide jobs to members of their social network, either at home as domestic helpers, or in some businesses that they are running in the informal sector (taxis, small shops, garment production, food processing, etc.). These businesses provide an outlet for their savings, which they rarely deposit with formal financial institutions. In fact, in the words of Aryeetey and Udry (1997): "the conclusion of virtually all studies of informal finance in both rural and urban Africa is that a substantial majority of lending occurs among friends, family and neighbors." Azam *et al.* (2001) support this view, using a sample of manufacturing firms in Côte d'Ivoire, showing that this is the cheapest way of getting funding for firms that have access to this type of credit.

The formal sector workers are supposed to earn a wage w^F, and to run simultaneously a small business in the informal sector. The production function for the latter is denoted $f(k,\ell)$, and is supposed to be well behaved, with constant returns to scale, and positive and decreasing marginal returns. Assume that the informal sector labor market is competitive, with a ruling wage w^I. The representative formal sector worker, assumed infinitely lived, seeks to maximize:

$$\int_0^\infty u(c)e^{-rt}dt, \tag{7.1}$$

subject to the following budget constraint:

$$dk/dt = w^F + f(k,\ell) - w^I\ell - c. \tag{7.2}$$

Applying Pontryagin's Maximum Principle, one can easily derive the following three optimality conditions, where subscripts again represent partial derivatives:

$$f_\ell(k,\ell) = w^I, \tag{7.3}$$

$$f_k(k,\ell) = r + \varepsilon d\log c/dt, \tag{7.4}$$

and

$$\lim_{t\to\infty} u'(c)ke^{-rt} = 0. \tag{7.5}$$

Condition (7.3) simply says that the informal sector firm will hire labor up to the point where its marginal productivity is equal to the ruling wage. Condition (7.4) is the standard Keynes–Ramsey formula, equating the marginal product of capital to the subjective rate of interest, where

$$\varepsilon = \frac{-cu''(c)}{u'(c)}$$

is the relative degree of risk aversion, more appropriately called here aversion to change, as the model is deterministic. Lastly, (7.5) is the transversality condition.

Given the condition on the marginal productivity of labor, and assuming a given supply of labor $\widetilde{\ell}$, equilibrium on the informal sector labor market allows us to define the profit function as:

$$\pi(k, \widetilde{\ell}) = f(k, \widetilde{\ell}) - \widetilde{\ell} f_\ell(k, \widetilde{\ell}). \qquad (7.6)$$

Moreover, after substituting the labor supply in (7.3), one can easily derive that the equilibrium wage rate in the informal sector is an increasing function of the capital stock, by differentiating it. This yields:

$$\frac{\partial w^I}{\partial k} = f_{lk}(k, \widetilde{\ell}) > 0. \qquad (7.7)$$

Therefore, there is a one-to-one correspondence between the dynamics of the informal sector wage rate and that of the capital stock invested in this sector. It is more convenient now to focus on the latter.

The dynamics of the model is governed by the following pair of differential equations:

$$\frac{dc}{dt} = \frac{c}{\varepsilon} \left(f_k(k, \widetilde{\ell}) - r \right), \qquad (7.8)$$

and

$$\frac{dk}{dt} = w^F + \pi(k, \widetilde{\ell}) - c. \qquad (7.9)$$

Notice that the function $\pi(k, \widetilde{\ell})$ is most likely to be increasing and concave in k. It is so for the CES production function, for example. However, this requires some conditions on second and third derivatives that need not detain us here.

For any given value of w^F, one can draw the phase diagram of figure 7.4. The vertical line is the locus $dc/dt = 0$. Consumption is moving upwards for all points located on the left-hand side of this vertical line, because the rate of return on capital is larger than the rate of time preference, and it is moving downwards on the right-hand side. The upward-sloping concave curve is the locus $dk/dt = 0$. Above it, consumption is too high, and the capital stock falls. Below it, the agent is saving, and capital is going up. The arrows drawn in the different zones of the phase space represent this dynamics.

If w^F were constant, then the agent would select the saddle path of figure 7.4, drawn with a dotted line. However, we are interested here

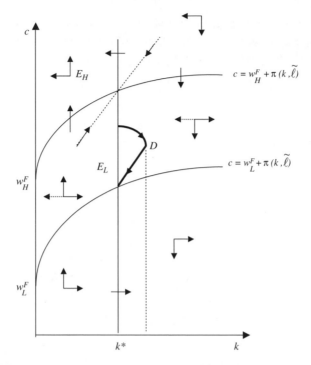

Figure 7.4. Dynamic response to an expected formal sector wage cut

in the case where the agent is predicting that w^F will fall in the future, either because of devaluation, or because of any other adjustment policy. Assume that the representative agent has initially reached the steady state corresponding to $w^F = w^F_H$, labeled E_H on figure 7.4. Now, she understands at date zero, for whatever reason, that this wage will be cut at a future date T. How is she going to respond? In order to deal with this question, assume that w^F follows the following path:

$$w^F = w^F_H, \text{ for } t < T, \tag{7.10}$$

and

$$w^F = w^F_L < w^F_H, \text{ for } t \geqslant T, \tag{7.11}$$

In this case, the locus $dk/dt = 0$ shifts downwards precisely at date T, and stays there for ever after. As we did in chapter 6, we must work backward to find the right trajectory. It is clear that the agent must choose a consumption path which lies on the saddle path after date T, aiming at the steady state E_L, for the usual reasons. The arbitrage condition (7.4) rules out any discontinuity in the trajectory of c at any future period. Therefore, she will cut her consumption at date zero immediately, in order to follow a trajectory heading to the south-east of the phase space, and reaching the saddle path at precisely date T. Such a trajectory is represented in figure 7.4 by the curvilinear downward-sloping curve, heading to the south-east. This is a divergent trajectory relative to the steady state labeled E_H, according to the dynamics prevailing prior to T. It reaches the saddle path at point D. In other words, the prospect of a future cut in her formal sector wage induces the representative formal sector worker to start saving as soon as she forms this prediction, for the sake of consumption smoothing. She invests these increased savings in her informal sector business, with a positive impact on the wages prevailing there, and she will gradually deplete this extra capital when the wage cut occurs, in order to slow down the fall in consumption.

The capital stock thus increases prior to the devaluation, as soon as the formal sector worker starts predicting the future wage cut, and decreases gradually after its occurrence. We know from (7.7) that the informal sector wage rate will follow suit, going up in the pre-devaluation phase, starting when the prediction of the future wage cut arises, and going down in the post-devaluation phase. This analysis thus predicts that the informal sector will thrive in the shadow of the devaluation, leading to the so-called "informalization" of the economy, but will begin to suffer when the light resumes.

Casual observation suggests that the process of "informalization" just described occurred in most CFA Zone countries as soon as the SAPs started. In the case of Niger, Azam *et al.* (1993) have described the expansion of the informal sector in the city of Niamey in the wake of the adoption of an SAP in 1982. This was made possible thanks to a pair of surveys of the informal sector performed by the local Statistical Office with the support of the International Labor Office (ILO) (i) in 1981, just before the change in policy, and (ii) in 1988. A point that was regarded by many as contentious at the time was that the wages in informal sector firms were going up in real terms by about 20% between these two dates. The number of established informal sector firms in Niamey – i.e. disregarding street vendors, door-to-door craftsmen, etc. – increased by 125% over this period, while the population increased by about 33%. The average number of employees per firm increased from 1 to 1.4. The local donor community was puzzled, but the model just presented offers a neat interpretation of this observation. As formal sector workers perceived their position in the formal sector under threat, especially in various state-owned enterprises (SOEs), they increased their saving and investment in informal sector firms. This had a positive impact on wages there.

I am not aware of similar data for Côte d'Ivoire, where only indirect evidence is available. The "informalization" process is nevertheless highly plausible there as well. According to Grootaert (1996), informal sector employment grew steadily between 1980, at the beginning of the adjustment process, and 1992 (Grootaert, 1996, p. 81). It increased over this twelve-year period by 153%, while employment increased in the whole country by only 52%. There is also some evidence of rural–urban migration over this period, as employment in agriculture grew by only 38%. This suggests that earnings in the informal sector became more attractive than in agriculture. In the meantime, employment in the "modern sector" fell by 14%, reflecting the effects of the two waves of adjustment programs (Azam and Morrisson, 1994). Another indirect look at this process can be derived from the Côte d'Ivoire Living Standard Survey (CILSS), which took place in four rounds in 1985–8. This shows that the incidence of extreme poverty fell in the informal sector, for both employees and self-employed, between 1985 and 1987 (Grootaert, 1996, p. 81). It then increased abruptly in 1988, in the wake of the TOT crash that occurred at the end of 1987. Nevertheless, the self-employed in this sector remained better off than in 1985, according to this criterion.

Section 7.4 presents some more systematic observations, using household surveys to look at the change in poverty that occurred in the wake of the devaluation.

7.4 Changing patterns of poverty in Côte d'Ivoire, 1993–1995, and Niger, 1994–1995

In this section, some results are presented on the decomposition of poverty among different socio-economic groups in Côte d'Ivoire and Niger, from Azam and Wane (2001). These two countries performed household surveys at two successive dates around 1994 that can help shed some light on the short-run impact of the devaluation on poverty. It should be emphasized that the resulting sample is not a panel, so that a transition analysis, as performed by Grootaert and

Kanbur (1995) is not possible. It is thus impossible to disentangle in the observed change in the distribution of income, as measured by consumption expenditures, what is due to the impact of the devaluation from what is due to a sampling problem, so that this distribution would be different even if the devaluation had not taken place. This remark is especially relevant for Côte d'Ivoire, whose two samples are different in significant ways, as described below. It is therefore important to check the validity of our results by going beyond the global figures, and looking at the "before–after" changes using different decompositions of the samples, in order to check that the results seem robust in this respect.

Only the Côte d'Ivoire surveys are really suitable for this exercise, as one took place just before the devaluation, in 1993, followed by a second one in 1995, after a full year of the post-devaluation era. However, even this pair of surveys raises problems, which have always stood in the way of a fully satisfactory analysis of poverty in this country, despite the large number of household surveys carried out. As emphasized by Grootaert and Kanbur (1995) and by Grootaert (1996), Côte d'Ivoire has had an inadequate price index for many years. The CPI collected by the statistical office has always been restricted to Abidjan, and a more comprehensive price index, covering some information about the countryside, is operational only for the analysis of the 1998 household survey (see Kouadio *et al.*, 2000). Here, the deflator used comes from the World Bank's tables (World Bank, 1997), from which an inflation of 44% can be computed over the two years. This is probably an over-estimate, as prices may possibly have increased more slowly outside Abidjan. The 1993 survey was a so-called "priority survey" on the social dimensions of adjustment, and interviewed a total of 10,080 households. In fact, 1,680 households from Abidjan were actually surveyed in 1992, and another 480 in 1993, while all the other households were surveyed in 1993 (see Ouattara, 1997). The 1995 survey was a living standards survey, with a more complete questionnaire but a much smaller sample. Only 1,200 households were surveyed in this round, 1,000 picked fully at random, and 200 among the households surveyed in 1993. This drastic difference in sample size between the two dates may legitimately raise some suspicion about how representative the second one is. This problem does not arise with the surveys of Niger.

Table 7.2 presents the contributions of different groups to poverty, using the Foster, Greer, and Thorbecke (FGT) (1984) measure. These computations for Côte d'Ivoire are made with respect to the poverty line $z = 144,800$ CFA Francs suggested by the World Bank. Three measures of poverty are presented: the Head Count ratio (P_0), the Poverty Gap (P_1), and the FGT2 (P_2), all derived from the so-called "FGT family" (Foster, Greer and Thorbeke, 1984). Its general formula is:

$$P_\alpha = \frac{1}{n} \sum_{i \leq q} \left(\frac{z - y_i}{z} \right) \qquad (7.12)$$

where z is the poverty line, and y_i is individual i's income, usually measured by consumption. Individuals are assumed to be ranked from the poorest to the richest, with i running from 1 to n, and q being the index of the individual whose income is just at the poverty line. This poverty measure has two attractive characteristics that explain its widespread use. First, it is decomposable, in that it can be computed for different sub-groups of the population, without changing the total. Second, it encompasses several widely used measures, depending on the value chosen for α. When $\alpha = 0$, it is in fact the headcount ratio q/n – i.e. the ratio of the number of poor to the total population. When $\alpha = 1$, we find the headcount ratio multiplied by the average income gap – i.e. the average distance of the incomes in the group of the poor to the poverty line – which can be written as follows, defining $\bar{y}$ as the average income of the group:

$$P_1 = \frac{q}{n} \frac{z - \bar{y}}{z}. \qquad (7.13)$$

Both of these versions of the FGT measure treat all the persons below the poverty line equally. The headcount ratio is the most widely used index, but it does not take into account the depth of poverty. The weighted poverty gap P_1 does this, but does not take into account the inequality among the poor, which it treats equally. For example, a mean-preserving spread of the income distribution among the poor, which would bring some of them coming closer to the poverty line, while others would move into deeper poverty, would not affect it. Some authors thus prefer to choose $\alpha = 2$, which amounts to weighting each person's poverty gap by itself, thus giving more weight

Table 7.2. Côte d'Ivoire: contribution to poverty of different groups before and after the devaluation, %

Poverty line z = 144,800 CFA Francs

	Headcount P_0		Poverty gap P_1		FGT P_2	
	1993	1995	1993	1995	1993	1995
Socio-economic category						
Unknown	44.5	55.4	1.73	2.96	0.105	0.252
Self-employed	65.4	75.8	3.23	5.04	0.237	0.472
Unskilled employee	40.9	57.0	1.57	2.51	0.100	0.167
Traders	38.1	57.4	1.43	2.74	0.086	0.186
Skilled employees	17.6	36.1	0.498	1.40	0.025	0.085
Others	36.1	52.5	1.56	2.69	0.108	0.203
Sector of activity						
Unknown	44.5	55.4	1.73	2.96	0.105	0.253
Primary	70.3	76.3	3.58	5.17	0.266	0.490
Public	18.9	39.5	0.56	1.47	0.028	0.086
Secondary	34.2	45.2	1.20	1.78	0.069	0.107
Commerce	37.6	54.7	1.46	2.58	0.092	0.176
Transportation	38.1	40.0	1.28	1.57	0.074	0.079
Others	31.0	56.9	1.08	2.49	0.066	0.161
Education level						
None	60.0	72.6	2.83	4.51	0.201	0.409
Primary	47.2	61.4	2.00	3.48	0.133	0.281
At least secondary	20.5	41.0	0.71	1.72	0.045	0.109
Farm						
None	51.3	74.1	2.29	4.63	0.157	0.419
Exporting	49.5	46.0	2.26	2.29	0.159	0.174
Food crop	49.7	48.1	2.33	2.19	0.169	0.150
Non-farm enterprise						
Yes	47.3	62.9	1.99	3.34	0.133	0.260
No	52.7	63.0	2.52	3.85	0.181	0.349
Region						
Abidjan	12.7	38.7	0.27	1.71	0.01	0.112
Other cities	44.6	58.7	1.73	2.73	0.10	0.189
East Forest	62.2	72.2	2.66	4.01	0.17	0.338
West Forest	70.3	76.2	3.77	5.47	0.29	0.531
Savannah	77.7	80.0	4.26	5.56	0.33	0.539

Table 7.2. Cont.

Poverty line z = 144,800 CFA Francs	Headcount P_0		Poverty gap P_1		FGT P_2	
	1993	1995	1993	1995	1993	1995
Ethnic group						
Akan	42.5	62.4	1.60	3.31	0.09	0.266
Krou or Voltaic	59.0	65.3	2.99	4.10	0.22	0.372
Mande	56.6	59.4	2.85	3.59	0.22	0.315
Non Ivoirian	46.7	63.5	2.02	3.56	0.13	0.296
Aggregate poverty	**50.4**	**62.9**	**2.29**	**3.65**	**0.16**	**0.313**

to the poorest of the poor. Table 7.2 shows the values of these three measures for Côte d'Ivoire, computed from the 1993 and the 1995 surveys, according to different partitions of the population.

The first partition aims at bringing out the different impact on different occupations. It shows that poverty increased in all occupational categories, whichever measure is used. In relative terms, it is undoubtedly the skilled employees, a typical formal sector category, who took the hardest blow. The second partition presented looks at the impact by industry. Here again, poverty goes up, according to all the measures; however, it is clear that poverty went up more strongly among the public sector workers and in the commerce sector. Transportation was more or less unaffected. The sector labeled "secondary" involves manufacturing industry and mining, and also displays a deterioration of the poverty situation.

The criterion of education also provides some interesting information. The incidence of poverty increased the most, in relative terms, among the persons with at least a secondary education level. Here again, this criterion points at the formal sector, as few educated persons work in the informal sector; people without any education were less affected by the deterioration, in terms of headcount. However, the use of the distribution-sensitive measures shows that all were affected. The next partition shows that people involved in farming were partly protected from the increase in poverty. This is true for the headcount index, and for the poverty gap measure as far as food crop growers are concerned, but it is not true for the last measure. By contrast, the fact of owning a non-farm enterprise has no discriminating power.

The next partition is especially interesting. Here, the geographic criterion is used, decomposing the population first according to the urban–rural distinction, and then among the rural people, according to the most relevant regional division: Savannah, in the north, and east and west forest zones, for the south. While the rural people were not shielded from the increase in poverty, whichever measure is used, it is clear that urbanites suffered the strongest deterioration. Abidjan, in particular saw its situation deteriorate massively. The West Forest and the Savannah zones suffered a much softer impact. The East Forest zone, the traditional Akan area, where cocoa and coffee have been grown since the beginning, also saw a non-negligible increase in poverty. Even among the relatively protected groups, in terms of headcount, the data show that the deterioration is worse the more distribution-sensitive is the measure used.

The last partition also gives some interesting clues. It is the traditionally dominant group, the Akan, who paid the greatest price, in terms of deteriorating poverty: its incidence is even larger than among the Mande, a northern group from the Savannah. The Akan were politically dominant between independence and the 1999 military *coup*, and they were the most numerous in the public sector and other segments of the formal sector.

The data are thus consistent with a story where the formal sector workers, and in particular those from the public sector, have seen their poverty situation deteriorate, and have brought down with them the living standards of other urbanites, mainly in the commerce sector, but in other sectors as well. Some spillover from the worsened urban situation to the rural one, to some extent in the Harris–Todaro spirit, probably followed.

Concerning the dates at which the household surveys have been performed, the data for Niger are not as suitable as the Ivorian ones, as they took place in 1994 and 1995, so that the post-devaluation era was observed *en route*. On the other hand, the sample size is more balanced, as the 1994 survey provides a sample of 3,823 households, and the 1995 one 4,067. Because the post-devaluation adjustment was already in progress when the first survey was done the inflation rate between the two rounds is smaller: 10.9%. This may be an underestimation of the true average increase in consumer prices that affected the sample households, because it refers to the change in prices between the two dates, at the end of the year. This is at variance with the Côte d'Ivoire case, where we may suspect an over-estimation. Nevertheless, the two before–after comparisons provide roughly the same picture. In fact, table 7.3 suggests that the increase in poverty in the wake of the devaluation was larger and deeper in Niger that in Côte d'Ivoire. Only the private sector employees, whichever the poverty measures used, and the administrative staff for P_2, seem to see their poverty situation improve. All the other socio-economic categories have seen poverty go up among their members, rather as in Côte d'Ivoire. In relative terms again, it is in the urban sector that the blow hit the hardest, and here even the farmers saw their poverty situation worsen.

The model presented above suggests that the temporary fall and subsequent rise in poverty observed before and after an expected devaluation are transitory phenomena. In the cases of Côte d'Ivoire and Niger, political instability inflicted new shocks on the economy around the turn of the century, so that nothing much can be learned from the disturbed series. However, the experience of Senegal provides a clear support to this view. There are no satisfactory surveys allowing us to analyze the short-run impact of the 1994 devaluation, as performed here for Côte d'Ivoire and Niger. However, a survey was performed in 1996 for the city of Dakar, suggesting that the same phenomenon was observed there, by comparison with the data of the ESAM 1 survey performed in 1994. No data are available for the rest of the country in the relevant period. However, a large-scale household survey was performed in 2001 that can be compared directly to a similar survey performed in 1994 (ESAM 1 and 2). A significant reduction of poverty occurred between these two surveys, in the wake of a remarkable run of rapid growth, by African standards (World Bank, 2005). Senegal avoided the regional recession that affected the whole WAEMU area around the turn of the century, following the *coup* in Côte d'Ivoire. It thus achieved nearly a decade of sustained GDP growth at an average rate above 5% per annum. After a lag, poverty responded very favorably, as the demand for labor in the urban formal sector thrived.

Table 7.4 describes how poverty changed in Senegal between the two ESAM surveys (1994–2001), using a breakdown by geographical areas.

The results show that urban poverty went down massively during that seven-year rapid-growth episode. These figures provide some

Table 7.3. Niger: contribution to poverty of different groups before and after the devaluation, %

Poverty line z = 150,000 CFA Francs	Headcount P_0		Poverty gap P_1		FGT P_2	
	1994	1995	1994	1995	1994	1995
Socio-economic category						
Idle	61.9	83.3	5.89	8.81	0.92	1.48
Management and professional	12.4	32.6	0.42	1.47	0.03	0.13
Administrative staff	23.4	52.7	1.96	2.30	0.33	0.16
Service staff	40.3	73.1	2.71	5.61	0.36	0.64
Unskilled workers	56.1	76.3	3.37	4.74	0.34	0.46
Traders	50.3	78.3	3.26	6.25	0.37	0.73
Craftsmen	47.3	77.0	3.52	7.12	0.47	0.97
Marabouts and other Religious	63.2	84.8	5.43	7.94	0.83	1.15
Farmers	84.7	96.2	8.02	13.5	1.14	2.47
Status in occupation						
Unknown	63.0	92.6	6.06	12.8	0.96	2.38
Entrepreneur	45.3	54.5	2.80	3.96	0.32	0.50
Self-employed	70.8	88.0	6.22	9.96	0.87	1.58
Public sector employees	26.4	55.6	1.22	3.13	0.10	0.28
Private sector employees	84.1	63.0	7.31	4.40	0.82	0.53
Family helpers	50.0	91.4	4.20	11.7	0.75	2.13
Others	56.6	78.6	3.16	6.94	0.23	0.99
Education level						
None	70.8	91.0	6.22	11.1	0.87	1.89
Primary	43.0	79.6	2.51	6.82	0.26	0.96
At least secondary	18.2	46.8	0.90	2.68	0.09	0.26
Farming						
None	55.9	74.7	4.64	6.34	0.66	0.84
Yes	77.8	95.2	6.76	13.0	0.89	2.37
Non-farm enterprise						
None	57.1	82.2	7.10	10.1	0.77	1.82
Yes	63.9	87.4	5.17	9.60	0.68	1.50
Region						
Urban	46.7	77.8	2.80	6.66	0.29	0.84
Rural	84.2	96.4	8.90	14.4	1.39	2.79
Aggregate poverty	**61.3**	**85.3**	**5.17**	**9.82**	**0.71**	**1.63**

Table 7.4. Change in poverty incidence: Senegal, 1994–2001, change in FGT P_0

Year	Dakar	Other towns	Rural sector	Total
2001	33.3	43.3	57.5	48.5
1994	49.7	62.6	61.4	61.4
Change	−16.4	−19.3	−3.9	−12.9

Source: World Bank (2005).

support for the view that sustained growth is a powerful instrument for reducing poverty, even if it acts with a lag. The impact was much less significant in the rural sector. During the same period, the share of agriculture in GDP went down significantly. Explaining how a sustained growth episode can thus lead to a fall in the relative importance of the rural sector is one of the main themes of chapter 8.

7.5 Conclusion

This chapter has analyzed the effects of the 1994 devaluation of the CFA Franc on growth and poverty in the WAEMU, with a medium-run horizon. Examination of the data has first shown that the crucial channel of impact is the fall in the real wages of the formal sector workers, which had not been achieved by any other means in most CFA Zone countries. Labor markets are known to be segmented in African economies, between the rural and the urban sector, on the one hand and, within the latter, between the formal and the informal sector, on the other hand. This is what the classic Harris–Todaro model is meant to capture. I did not follow this path here, and instead modeled the stratification of the labor market between formal and informal sectors. The crucial link is through the fact that formal sector workers, who are much more affluent than other workers, in most countries of the CFA Zone, are running businesses in the informal sector. They invest their savings in small firms, where they generally employ people from their own social network. It is the increase in saving induced by the prospect of a future wage cut, due to an expected devaluation or to other reasons, that therefore drives the predicted dynamics of the model. For the sake of smoothing consumption, formal sector workers begin to increase their saving in anticipation of a cut in their purchasing power, and invest more in their informal sector firms. This involves an increase in informal sector wages in the pre-devaluation period, as capital intensity increases in equilibrium. However, when the cut comes, as it did after the 1994 devaluation, then savers are gradually running down their assets, and informal sector wages go down. This is thus a medium-run model of a stratified labor market, as it takes into account capital accumulation and decumulation, but does not take on board longer-term processes such as technical progress and the accumulation of human capital.

This provides a rationale for an observation which seems puzzling at first, namely that poverty increased significantly in the wake of the 1994 devaluation in Côte d'Ivoire and Niger, and most probably in other CFA Zone countries. The designers of this measure were expecting a response in the other direction, hoping that the depreciation would mainly entail an improvement in agricultural prices, boosting the incomes of the rural poor. The results found by looking at the change in various standard measures of poverty before and after the devaluation in Côte d'Ivoire and Niger in fact show a marked deepening of poverty, despite the resumption of GDP growth. Only the people in some way related to agriculture in Côte d'Ivoire got some relative protection from the cut in living standards. Preliminary results using the 1998 survey by Kouadio *et al.* (2000) and by Grimm (2001), while using different approaches, confirm that urban poverty increased in Côte d'Ivoire in the wake of the devaluation, while they show that some recovery took place in the rural sector, especially among food crop farmers and export crop farmers from the West Forest area. This was in part a result of the improvement in world prices for export crops. While unexpected at the time of the decision, this type of delinking of growth and poverty is not unheard of. Deaton (2001, p. 125) concludes: "Thus economic growth, as measured, has at best a weak relationship with poverty, as measured." The story presented here suggests that the standard favorable impact should be expected only from an unexpected devaluation.

These results are not perfectly satisfactory, insofar as the data are not ideally suited for this exercise. In both countries, there are problems with the CPI, while the 1995 survey in Côte d'Ivoire has a small sample and the 1994 survey in Niger was performed after the devaluation had already been carried out. The convergent results of these two before–after comparisons, for two very different countries, at a drastically different level of income *per capita*, suggest either of two conclusions (i) the labor earnings of the poor really have fallen behind the devaluation-induced price rises, creating a fall in their real incomes, or (ii) we have a more fundamental methodological problem, namely that consumption expenditures are in this case a misleading indicator of incomes because, despite some increase in labor earnings, households have decided to reduce consumption in order to restore the level of their assets. After all, the real balance effect is one of the standard mechanisms whereby devaluation is supposed to help cut absorption, in standard open-economy macroeconomics. Only a detailed study of the evolution of earnings in different segments of the labor market, which falls outside the scope of the present chapter, can hope to shed some light on this issue. Nevertheless, it seems unlikely that the poor held substantial nominal assets whose real value was cut by the devaluation, beside the wages of their relatives working in the formal sector.

8 *Export crops, human capital, and endogenous growth*

8.1 Introduction

Côte d'Ivoire was up to the 1980s one of the few African success stories. At independence, it was a low-income country, raising no special hopes for fast growth. There were no mineral reserves, and agriculture was the only basis for economic development. Growth was driven by the rapid expansion of export revenues, mainly cocoa and coffee. By the end of the 1970s, Côte d'Ivoire was one of the wealthiest countries in Africa, exporting some manufactured goods. It then suffered like many other countries from a public investment explosion in the wake of the export boom of the late 1970s (Berthélemy and Bourguignon, 1996; Ghanem, 1999). Unsustainable macroeconomic imbalances and mounting indebtedness, aggravated by the high interest rates and the appreciation of the US dollar in terms of CFA Francs, making debt service obligations heavier, demanded an adjustment process, which began in 1980. By 1986, the adjustment process was complete, and the World Bank was optimistic (World Bank, 1987a). The success story, however, collapsed at the end of 1986 when the world prices of coffee and cocoa fell to historically low levels in real terms. The economy also took a long time to show any sign of recovery from what seemed, until the mid-1990s, a permanent adverse shift of its TOT. Unfortunately, after a *coup* at the end of 1999 and a civil war starting in September 2002, the economy was eventually wrecked by political violence. Chapter 9

Most of this chapter has been presented in seminars in Clermont-Ferrand and Oxford, as well as in Liège in a French version. It has also been presented in Dublin at the European Economic Association 7th Annual Congress, in 1992. It owes much to stimulating discussions with Allechi M'Bet, Jacques Pégatienan, and Joseph Yao Yao, and to useful comments by Chris Allen, Tim Besley, François Bourguignon, Paul Collier, and Jan Gunning. It draws on Azam (1993) and to some extent on Azam and Djimtoingar (2004).

offers a framework for understanding the economic dimension of the kind of political constraints that Côte d'Ivoire had to face.

The aim of the present chapter is to provide a framework for analyzing some stylized facts of the Ivoirian long-run growth experience, including its extreme sensitivity to TOT shocks. But the TOT cannot explain everything, as many other African countries have faced similar TOT as Côte d'Ivoire without achieving the same performance in the 1960s and 1970s. It is therefore interesting to identify the specifics of Côte d'Ivoire's development strategy, in order to draw some lessons which might be valid for other African countries with similar features. Some comments about the extension of this framework to other African countries are offered in section 8.5.

The first stylized fact is an open-door policy for both labor and capital. In the late 1980s, immigrants accounted for about 25% of the population, and this share increased slightly in the 1990s. They came mainly from Burkina Faso and Mali in the North, and from Ghana. This massive immigration was handled peacefully by President Houphouët-Boigny. Unfortunately, it was later used by several political entrepreneurs who based their strategy on xenophobia, creating various political parties along ethnic lines, following the movement of democratization forced upon Francophone African countries by Mitterrand's famous "La Baule Speech," which made democratization a condition for continued French aid. Xenophobia could then be extended to a north–south division of the country, which led naturally to civil war, discussed in more detail in chapter 9.

The second salient feature is the heavy taxation of the main export products, coffee and cocoa. This tax was mainly levied through a stabilization fund known as the *Caisse de stabilisation* (Ridler, 1988; Schiller, 1989; McIntire and Varangis, 1999), whose task was to stabilize producer prices. Pegatienan (1988) has calculated that the rate of this tax was on average about 50%. Despite this anti-export incentive, reinforced by the protection of the import-competing manufacturing sector by tariffs or quotas, export revenues remained buoyant until the late 1980s. Export crops remained lucrative over most of the period, and the doubling of the Ivorian crop over the 1970s and 1980s played a significant role in depressing the TOT, which collapsed at the end of 1987. Cocoa farming is a kind of frontier agriculture, with new land being continually brought into cultivation at the expense of the forest, and migrant workers providing cheap labor (Gastellu, 1989). People are richer in the Forest Zone, where export crops are grown, than in the northern Savannah Zone, which relies on subsistence agriculture (Kanbur, 1990). This sector was liberalized in 1999, and it is not clear yet how the government will make up for the lost revenues.

The third and most original fact of the development policy was the structure of government expenditures. It is appropriate in Côte d'Ivoire to speak of a strategy of "human capital accumulation." The share of public expenditures on education has been around 30% of the government budget (Pegatienan, 1988); in 1983, this amounted to more than 9% of GDP, a higher share than in any comparable country. Education has been favored by the government over most of the post-independence period, and students and teachers became the most vocal political opponents during the adjustment phase. Yao (1988) has tested econometrically the impact of human capital on wages in Côte d'Ivoire, concluding that it has a positive rate of return; this suggests that the sustained accumulation of human capital has been productive. This is interesting to analyze in the light of the new endogenous growth literature, which emphasizes the role of human capital accumulation, viewed partly as an unplanned by-product of investment in physical capital (as in Arrow's 1962 model of learning-by-doing), and partly as the result of a conscious choice by households (Becker, Murphy, and Tamura, 1990). In most of these analyses (e.g. Lucas, 1988), human capital accumulation is viewed as involving externalities, entailing some inefficiency in the competitive equilibrium. Government intervention may therefore be defensible.

As noted by Barro (1990), a number of these papers are extensions of pre-Solowian Harrod–Domar models. They assume constant (or increasing) returns to a broadly defined capital stock (Rebelo, 1991). This is not the case here, and the intellectual origin of this growth model should be traced back to Lewis (1954). It assumes unlimited supplies of labor and capital from abroad, which is acceptable in the case of Côte d'Ivoire. This country has a small population compared to the whole of West Africa, where populations are traditionally mobile (e.g. Ajayi, 1990). It is therefore reasonable to regard its supplies of migrant labor as infinitely elastic. Moreover, the Franc Zone guarantees currency convertibility and free capital movements, providing a large access to capital inflows (Guillaumont and Guillaumont, 1984).

It is assumed that the limiting factor is local human capital, regarded as an imperfect substitute for human capital embodied in expatriate professionals. This is especially true for supporting activities provided by the local administration, predominantly staffed by nationals. Even in private firms, a significant share of the knowledge used is mastered better by local people than by foreigners. The appropriate way to deal with local workers or civil servants requires a subtle blend of modern and traditional knowledge, which is also true for adapting a foreign technology to local conditions. This assumption is combined with that of a public sector devoted to the production of human capital for capturing the stylized facts sketched above in a generalized Lewis-type model, driven by human capital accumulation. Unlike many of the endogenous growth models, it has a non-degenerate transitional dynamics, and reaches its steady-growth path only asymptotically. This model is therefore consistent with the so-called "convergence hypothesis," which predicts that poor countries should catch-up on richer ones. Human capital is then the "core capital good," as defined by Rebelo (1991), because its production does not involve non-reproducible factors. But here, physical capital and labor are "produced" by foreign investment and migration.

The private production sectors are described in section 8.2. Section 8.3 analyzes the public sector, which produces new human capital. These elements are drawn together in section 8.4, where the determination of GDP and its growth rate is presented. Two caveats are discussed in section 8.5, in order to assess the possibility of extending the lessons of the model to other African countries.

8.2 The private production sectors

I model the engine of growth as the transformation by the state of agricultural surpluses into productive human capital: a full-blown analysis of the dynamics of export crops in West Africa lies outside the scope of this chapter. The development of coffee and cocoa production is based on the destruction of the common-property forest, and its replacement by privately owned coffee and cocoa trees, planted by migrant farmers. It thus calls for a dynamic analysis based on the theory of the depletion of exhaustible resources (Dasgupta and Heal, 1979). I leave such an analysis for further research, and focus here on the effects of human capital accumulation in an economy with infinite supplies of the other factors of production.

Let $X = J(L^x)$ be the output of the export crop, where L^x is the quantity of labor employed in this sector, and $J(\cdot)$ is a standard production function ($J' > 0$, $J'' < 0$). The assumption of decreasing returns to scale in the agricultural sector has been traditional since David Ricardo in the early nineteenth century, and captures the fact that the supply of land is fixed, neglecting the dynamics sketched above. This crop sells on the world market at the price p, in terms of the numéraire good, and is taxed by the government at the rate t^x. The supply of labor is infinitely elastic, with a fixed reservation wage R. In Côte d'Ivoire, wage payment for migrant labor is a transient phenomenon in agriculture; when the migrant worker has accumulated enough money to support his family while waiting for the crop to be sold, the labor contract is turned into a sharecropping agreement. This is called *abusan* in Côte d'Ivoire (Gastellu, 1989), and it allocates one-third of the crop to the laborer, and two-thirds to the planter. This contract can be found also across the border in Ghana, where it is called *abusa* (Hill, 1963), and seems to be typical of the Akan ethnic group. For the sake of simplicity, I neglect these details and assume that all the farmers are self-employed. The migration equilibrium then implies the following arbitrage condition:

$$R = (1 - t^x)\frac{PX}{L^x} \tag{8.1}$$

This assumes that the representative farmer gets the whole after-tax value of the crop, and makes the migration decision by comparing the average farm income to his reservation wage. This is a crude assumption, which is defensible only because of its simplicity. Stark (1991) has shown that migrations are more complex, but taking his points into account would make the model untractable.

By inverting (8.1), output of the export crop can be written as:

$$X = X\left(\frac{(1 - t^x)p}{R}\right), X' > 0. \tag{8.2}$$

It is thus an increasing function of its world price p, and a decreasing function of the tax rate t^x and the reservation wage R.

The second private production sector produces a quantity Q of a tradable good, taken as the numéraire. As this sector uses human capital, I regard it as "modern," and call it "manufacturing," for short. It can also encompass modern services, insofar as the latter are using significant human capital. It uses also a quantity K of physical capital, a quantity L^M of labor, and a quantity S^M of local skilled labor, embodying some local human capital. The stock of physical capital K can be owned by local residents or by foreigners. As I assume perfect capital mobility, it is endogenous, and not pre-determined as in most growth models. Modeling it more con-ventionally as a state variable would complicate the model, without providing any additional insight. Foreign human capital is aggregated with K. I assume the following "well-behaved" production function:

$$Q = F(K, L^M, S^M). \tag{8.3}$$

In order to capture the idea that local human capital is necessary for the development of the manufacturing sector, I assume that:

$$F(K, L^S, 0) = 0. \tag{8.4}$$

The representative firm of this sector is competitive, so that profit maximization equates the marginal product of each input to the relevant price, r for capital, w for labor, and w^S for skilled labor. Denoting partial derivatives by a subscript, this means that:

$$F_K = r, F_L = w, F_S = w^S. \tag{8.5}$$

I regard r and w as exogenous, determined by perfect capital mobility and by the migration equilibrium ($w = R$). Because of con-stant returns to scale of the production function $F(.)$, one can then derive from (8.5) w^S as a function of R and r:

$$w^S = w^S(R, r), w^S_R = -\left(\frac{L^M}{S^M}\right) < 0, w^S_r = -\left(\frac{K}{S^M}\right) < 0 \tag{8.6}$$

Equation (8.6) is a generalized factor-price frontier, whose partial derivatives are again denoted by subscripts. The manufacturing sector can develop only if the net-of-tax salary of skilled workers is above their opportunity cost. If skilled labor is allowed to accept an unskilled job, at the cost of a social stigma σ, or if local skilled labor can emigrate to get a (net-of-tax) salary w^{SF} abroad, at a cost γ, then denoting t^S the tax rate on skilled labor wages, it is natural to require that:

$$(1 - t^S)w^S \geq \max\{R - \sigma, w^{SF} - \gamma\} \text{ if } S^M > 0. \tag{8.7}$$

As w^S is a decreasing function of R, condition (8.7) implies that one can define $R^{\max}(t^S, r, \sigma)(R^{\max}_{t^S} < 0, R^{\max}_r < 0, R^{\max}_\sigma > 0)$, such that the manufacturing sector cannot develop unless $R < R^{\max}(t^S \gamma, \sigma)$. One can similarly define $w^{S\min}(t^S, r, \sigma) = \frac{R^{\max}(\cdot) - \sigma}{1 - t^S}$, as the minimum level of the skilled labor wage rate consistent with the existence of the manufacturing sector. Thus, for any given reservation wage R, there exist some maximum levels of the interest rate r and the tax rate t^S beyond which the manufacturing sector has to close down. Figure 8.1 helps us to understand this reasoning. The downward-sloping curve represents the skilled labor wage rate (8.6), while the upward-sloping line shows the minimum value of this wage given by (8.7), below which all the educated workers emigrate. I assume that R, r and t^S are such that this does not arise. An analogous reasoning could be made regarding w^{SF}, and this is left as an exercise. The latter can thus provide a useful analysis of the "brain drain," showing that, beyond a point, the "modern" sector is unable to develop if the international market for educated labor is offering opportunities so attractive that they trigger a massive emigration of human capital.

As $F(.)$ is homogenous of degree one, it is easily derived from (8.5) that manufacturing sector output may be written as:

$$Q = v(R, r)S^M, \quad v_R < 0, \quad v_r < 0. \tag{8.8}$$

This clarifies the relationship between the present model and the class of endogenous growth models described by Rebelo (1991). As the manufacturing sector output is produced under constant returns

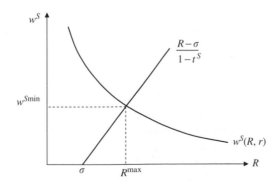

Figure 8.1. Conditions for manufacturing development

to scale with respect to the three production factors, and as the supplies of labor and physical capital are infinitely elastic, it is in fact proportional to the human capital stock. We are back to a fixed-coefficient sort of Harrod–Domar model in the manufacturing sector, where this coefficient depends on the supply prices of migrant labor and capital inflow.

A similar result holds for the public sector, as I now establish.

8.3 The public sector

The government raises taxes and produces local human capital. Denote by S^G the quantity of skilled labor employed by the government and define $S = S^M + S^G$. Then, under the assumptions already stated, tax revenues can be written:

$$T(t^X, t^S p, R, r, S) = t^X p X(.) + t^S w^S(.) S. \tag{8.9}$$

This equation assumes away any tax on physical capital and unskilled labor, but including these items in the model would not raise any difficulty. Again denoting partial derivatives by subscripts, and defining the elasticity of the export crop supply function as:

$$\xi = \frac{(1 - t^X) p X'}{R X}$$

one can easily find:

$$T_{t^X} = pX \left(\frac{1 - t^X \xi}{1 - t^X} \right), \; T_{t^S} = w^S S > 0, \; T_p = t^X X (1 + \xi) > 0,$$

$$T_R = -t^X \xi \frac{pX}{R} + t^S w_R^S < 0, \; T_r = t^S w_r^S S < 0, \; T_S = t^S w^S > 0. \tag{8.9'}$$

The impact of the tax rate on the export crop t^X is the only ambiguous result. This is a Dupuit–Laffer effect, as tax revenues are first rising with increasing t^X, and then declining:

$$T_{t^X} \lessgtr 0 \text{ as } t^X \underset{>}{\overset{<}{}} \frac{1}{1 + \xi} \tag{8.9''}$$

The government uses a quantity L^G of labor and a quantity S^G of skilled labor to produce human capital. L^G is thus the number of students in the education system. They are paid a policy-determined wage $w^G (w < w^G < w^S)$, which in fact represents the scholarship that is granted by the government to fund their course of study. In Côte d'Ivoire, scholarships used to compare well with the salaries of civil servants. This is consistent with an infinitely elastic supply of students. Let the time-derivative of S be denoted by dS/dt, and $G(.)$ be a well-behaved production function. Neglecting the depreciation of human capital, the growth of the stock of local skilled labor can be written:

$$\frac{dS}{dt} = G(L^G, S^G).$$ (8.10)

When modeling a developed-country government, one generally assumes either that it maximizes some ethically determined social welfare function, or that it maximizes the welfare of the median voter. These assumptions are not attractive when dealing with most LDCs. The political economy of LDCs government behavior has not been studied as much as that of western democracies, but Findlay (1991) provides interesting analyses in this direction, including a typology of the appropriate assumptions, ranging from the surplus-maximizing predatory state to the expenditure-maximizing bureaucratic state. Here, we model the government's decision as follows.

Assume that the government is divided into a taxing agency and a spending agency, the decisions regarding t^x and t^s being taken separately from the others. The impacts of the tax rates are discussed later. The spending agency maximizes dS/dt subject to the budget constraint:

$$w^G L^G + w^S S^G \leq T.$$ (8.11)

This assumption may seem optimistic on the efficiency of public expenditures. However, the maximization of any strictly increasing, quasi-concave and homothetic function of L^G and S^G under the revenue constraint (8.11) will result in basically the same outcome. One may imagine that the parameters of $G(.)$ embody any level of X-inefficiency that one may find realistic, without drastically modifying the results. Maximizing (8.10) subject to (8.11) then yields:

$$\mu = \frac{G_L}{w^G} = \frac{G_S}{w^S},$$ (8.12)

where μ is the marginal product of tax revenues in terms of human capital. Moreover, (8.11) holds with equality, as the spending agency is not wasting any of its budget. From (8.12), μ is a function of w^G and w^S, and thus, using the factor price frontier (8.6), one can write:

$$\mu = \mu(R, r, w^G).$$ (8.13)

One can prove unambiguously that $\mu_r > 0$, $\mu_R > 0$ and $\mu_w{}^G < 0$. Then, using (8.11), (8.12), and Euler's theorem, one can transform (8.10) into the following expression:

$$\frac{dS}{dt} = \mu(R, r, w^G)T. \tag{8.14}$$

A constant-coefficient relation is again found. The marginal product of tax revenues in terms of human capital μ is thus also the average product, because of constant returns to scale. Similarly, the demand for skilled labor by the public sector is proportional to the level of tax revenues:

$$T = g(R, r, w^G)S^G. \tag{8.15}$$

This ratio T/S^G is the average product of skilled labor in the public sector, whose value added is evaluated at its production cost, as in standard national accounting.

The results of sections 8.2 and 8.3 can now be put together, in order to analyze the determination of GDP and its growth rate.

8.4 GDP and growth

Evaluating public output at cost, one can define GDP as:

$$Y = pX + Q + T. \tag{8.16}$$

This is thus the sum of agricultural output, manufacturing output, and the wage cost of the public sector. Then, using (8.8), (8.9), and (8.15), one can transform (8.16) into:

$$Y = ApX + BS, \tag{8.17}$$

where $A = 1 + t^X(1 - v/g)$ and $B = v + t^S w^S(1 - v/g)$. This expression brings out how GDP depends on the export crop and the stock of human capital. As noted above, v and g are the average productivity of skilled labor in manufacturing and public production, respectively. It is therefore natural to assume that $v/g > 1$. This is related to the relative intensity assumption made by Becker, Murphy, and Tamura (1990). Hence, it is possible to have t^X or t^S so high as to make either A or B negative. However, as these tax rates are necessarily less than one, a sufficient condition for these coefficients to be positive is that $v/g < 2$. Even if the average productivity of skilled labor was three times as high in the manufacturing sector as in the public sector, then A

and B would still be positive provided the two tax rates were less than 1/2. However, A and B are decreasing functions of the relevant tax rates, provided $v > g$.

Notice that if $t^X = \frac{g}{v-g}$, then $Y = BS$, and we are back to a fixed-coefficient model, as in Barro (1990) and Rebelo (1991). But then GDP is proportional to the human capital stock embodied in local skilled labor, and not to the stock of physical capital. Assuming that t^X is below this value, (8.17) implies that GDP is a non-homogeneous function of S. It follows that the steady-growth path, with a constant growth rate of Y, will be reached only asymptotically.

By differentiating (8.17) with respect to time, and using (8.14), one gets:

$$\frac{dY}{dt} = \mu BT. \tag{8.18}$$

Then, using (8.9) and (8.17) again, we get an expression for the growth rate $g^Y = d \log Y/dt$:

$$g^Y = \frac{\mu B}{A}(t^X + (t^S w^S - t^X v)s), \tag{8.19}$$

where $s = S/Y$. The growth rate of GDP is thus a decreasing linear function of the latter ratio, provided: $\frac{t^S - t^X}{t^X} < \frac{rK + wL^M}{w^S s^M}$

In the case of Côte d'Ivoire, where the implicit tax rate on export crops has been around 50% over most of the period under study (Pegatienan, 1988), this condition seems realistic. It also seems acceptable for most other African countries. This economy therefore converges to a steady-growth path if s converges to a constant value. We analyze this question now.

Defining $g^S = d \log S/dt$, one can write the change in s over time as:

$$\frac{ds}{dt} = (g^S - g^Y)s. \tag{8.20}$$

Then using (8.9), (8.14), and (8.17) we can compute the value of g^S as:

$$g^S = \frac{\mu}{A}\left([t^S w^S - t^X v] + \frac{t^X}{s}\right). \tag{8.21}$$

As discussed above, the difference between square brackets is negative.

Figure 8.2 may be used to analyze the dynamics of this model. The downward-sloping straight line represents g^Y, from (8.19). The

rectangular hyperbola represents g^S, from (8.21). These curves intersect for $s^* = 1/B$ and $s^o = \frac{t^X}{t^X v - t^S w^S}$.

But it can be checked by looking at (8.17) that $s > 1/B$ is mean-
ingless if $A > 0$. We know from (8.20) that s grows when $g^S > g^Y$, i.e.
for any point located below the rectangular hyperbola. The transitional dynamics of the growth rate of GDP can therefore be represented by the arrow borne by the g^Y line, and pointing to the right. Its
negative slope shows that growth is slowing down as the economy
gradually substitutes manufacturing production for an export crop.
Figure 8.2 thus shows that for any initial value of $s < 1/B$, this
economy converges eventually to a steady-growth path with $s^* = 1/B$
and the long-run GDP growth rate:

$$g^{Y*} = \mu t^S w^S. \tag{8.22}$$

Using (8.6) and (8.14), one can derive from (8.22) that this is an
increasing function of the tax rate on skilled labor wages t^S, and a
decreasing function of the student wage w^G and the factor prices R
and r. One can prove that it does not depend on the tax rate on the
export crop t^X, nor on the terms of trade p. But these parameters play
a part in this model. First, it is clear from (8.17) that they affect the
level of GDP, for any given value of S. They thus have an impact on
the growth rates in the transitional dynamics. To show this, it
is convenient to use (8.22) to transform (8.19) and (8.21) into the

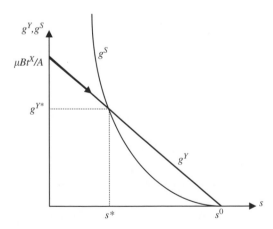

Figure 8.2. Transitional convergence

following pair of equations:

$$g^Y = \left(\frac{s}{s^*}\right)\left(g^{Y*} + \frac{\mu t^X pX}{S}\right), \qquad (8.23)$$

$$g^S = g^{Y*} + \frac{\mu t^X pX}{S}. \qquad (8.24)$$

Given s and S, the tax revenues on the export crop thus determine the speed of the transitional dynamics: the higher the former, the faster the economy converges to its steady-growth path, where their role vanishes. Remember that a Dupuit–Laffer curve was found with respect to t^X, when discussing (8.9″). There thus exists a value of $t^X = 1/(1+\xi)$ which maximizes the speed of convergence, given μ. This value is consistent with the assumed condition $A > 0$ provided $v/g < 2 + \xi$.

Equation (8.19), together with figure 8.2, sheds some interesting light on the β convergence hypothesis, made popular by the cross-country empirical analysis presented by Barro (1991), and numerous followers. It predicts that, *ceteris paribus*, poorer countries should grow faster than richer ones. The present model offers a similar prediction, suggesting that the growth rate of GDP goes down gradually as the economy develops, with both income and the ratio of skilled labor to income increasing in the transitional dynamics. Primary exports also play an important part in the early phase of this dynamics, while their relative importance decreases as income grows. However, (8.23) shows that a large export crop is an important asset for a country to have if it is to benefit from accelerated development. This observation is consistent with the case of Côte d'Ivoire, where cocoa and coffee were initially the engine of growth. This discussion is thus leading to a qualification of the convergence hypothesis, such that crop-rich developing countries should converge faster than crop-poor ones. This model also emphasizes education as the engine of growth, as does most of this empirical literature.

8.5 Two caveats

This model is heavily dependent on the institutional setting prevailing in the Francophone countries, with a pervasive involvement of the state in education, as well as a heavy taxation of export agriculture and a convertible currency that provides some support to capital mobility. However, in many Anglophone countries, the education system depends much more on private initiative. An especially interesting case is that of Kenya, where the government has restricted entry in the education system for a long time, under the cover of a "manpower planning" policy. Even Michael Todaro has been caught supporting this policy (Todaro, 1976). The result of this openly restrictive policy turned out quite spectacularly: a non-governmental organization called *Harambee* developed countrywide, helping parents to get their children educated (Azam and Daubrée, 1997). At one point, about two-thirds of the children in secondary education were in the *Harambee* movement. The supply of education had to adjust to demand, and the outcome was an accumulation of human capital which made a significant impact on growth. Azam and Daubrée (1997) test four different and independent measures of the educational effort in a production function, and find them all highly significant. By contrast, Berthélemy, Seck, and Vourc'h (1996) perform a similar test using data from Senegal and fail to find any significant impact. Publicly provided education in Senegal was a declared priority of President Léopold Sédar Senghor. As a poet, and philosopher of "Negritude," the President was very keen to prove that Africans could become highly literate, and become at least as good as the French at classical Greek and Latin. He undoubtedly succeeded, and this massive investment in education paid off later, even when the emphasis on classical studies had waned.

It takes only a limited effort of imagination to see how this model can be adapted to include a private sector-led education rather than a supply-driven, public education system: the tax rates on the export crop and on the earnings of skilled workers can be interpreted as the share of their incomes that the people from these two occupational categories are investing in the education of their children. Various refinements immediately come to mind without changing the basic structure of the model.

The second caveat is that the emphasis in the mechanics of the model is put on the educational sector, and the efficiency with which the revenues from the export crop are transformed into human capital. However, (8.23) makes it clear that export crop production does play a dominant role in the growth process at low levels of human capital. When S is very low, the second term becomes dominant in this equation, even if μ is quite low. In other words, at very low levels of development, growth is mainly explained by looking at the output of the export crop sector. This comes out quite clearly from the following exercise.

Using data from Chad, one of the poorest countries in the world, after several years of civil war at the end of the 1970s and the beginning of the 1980s, Azam and Djimtoingar (2004) have estimated the following growth equation, for the period 1963–95:

$$\Delta \log Y = -0.2 \, War + 0.11 \Delta \log Cot + 0.20 \log Cot(-1) - 0.88$$
$$(5.66) \qquad (2.90) \qquad\qquad (3.66) \qquad\qquad\qquad (6.02)$$
$$\log Y(-1) + 0.39 \log Pop(-1) - 0.14 \log Tot(-1) + 0.73 AR(1)$$
$$(3.87) \qquad\qquad (2.06) \qquad\qquad (5.00)$$
$$R^2 = 0.74, \quad LM2 - F = 1.53.$$

$$(8.25)$$

In this equation, Y is GDP, War is a dummy variable for the years of the civil war (1979–84), Cot measures the output of cotton, Pop is population, and Tot are the terms of trade. The residuals are modeled as following an autoregressive process of order one, and no auto-correlation is left up to the second order, according to the LM-test presented. Here again, as in previous chapters, there is an implicit error-correction representation, as both the lagged levels and the growth rates are included in the equation, *à la* Banerjee *et al.* (1993). The fit is quite good given the profile of growth in the country. It is clear that cotton output is one of the main drivers of GDP growth in Chad, according to this equation. The long-run relation implicit in (8.25) shows that GDP is an increasing function of cotton output and population, and a decreasing function of the TOT. The latter effect is rather surprising and can be explained by the following mechanism. In the cotton sector, the producer price is stabilized by a parastatal, Cotontchad, and the profits are levied by the state, by different channels (see Azam and Djimtoingar, 2004). So, when the TOT improve, due to an increase in the price of cotton, the whole improvement is captured by the government, which expands public expenditures, and especially public employment. The latter takes away some labor from productive employment elsewhere in the economy, with a negative output effect. Similarly, when the TOT improve in response to a fall in import prices – i.e. mainly oil prices – the improvement is not passed on to consumers, but taxed away by the government, with the same impact.

8.6 Conclusion

This chapter has analyzed a model of endogenous growth driven by the accumulation of human capital, funded in the transitional phase by the taxation of export crops. It bears some resemblance to Lewis' analysis of economic development with unlimited supplies of labor. This analysis is motivated by three stylized facts of the long-run growth experience of Côte d'Ivoire: (i) an open-door policy for both labor and capital inflows, (ii) heavy taxation of export crops, and (iii) government expenditures skewed in favor of education. No attempt has been made to calibrate it to the actual data. Other features of the Ivoirian development policy, which this country shares with other relatively successful African countries, such as the sustained public investment in infrastructure, have been left out of the analysis. Nothing substantial would be changed in this model if the public sector were assumed to produce infrastructural capital along with human capital. Under some conditions, this economy converges asymptotically to a steady-growth path. The long-run growth rate of GDP is an increasing function of the tax rate on skilled-labor wages, and a decreasing function of the interest rate and the reservation wage of migrant workers. The tax revenues on the export crop affect the convergence speed. A crucial parameter in the determination of the GDP growth rate is the marginal productivity of tax revenues in terms of human capital: the more efficiently tax revenues are transformed into human capital, the faster is GDP growth.

This model should be viewed as a "parable," which drastically simplifies some features of the real world. A more satisfactory version of this model should (i) extend the analysis of export crop development using the theory of exhaustible resources, (ii) take into account the private production of human capital, (iii) draw the welfare consequences of such an analysis, and lastly (iv) test empirically the relevance of the main results. This list opens the agenda for further research.

9 | Ethnic rents and the politics of redistribution

9.1 Introduction

Poor countries are not uniformly poor. In many African countries there is generally a simple mapping between the allocation of wealth across ethnic groups and their geographical distribution. The cultural or religious divisions between ethnic groups in West African countries, for example, are strongly correlated with the difference in wealth between them: there is a sharp contrast between a relatively affluent south and a poorer north in most of the countries of the area. For instance, in Chad, the southerners produce cotton, while the northerners are poor nomadic herdsmen. A similar distribution of activities can be found in Mali and Niger, where southerners are agriculturists and northerners are nomadic herdsmen. In Côte d'Ivoire, the northerners produce also cotton, but it is a poorer crop than the coffee and cocoa produced by the southerners. In Nigeria, the northerners rely on a typical Sahelian agriculture, growing cotton and millet, while oil dominates the southern economy.

In these countries, a typical political pattern seems to emerge: a military regime often prevails when the northerners are in power, while civilian rule seems to be the dominant mode of government when the southerners are in power. Tombalbaye in Chad and Houphouët-Boigny in Côte d'Ivoire were from the south of their countries, and ran civilian governments. The Hausa generals from northern Nigeria came to power time and again, while the southerner

This chapter draws on a paper presented at the AERC/Harvard University workshop on "Explaining African Economic Growth, 1960–2000" (Weatherhead Center for International Affairs, March 18–19, 2005). It benefited from the comments by Nahomi Ichino, who was the discussant, and by Robert Bates, who also offered editorial remarks, and by Chinyamata Chipeta, Paul Collier, Augustin Fosu, Christine de Mariz, Benno Ndulu, Dominique Njinkeu, Janvier Nkurunziza, Steve O'Connell, and Nicolas van de Walle; these comments are gratefully acknowledged, without implicating their authors.

Obasanjo led the return to civilian rule in that country (see Zartman *et al.*, 1997). This pattern allows for some exceptions. For example, in Mali, the military rulers, Modibo Keita and Moussa Traoré, were also from the south, like the civilian governments that were in power either before or after them. No northerner has ever ruled Mali. Nevertheless, the pattern sketched above seems to occur often enough to warrant some further analysis. Azam and Mesnard (2003) and Azam (2006) analyze the theoretical foundations of such a pattern. This analysis is sketched below, spelling out the kind of political determinism that the latter seems to reveal. The natural endowments of the different ethno-regional groups that live together in some African countries, for historical reasons, impose some significant constraints on the sustainable political regimes that can be found there.

Sometimes, a more complex pattern emerges, as in Ghana, where the rich cocoa growers have poorer neighbors in both the north and in the south. Nevertheless, a related pattern emerges, as the civilian leader Busia, for example, came from the richest Akan group, while some of the military rulers, including in particular Jerry Rawlings, came from poorer groups. In East Africa, the pattern is slightly different, with a rough east–west division, corresponding mostly to altitude. The rich crops grow mainly on the hills, above 3,000 ft, while herdsmen are found mostly below that level. In all these cases, these geographical differences give rise to some form of "ethnic rent," as migration from the poorer areas to the richer ones is largely precluded by the rules of land ownership. A fairly tight mapping thus exists between ethnicity and regional location of the groups. Politics is to a large extent devoted to the redistribution of these rents across groups. Sometimes, a civil war breaks out between them. In Chad, for example, in the late 1970s, or in Nigeria a few years earlier, the civil wars opposed the rich groups to the poorer ones. In other cases, peace prevails despite this type of inter-group inequality.

As proved by the later events starting in September 2002, Côte d'Ivoire was clearly exposed to such a risk. The north–south divide there involves both ethnic and religious aspects. The Djula and the Senufo in the north are Muslim, and grow cotton and millet; in fact, the land of the Djula is so poor that they are found mainly in trade, rather than in agriculture. The Akan and the Kru in the south are Christian or Animist and they grow cocoa and coffee, as well as palm oil and exportable vegetables. However, peace was purchased by redistribution for several decades. President Houphouët-Boigny tried explicitly to build national unity by taxing his own ethnic group, the Akan cocoa and coffee growers, in order to fund visible public investments in infrastructure in the other regions and some other redistributive public expenditure, such as the public provision of health and education. This strategy was quite successful until his death. After 1993, his successors have changed the general orientation of the country's public expenditure strategy, keeping the northerners out of the game. There was a *coup* in 1999, which brought General Gueï to power for a year. He was a western Mandé, a group related to the northern ones. A mutiny split the country into two parts in 2002, the northern part falling under the mutineers' control. The history of Côte d'Ivoire thus seems to suggest that this type of country has the choice between orderly redistribution between groups, organized by peaceful means, or violent appropriation. Viewed in this light, the type of redistributive policies that Houphouët-Boigny used consistently from the 1970s until his death played a fundamental part in purchasing peace. This strategy seems to have a wider domain of application in Africa. Azam *et al.* (1996), for example, using panel data from a series of African countries, find a significant negative impact of public expenditures with a strong redistributive content, such as education and health, on the probability of the outbreak of political violence.

The "redistribution syndrome" which has been identified in many African countries is probably a response to some deeper parameters, which are in some way rooted in the colonial origins of national borders. As in medicine, one should in political economy never confuse the syndrome with the disease that it reveals. African countries have been either delineated by agreements between competing colonial powers, or by a colonial administration, for fiscal or economic reasons, within the ambit of one of them. Modern-day Burkina Faso was twice split between neighboring countries by the French, in order to provide the richer neighbors with a reserve of manpower to enhance their development potentials. No attention was paid at all to the deep cultural unity of the Mossi Empire, rooted in a long and rich common history. Twice, the Moro Naba got his country back together by providing the French with highly organized military units for fighting its two world wars. The northern tip of the then Ubangui Shari territory was similarly grafted onto Chad in 1936 by the French

Popular Front government, in order to provide the local colonial administration with some fiscal revenues. The civil war that took place in Chad in the second half of the 1970s in fact pitted the original Chadian groups against the people from the grafted-on south. These examples suggest that some countries have inherited a polarized ethnic division from the past, and have been left with a fairly radical choice of political strategy. They can either buy peace, by the means described below, or go for a civil war instead. Redistribution and state breakdown may thus be the possible syndromes of a common disease, related to ethnic division and the polarization of wealth across groups.

The present chapter sheds some light on this type of behavior, using the recent development of the economic theory of conflict. Section 9.2 presents the relations between ethnicity, the geographic allocation of resources, and the resulting polarization of the distribution of wealth across groups. Section 9.3 discusses how redistribution and deterrence can be used for buying peace in this type of country. Section 9.4 goes deeper into the social mechanisms involved in this type of redistribution, against the background of the rural–urban migration flows that necessarily come with economic development. Section 9.5 briefly concludes.

9.2 Ethnicity and the polarization of wealth

The mapping between the unequal levels of affluence of different ethnic groups and the natural resources available in their territory is determined by the history of their migration and settlements. Most African ethnic groups have a long memory of the different places from where they came, before they settled in their current location. Most of the people in Central and Eastern Africa, and a large part of Southern Africa, are descendants of the Bantu migrants. Similarly, in West Africa, some of the forest groups, such as the Akan, can claim some ancestors that came from the Sahelian region. They sometimes conquered their current territory by force, but they often found an empty land. In some cases, the germs that they brought with them decimated the previous occupants (Diamond, 1997). Some ethnic groups have moved in a more recent past, and are currently found in recently conquered land. For example, the Djulas from northern Côte d'Ivoire arrived there under the leadership of Samory Touré, at the beginning of the twentieth century. They evicted the Animist Senufo farmers, killing many of them and converting the survivors to Islam. However, these historical roots are now sufficient to found the perceived legitimacy of the collective ownership of their land by many ethnic groups in Africa. As a result, only farmers from some well-defined ethnic groups are entitled to get some land in some areas. The resulting exclusion of migrants from other groups may create some inefficiency and some inequality of wealth across groups.

Figure 9.1 describes the type of rent that may result in Africa from the restrictions on labor mobility imposed by ethnicity and collective land ownership. The quantity of labor used on the land owned collectively by group R is measured from left to right. From right to left, the quantity of labor measured is that used on group P's land. The vertical line through points R and P represents the natural allocation of labor between the two groups, in the absence of migration. Maybe because group R's land is more fertile, or because this group also owns other assets that enhance the productivity of its labor, or because it has a lower population density on a similar land, its marginal productivity is larger than group P's. Given the supply of labor in each group, the marginal product of labor in group R is at R, located above group P's marginal product measured at P. The area of the rectangle so labeled measures the "ethnic rent" that accrues to the members of group R. This is akin to a monopsony rent, insofar as the restriction on hiring labor from the other group allows them to drive a wedge between the marginal product of labor and its opportunity cost. In the case depicted in figure 9.1, the market equilibrium involves a distortion, as the marginal productivity of labor is not equalized across groups. The social cost of the resulting inefficient allocation of labor is measured by the area of the triangle REP, which measures the deadweight loss.

In order to restore productive efficiency, the quantity M of labor would have to migrate from the land of group P to that of group R. The marginal product of labor would then be equalized across groups, and output would reach its maximum. The large discrepancies that can be observed in some African countries between the marginal productivities of labor across different ethno-regional groups can therefore be ascribed to a labor market failure or to a land market failure. However, the latter diagnosis seems more accurate, as it pinpoints the root cause of the problem, namely the collective

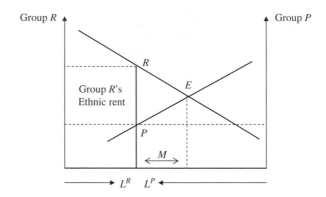

Figure 9.1. Ethnic rent and migration failure

ownership of land by the whole ethnic group. In fact, the expression "migration failure" encapsulates these two ideas at once. Efficiency could be restored, for example, if M units of group P's labor were allowed to migrate to group R's land, and work there for an income equal to the height of point E, while the rest of the "Harberger triangle" would be paid to some group R members as rent. Such a move could be Pareto improving, depending on the initial distribution of income within group R, and in particular on the functioning of the labor market within that group. It would undoubtedly be socially desirable from a utilitarian point of view.

The distortion described above does not necessarily occur all over Africa. Many ethnic groups have developed a well-functioning market for land, where some form of sharecropping contracts have existed for centuries, allowing migrants to make a living on rented land. Polly Hill (1963) has described in detail the *abusa* contract, which solves this problem among the Akan cocoa planters in Ghana. As we saw in chapter 8, the same contract exists, called *abusan*, in neighboring Côte d'Ivoire. It gives one-third of the crop to the migrant farmer, and two-thirds to the planter (Gastellu, 1989). Some marginal adjustments are made by allocating some land to the migrant's wife(ves), and by allowing for the gift of some free meals to the planter. Nothing is paid to the collective owner of the land, i.e. the ethnic group. Among the Akan, in both countries, the planter traditionally owns the trees, but has only usufruct rights on the land for the duration of the life of the trees. This system has worked smoothly for a long time, and largely explains the early success of post-independence Côte d'Ivoire. Azam (1993) shows how smooth immigration allowed Côte d'Ivoire to engage in a process of endogenous growth; however, events leading to the civil war which began in 2002 suggest that this migration process could be turned into a time bomb by some simple manipulation of the laws governing land ownership. The 1998 "*Reforme foncière*" (Land reform), enacted by President Konan Bedié, himself from the Akan group, engineered a massive expropriation of many of the migrants, who had bought the orchards from the planters. The distinction between the ownership of the land and that of the trees became blurred, resulting in massive violence, as alien migrants were then seen as occupying Akan ethnic land. This came with a vengeance, as some Akan migrants had also planted cocoa on Kru land, in the south-west of Côte d'Ivoire, and have been expelled as well. President Konan Bedié was ousted by a *coup* in December 1999, but the smooth functioning of the land market has not been restored.

Land markets seem to be working more efficiently in Muslim countries than in Animist or Christian ones, at least when Islam has been present for a long time. For example, Manchuelle (1997) shows how the flow of migrants from the Soninke group, in the Upper Senegal Valley, was primed in the nineteenth century by the possibility of renting some land downstream near the French trading post of Bakel. Since then, this ethnic group has been very successful at making up for the secular impoverishment of its land by migration. Inheritance laws force people to define land ownership individually in Muslim societies, although some hybrid systems are still in force in some Muslim African countries.

Several post-independence African rulers did attempt to alleviate such migration failures. For example, Houphouët-Boigny knew very well that Côte d'Ivoire needed massive imports of manpower from Burkina Faso (then Upper Volta) and Mali, to produce the coffee and cocoa that would earn his country the foreign exchange required for development. The colonial French had understood this, and Upper Volta had been divided between the neighboring countries from 1936 to 1945. Côte d'Ivoire had a pool of manpower available in its northern part, cut off from the Mossi Empire. However, the Moro Naba, the Mossi emperor, recovered his country after the Second World War, in return for raising an army that joined the Free France Forces in the Gold Coast during the war. Houphouët-Boigny wanted to make the massive immigration from the north irreversible by granting dual citizenship to the migrants. However, this is one of the few policy decisions that he was unable to get through parliament. Part of the current problems faced by Côte d'Ivoire since the turn of the century stems from this failure. However, in some cases, the migration of people from the poorest group follows the military defeat of the rich, and does not ensure an optimal use of the land. For example, in Chad after 1990, the northern herdsmen often trespass in the cotton fields of the southern cotton growers, which they use as grazing land, and do not hesitate to kill the complaining farmer. This is done with perfect impunity, since the northerners won the civil war and now rule the country. This example epitomizes how the existence of a glaring inequality of wealth across groups is likely to be ended, sometimes violently, unless policies are consciously chosen to manage the potential distributional conflict in an orderly fashion. Group P may take over, probably by violent means, and then impose some sharing of the rent under some form of threat. The Chadian example just described shows that this is not necessarily done by efficient means. Section 9.3 describes how this can be prevented, if group R is prepared to pay the price of peace.

"Ethnic rent" does not arise only from agriculture; the collective ownership of the land extends to the traditional ownership of its mineral wealth. In Côte d'Ivoire and Mali, for example, there are substantial gold mines scattered on ethnic land. Modern governments have usually found ways of appropriating these mines, often by compensating some traditional ethnic authority. This is not necessarily easy to enforce, and Sierra Leone provides a sad example where alluvial diamonds have given rise to state breakdown, with extreme violence. This type of violent expropriation occurs more often with mineral wealth than with agricultural production, although Zimbabwe has provided a recent example to the contrary. The main reason for this fact, which the case of Zimbabwe supports equally, is that farmers are needed for production as much as the land itself. Their know-how is part of the wealth, and cannot be expropriated as easily as mineral wealth. Leonard and Straus (2003) use the expression "enclave production" to indicate the latter type of resources, which seems to increase the probability of violent expropriation. These examples illustrate the link that exists between wealth inequality across groups and the incentives that they create for violent appropriation.

However, political violence or civil war does not necessarily follow from the polarization of wealth across groups. In most cases, the two sides have an incentive to avoid the outbreak of political violence as it is bound to destroy both resources and lives. This is where politics comes in, understood as a way to solve the distributional problem without violence, and to prevent the outbreak of war. Section 9.3 describes how the richest group might prevent war by choosing the right combination of redistribution of wealth and accumulation of weapons, for the sake of deterrence.

9.3 How to pay for peace

When the initial distribution of wealth is too polarized, the richest group has the choice between running the risk of a war, with all the destruction that this implies, and paying some price for securing the peace. This section sketches how the price of peace can be determined, within a simple graphical setting. Further analysis can be found in Azam and Mesnard (2003) and Azam (2006).

Figure 9.2 depicts how the richer group can pay for peace. The setting is similar to that of a standard analysis of the bargaining problem. Point *B* represents the break point, which describes the allocation of wealth that would prevail in case of civil war. Because of

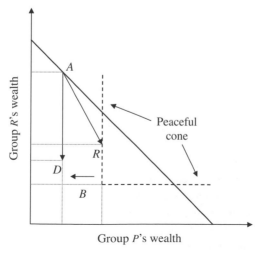

Figure 9.2. Paying for peace

the intrinsic uncertainty of the outcome of a war, this point may be interpreted as representing the allocation of *expected* wealth across the two groups in case of war. Then, the efficiency frontier is represented by the downward sloping line with a slope equal to one. It is the locus of all the possible allocations of a given wealth between the two groups. Peace occurs only if the final allocation of wealth is chosen within the cone located to the north-east of point B, or on its frontier. Otherwise, one group or the other will choose war, which will then promise a higher expected wealth than peace. Call this the "peaceful cone." If the initial allocation of wealth falls within that cone, then the analysis can stop here, as no further policy choice is required to establish the peace. However, the discussion above has shown that many African countries are in fact characterized by a highly unequal initial distribution of wealth across groups, creating a rent for the lucky ethno-regional groups. As mentioned above, this typical case poses the problem of politics, understood as the collective search for a peaceful equilibrium. Politics then boils down to either the conscious reduction of the polarized distribution of wealth between the two groups, or to the modification of their aspirations by some form of military threat. Figure 9.2 illustrates the two pure methods that can be used for buying peace.

Point A represents the initial allocation of wealth between the two groups, which is assumed to fall outside the peaceful cone. The status quo at A is not an equilibrium outcome, as group P would get a higher expected wealth by choosing to wage a war against group R, thus getting to point B. The first possible strategy for buying peace is for group R to give away some of its wealth to group P. If no resource cost is involved in such a move, then the allocation of wealth is shifted along the efficiency frontier, up to the point where group R's wealth lies on the vertical line above B, maybe with a minute addition for breaking the tie between the two points. Peace is then Pareto-improving over B, as both players get a higher payoff in the resulting equilibrium. However, it is realistic to assume that some resource cost might be incurred for making such a transfer of wealth. For example, some taxes might have to be levied on group R's members by its leader, possibly involving some incentive effects. Some output might be lost if the taxes so levied reduce the marginal reward to labor. However, as discussed above, there are many rents existing in Africa, so that the social cost of taxation might be negligible in some cases.

This would require a careful targeting of these rents, as advocated by David Ricardo nearly two centuries ago. For example, the massive implicit taxation of the cocoa crop in Côte d'Ivoire in the 1970s and 1980s, whereby the "Stabilization Fund" was on average taking about 50% of the export value of the crop, did not impose much distortion. In fact, the cocoa growers remained by far the best-off group in the country, and the quantity exported doubled over about a decade, resulting in a glut that depressed the world market at the end of 1987. Nevertheless, the present framework can easily accommodate such transaction costs. The resulting deadweight loss might then involve a move below the efficiency frontier, as depicted in figure 9.2 by the move from A to R. As long as R is located above B, the resulting equilibrium outcome is unanimously preferred to war.

The redistributive policy sketched above, however, raises a fundamental problem of credibility, described by Azam (2001c) and Azam and Mesnard (2003). It is in fact based on the offer by group R of an implicit or explicit contract of the type: "I will give you a transfer T if you do not get armed and engage in a war against me." However, once group P has refrained from arming and engaging in the war, then the latter is in a much weaker position, and the incentives for group R to deliver the promised transfer are much weakened. Knowing this, group P might be deterred from accepting the contract, and might go for the war instead, despite the peaceful offer made by group R. This type of commitment problem lies at the heart of the economic analysis of institutions, as developed in particular by North (1990), and has a wide-ranging application. In Africa, the historical record suggests that two types of systems have been used by rulers for securing peace by such a redistribution strategy. The first is typically based on reputation: the ruler acquires gradually a reputation for keeping his word, and never reneges on his promises. This was the course of action chosen by Houphouët-Boigny; the drawback of this approach is that his reputation died with him, leaving the subsequent governments in a delicate position.

Léopold Sédar Senghor of Senegal used a different approach, of a more institutional kind, related to the analysis of the universal franchise adopted in nineteenth-century Europe made by Acemoglu and Robinson (2000). Senghor came from a minority group, the Serer, and was a Christian, in a predominantly Muslim country (Boone, 2003). He very early on relied on democracy, with universal franchise, but the secret ballot was not enforced until 1993 (Schaffer, 1998). The Sufi brotherhoods, and in particular the Mourides, really controlled the votes, at least in the rural areas; during this whole period, the modernizing government was using the traditional brotherhoods as guarantors, making promises credible by their ability to defeat it in the elections. The brotherhoods thus served as political inter-mediaries, voicing the demands of the people and mobilizing popular support in return for promises kept. However, in most other cases, the credibility of the promises made will be less than perfectly credible. The promised transfer will have to be larger, the less credible is the promise, in order to compensate group *P* for the risk of default. However, there are limits to this type of compensation, as the ruling group cannot promise more than its available resources. Azam (2001c, 2006) and Azam and Mesnard (2003) show how a civil war might break out because of such commitment failure, while the ruling group has the resources and is willing to share them. Hence, the commitment technology is a crucial ingredient in a strategy aiming at buying peace by redistributing wealth. This suggests that when in power, group *R* has an incentive to build credible political institu-tions, and to tie its own hands by creating some system of checks and balances, in order to reduce its probability of reneging on its own promises.

When group *R* does not have a credible enough commitment technology, then it might be profitable to simply hand over the poli-tical power to group *P*. The latter might take over the ability to tax group *R*, and to engineer the required redistribution in an orderly fashion. However, nothing would then prevent the ruling group *P* going beyond the necessary redistribution level, described in figure 9.2. When in power, group *P* would have an incentive to tax group *R* up to the point where the latter is just indifferent between peace and war – i.e. where group *R*'s wealth falls to the level of *B*, or minutely above it. Because of this prospect, group *R* might in fact prefer to take a chance and go for war. If the latter is lost, then political power changes hands, and the analysis just made can be repeated, with group *P* in power. Here again, building some political institutions for reducing the ruling group's ability to tax the other one might be the solution for peace to be credible.

The alternative strategy to redistribution is based on deterrence. The latter consists of accumulating weapons in peacetime with a view to reducing the potential opponent's payoff in case of war, to such an extent that the latter will prefer peace. In figure 9.2, such a move is represented by a shift from point *A* to point *D*. Group *R* sacrifices a quantity *AD* of resources, invested irreversibly in weaponry, in order to reduce group *P*'s expected payoff in case of war. In the case of figure 9.2, this is supposed to shift group *P*'s expected payoff in case of war to the vertical of point *A*. *D* will then secure peace, if it lies above the resulting expected payoff that group *R* would get in case of war. Deterrence is thus socially costly, as it involves the sacrifice of productive resources in equilibrium in order to prevent the occurrence of a state of nature where the accumulated weaponry could be used for fighting, on the off-equilibrium path. Nevertheless, it might be preferable to the outbreak of a war, if the resource cost implied is lower than the expected cost of the war – i.e. if point *D* lies above point *B*, as in figure 9.2. In many cases, group *R* may choose a blend of the two pure strategies described above. For example, in the case of figure 9.2, group *R* could invest some resources in deterrence, in order to shift the break point to the left, but not all the way to the vertical of point *A*. The remaining gap would then be filled by redistribution. Such a strategy mix might be optimal, for example, if the marginal cost of deterrence or redistribution is increasing.

In general, then, there exists a locus that describes all the combinations of redistribution and deterrence that provide group *P* with the same expected payoff in case of peace as the expected payoff from war. Call this "group *P*'s participation constraint" (Azam and Mesnard, 2003; Azam, 2006). The position of this curve in this space depends on the relative efficiency at fighting and at producing of the two groups. If group *P* is very efficient at fighting, relative to group *R*, then this participation constraint will be located quite far to the right, as group *R* would have then to invest more on deterrence, for any given level of redistribution. Similarly, if group *R* is highly productive, relative to group *P*, the latter's participation constraint will be located high up in this space, as the stakes of the potential fighting would be high. Peace is secured if group *P* is faced with a combination of redistribution and deterrence that yields a higher payoff than this benchmark, even minutely so, while war occurs otherwise. Figure 9.3 represents a plausible shape of this locus, as the convex curve. All the points located above that locus are consistent with peace, as they give more redistribution for any level of deterrence, or vice versa. Then,

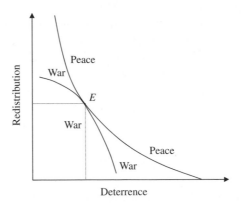

Figure 9.3. The redistribution/deterrence trade-off

the peace-seeking government will choose a point on this locus that minimizes the price paid for peace. The case described in figure 9.3 assumes that the marginal cost of redistribution or deterrence incurred by group R is increasing, so that the iso-cost contours are concave. The equilibrium mix of deterrence and redistribution is then found where an iso-cost contour is tangent to group P's participation constraint, labeled E in figure 9.3. The location of E on this locus depends on the efficiency of group R at producing or fighting. If its labor is highly productive, then the opportunity cost of diverting resources for military deterrence is also high, and it will rely more on redistribution. If its soldiers are very efficient at fighting, then any given level of deterrence can be achieved by diverting a small quantity of resources from production, making this solution more attractive. Therefore, the exact location of the equilibrium mix of deterrence and redistribution will be determined by the comparative advantage of the two groups at fighting and at producing. A more precise analysis of this point is presented in Azam (2006), which yields a typology of political regimes as a function of these comparative advantages.

However, group R might choose not to pay for peace, and to go for war instead. This would occur if point E turned out to be more expensive than the expected cost of war. Then, group R would be tempted to take a chance at the latter. The analysis presented above thus gives group R the choice first between war and peace, and then between redistribution and deterrence. From a utilitarian point of view, the redistributive solution for buying peace is the best one, unless there are huge transaction costs involved. The other two solutions, based on deterrence or civil war, are socially more costly, as they require that some resources be diverted from production into defense expenditures or outright fighting.

One of the crucial issues to be faced when choosing the redistribution strategy is to determine who in group P should be the recipient of the transfer. Should it be broad-based, aiming at giving some benefit of peace to a large number of group P's members, or should it be delegated to some key players from group P, who could then optimize its distribution within their own group? The answer to this question depends largely on the pre-existing social structure of the target ethnic group. Redistribution can be at times highly efficient. For example, Houphouët-Boigny used the traditional leader Gbon Coulibaly, and then his family, to exert social control over the Senufo, in northern Côte d'Ivoire. There was then no need to establish a heavy public administration in the north, as traditional institutions were doing their job. Similarly, as described above, Léopold Sédar Senghor used the traditional authority of the Sufi brotherhoods to manage the redistribution flows. However, this turns out to be very difficult when the target group has a very loose social structure, a problem arising in particular among the forest people including, for example, the Diola from Casamance, in Senegal (Boone, 2003). There, a low-intensity civil war erupted until a credible leader emerged, permitting some political settlement to be found. Similarly, the Bété from southwestern Côte d'Ivoire have also been regarded as a politically amorphous group, with no traditional authority with which to negotiate. Section 9.5 aims to provide a framework for thinking about this issue.

9.4 Triangular redistribution and political control

The redistribution problem must be analyzed against the background of the rural–urban migration flows that result necessarily from economic and political development (Bates, 2000). Village communities send the most promising of their offspring to the urban sector, equipped with the required education for obtaining hopefully good positions in the formal sector, and preferably in government. They can thus have access to high and regular incomes, so that they can in turn remit back some money to the village community which has funded the initial investment in education, or fund some investments

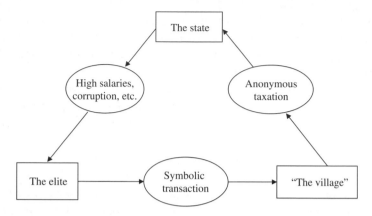

Figure 9.4. The triangular redistribution game

in local infrastructure. The most talented will climb the social ladder, and acquire powerful positions that will give them the opportunity to influence the regional allocation of public investments (Ayogu, 2000). The migrants to the urban sector thus function as "delegates" of their group of origin, in charge of earning there the means for supporting themselves and returning a share of this income back to the village. Sometimes the resulting transfers come as contingent remittances, triggered by the occurrence of some shock, within an implicit insurance contract (Azam and Gubert, forthcoming). In a more indirect fashion, they can also direct public spending in social or physical infrastructure to the benefit of their village of origin. However, as mentioned above, some of the resources that are redistributed by this system are levied in a distortionary way, in particular when they are channeled by the public sector. These distortions are liable to impose some cost on the ordinary people, and help maintain them in poverty.

Collectively, part of the African elite can therefore be viewed as redistributing a share of the resources that have been collected through the state apparatus or the public sector, in a way that may cause a lot of distortion. A reflection of this redistribution has been highlighted in chapter 7, as the channel whereby the cut in formal sector wages spilled over to informal sector earnings. This "triangular redistribution" system is illustrated in figure 9.4. As discussed above, the personalized relationships between the elite and the people from their village of origin involve the repayment of some initial investment made by the villagers in the education and the migration of their offspring. However, some enforcement mechanisms are used by the villagers to secure the inflow of remittances. The precise mechanism involved depends on the ethnic group, and calls for more research. As a first approximation, the exchange between the migrant and the villagers may be understood as an exchange of gift for prestige and support (Azam, 1995b). This is captured in figure 9.4 by the expression "symbolic transaction." The urban elite will eventually be responsible for the development of the state apparatus, which lives to a large extent off the taxes levied on the villagers through the taxation of agricultural exports or the distortions imposed on food markets. Chapter 8 has brought out the macroeconomic importance of the taxation of export crops, at least in the early phase of the development process. Similarly, chapter 4 has shown how the official market for foreign exchange can be used to collect the inflation tax and distribute the proceeds to selected agents. However, the burden of the latter will probably fall more on urbanites than on village folk, whose economy is less reliant on monetary transactions.

Nonetheless, one should not regard the villagers as the victims of this triangular redistribution system. Given that all the other groups in the country have similarly sent some "delegates" to participate in the urban economy and in the political appropriation game, it is optimal for the group to invest in the migration of its best offspring to participate in the scrum, and try to get hold of a good share. This can be analyzed as an inefficient Nash equilibrium, of the "prisoner's dilemma" type: given that all the other groups are engaged in the taxation game, it is best for them to have some delegates engaged in this game as well. Otherwise, the burden of the political game that is bearing on them would basically be the same, while the probability of getting some reward would be zero. Inefficiency results from the fact that none of them takes into account the distortions imposed on the economy by their collective behavior.

The main point of this analysis can be captured by an extremely simple model. Assume that there are two kin groups, each composed of a farmer and an urbanite. The game takes place in two stages, and is solved by backward induction. In stage one, the two urbanites decide collectively through the political process the tax rate t that the government is going to impose on the farmers; this political process also determines the shares of the expected proceeds that each of them will obtain. This determination is modeled here in a fairly general way, in some manner related to a bargaining process. The assumed uniform tax rate imposed on the two groups may be regarded as a political or administrative constraint, which is assumed to prevent the tax system from tailoring a different tax rate for each group. This might also reflect a built-in equity consideration characterizing the tax law of this country. For the sake of simplicity, assume that the intra-group redistribution, through the "symbolic transaction" mentioned above, functions extremely well. Assume that the urbanites remit their entire share as remittances g_i, $i \in \{1, 2\}$, to the farmers. In the real world, the reward that the groups get from their urban "delegates" does not only take the form of remittances. Ayogu (2000), for example, has shown how the most successful migrants to the city are able to influence the regional allocation of public investment, and get political support from their group for that. However, there is no need to go into these details here, as the main point to capture in the model is that the urbanites will return some resources for the benefit of their village of origin. No risk of default is assumed regarding these remittances. This might result from the "gift-for-prestige" redis-tribution system analyzed by Azam (1995b). For the sake of simpli-city, assume that the urbanites do remit voluntarily the whole share that they have got from the political process, and derive a utility g_i from doing it. This captures all the symbolic and social rewards that they get from the villagers. It could also be interpreted as an extreme form of altruism, of the kind labeled "warm glow" in the theoretical public economics literature.

In the second stage, the farmer from group $i \in \{1, 2\}$ puts an effort level e_i into production, with a unitary productivity (i.e. output is also e_i). The farmer's utility function is assumed quasi-linear in con-sumption c_i and effort e_i. The disutility of effort is assumed increasing and convex, and, for the sake of simplicity, is specified as $1/2\ e_i^2$. The farmer decides on the effort level knowing the amount of remittances received from the urbanite g_i, as well as the tax rate t that bears on output. Therefore, in stage 2, the farmer from group i will seek to solve the following maximization problem:

$$\max c_i - \frac{1}{2}e_i^2,$$
$$\text{s.t. } c_i = g_i + (1 - t)e_i.$$

The following effort and output supply function can be derived easily from the first-order condition of this maximization problem:

$$e_i = 1 - t, \ i \in \{1, 2\}. \tag{9.1}$$

This supply function shows very clearly the disincentive effect of taxation.

Now, the backward induction solution requires that this function be taken into account when analyzing the political process that takes place in stage one. For the outcome to be sub-game perfect, we need to assume that the two urbanites correctly anticipate the best-response functions described by (9.1). The political process is modeled in the simplest and most general way, which encompasses the Nash bargaining solution, generalized or not, as a special case. As suggested above, this political solution should take due account of the two groups' participation constraints – i.e. that no group should get less in the peaceful outcome than its expected gain from a potential war. Now that the ethnic groups are disaggregated, by distinguishing the urban elite from the villagers that they represent in the political process, the latter must be defined accordingly.

It is natural in this simple setting to assume that in case of war, the urban "delegates" would fight over the power to tax the farmers. The expected payoff from the conflict can then simply be modeled for each group's representative as the total value of the tax proceeds at the end of the conflict multiplied by their probability of winning the war. Denote B_1 and B_2 each group's expected payoff from a potential war, so defined. It is natural to assume that the sum $B_1 + B_2$ is smaller than the fiscal revenues collected in case of peace.

The political solution will then be a triplet $\{t, g_1, g_2\}$ that maximizes some function $v\,(g_1, g_2)$, assumed increasing and quasi-concave in its two arguments.[1] For example, the generalized Nash bargaining solution would maximize $(g_1 - B_1)^\eta (g_2 - B_2)^{1-\eta}$. If the outcome were determined by some random allocation mechanism, after the tax revenues had been chosen, such that group 1 would win the fiscal pot with probability p and group 2 with probability $1-p$, then $g_1 + g_2$ would be maximized. There is no need to specify so precisely how the political process is solved. However, the following constraints would

---

[1] See Anbarci, Skaperdas, and Syropoulos (2002) for a discussion of various bargaining solutions "in the shadow of conflict."

clearly be taken into account. First, the urbanites cannot deliver back to their kinfolks in the village more than is available in the fiscal revenues. This requires:

$$g_1 + g_2 = t \cdot (e_1 + e_2). \qquad (9.2)$$

This assumes that there are no other sources of finance than the taxes levied on the farmers, but it would be extremely easy to add some exogenous flow of resources. Then, of course, for the equilibrium outcome to be sub-game perfect, the urbanites should take (9.1) into account, for substituting into (9.2).

In addition, if war is to be avoided, the following two participation constraints should be taken into account:

$$g_1 \geq B_1 \quad \text{and} \quad g_2 \geq B_2. \qquad (9.3)$$

From the first-order conditions of this very general maximization program, one finds that $t = 1/2$. This is the main result coming out of this exercise. The intuition for it is simply that the urbanites will select the maximum of the Laffer curve, in order to extract collectively the maximum possible resources from the farmers. The Laffer curve here reads: $2t(1- t)$, as can be seen by substituting (9.1) into the budget constraint (9.2). In other words, to maximize the amount of money that they can remit back to the village, the urbanites have an incentive to impose the tax distortion that maximizes the tax revenue. This is found here in a simple model where the urbanites are assumed to be the most altruistic and devoted to their group's welfare, as they give back their entire income from the urban game. This result goes at the crucial point about the redistribution syndrome: even if the behavior of the elites is driven entirely by altruism and the desire to remit their whole income for the sake of their kinfolks, they will choose a tax rate as high as if they were driven by a pure predatory objective. This allows us to shed some light on the behavior of the customs officers described in part I of this volume. The latter has emphasized the roles of tariffs and corruption in collecting these resources at the customs, and drawn some of its macroeconomic consequences. The argument developed here suggests that corruption at the customs can be viewed as the result of the overlapping loyalties that link the officers to the formal institutions of the modern bureaucracy, on the one hand, and to the informal institutions of kinship and family ties, on the other hand. Similarly, chapter 4 has shown how the official market for foreign exchange, when a parallel market is active, can also be used to distribute some resources in a covert fashion, with some consequences for the inflation tax. It follows from (9.1) that $e_i = 1/2$, $i \in \{1, 2\}$, while the optimum would be one, were the farmers not to reward as they do the remittances that they receive from the urbanites.[2] This captures the distortion entailed by the triangular redistribution game described in this section. Then, from (9.2), it follows that the fiscal pot to be allocated is equal to 1/2 also.

Lastly, the sub-game perfect equilibrium of this game is characterized by the allocation of remittances to the two farmers. It is clearly influenced by the expected gains that the two groups would get from a potential war. It is also influenced to a large extent by the precise specification of the function $V(g_1, g_2)$ that the political process is supposed to maximize. Here, the simplest effect comes out of the solution of the game. Define $v = (V_1/V_2)$ as the marginal rate of substitution between the two urbanites' payoffs – i.e. the ratio of the partial derivatives of $V(g_1, g_2)$ with respect to its first and second argument, respectively.[3] There are three possible outcomes, where each group gets the following allocation, for some $\alpha \in [0,1]$ depending on the specification of the function $V(g_1, g_2)$:

$$g_1 = B_1 + \alpha[1/2 - (B_1 + B_2)] \quad \text{and}$$
$$g_2 = B_2 + (1 - \alpha)[1/2 - (B_1 + B_2)],$$

where $\alpha = 0$ if $v > 1$, $0 < \alpha < 1$ if $v = 1$, and $\alpha = 1$ if $v < 1$.

This expression brings out nicely both the stakes of – and the constraints bearing on – the peaceful political process, namely that the allocation between the two groups of the benefit from the peace cannot fall below the expected payoff that each would get from the war. Each group gets first the equivalent of its expected gain from the war, and then additionally a share of the incremental social gain from the peace: $1/2 - (B_1 + B_2)$. That share may be zero in the two corner solutions. This completes the formal description of the sub-game perfect equilibrium of this game.

---

[2] In that case, the villagers would have no incentives to invest in their offspring's migration, and the political game described here would be stillborn. In a sense, then, the inefficiency identified in this model is simply the price to pay for triggering development, insofar as the latter requires a flow of rural–urban migration.

[3] This formulation can encompass the Rawlsian function $V(g_1, g_2) = \min \}g_1, g_2\}$, provided that v is defined as the ratio of the two *left-hand* derivatives.

This simple game-theoretic model therefore helps us to understand the main features of the "triangular redistribution game" described above: in order to acquire prestige and support from their kinfolks remained in the village, the group's "delegates," the urban migrants participating in the political process, have an incentive to extract as many resources as possible from the country, in an anonymous fashion. This analysis does not contain any moral overtones that would blame the redistribution game that can be observed on some kind of "evil nature" of the African elite, but traces it instead to the incentives created by the structure of the game. It identifies its root cause in the redistribution system that links the elite to the ordinary people.[4] As discussed elsewhere (Azam, 1995b, 2001c, 2006), this redistribution system is crucial to maintain civil peace in the ethnically divided African countries. Hence, it will remain in force for the foreseeable future, at least in peaceful societies.

Houphouët-Boigny of Côte d'Ivoire was probably the master of this type of strategy. Using all the tools made available to him by a relatively well-functioning state, he systematically coopted rising politicians as a way to remain in power, by getting them involved in the government or at the highest levels of the bureaucracy, often in lucrative positions (Azam and Morrisson, 1994; Azam, 1995b). He knew how selectively to turn a blind eye to some forms of corruption. The aim of this policy was to deprive any potential opposition movement of any effective leader, by attracting the latter into the circles of power, and even turning their political clout into an asset for the government. In only one occasion, in 1970, when the Bété Kragbé Gniagbé proved to be insensitive to this type of gifts, did he reluctantly let the army suppress the nascent movement. Moreover, he based his redistribution policy on the implicit taxation of his own unconditional supporters, the Baule cocoa and coffee growers, to fund highly visible public investment in the other regions of the country. Example of the latter are given by the San Pedro harbor and the related infrastructure in the South-Western Bété area, or the sugar complexes, in the northern Senufo area. In so doing, he was making more difficult, and therefore more costly, the mobilization of the local

---

[4] The inefficiency brought out here would be mitigated were the migrants rewarded for the welfare level achieved by their kinfolk rather than for the resources that they bring back. Then, however, it is doubtful that the villagers would have an incentive to invest in their offspring out-migration.

people along ethnic lines, by investing public capital to increase labor productivity in these areas. Lastly, his education policy, one of the most generous in the world relative to GDP, explicitly aimed at creating "national unity" by helping elites from all the ethno-regional groups to emerge, ensuring political participation and inclusion for all of them (Azam, 1993; Azam and Morrisson, 1994). Chapter 8 has demonstrated the consequences of such an education policy for long-run growth in an African country. In sum, Houphouët-Boigny was pursuing a strategy aiming at increasing the opportunity cost of opposition or rebellion at the level both of the potential leaders and that of ordinary supporters.

Indeed, when some groups are excluded from the game, they may engage in political violence, trying to acquire by rebellion what is denied to them by the political system (Azam, 2001a). This can occur either because the government excludes them consciously, preferring to reserve the benefit of participation to its own supporters, or because the social ladder is cut by a shortage of education services, precluding the initial investment in human capital that is the prerequisite for joining the urban elite. Uganda under Idi Amin or Obote provides an example of the first case, while Mali under Moussa Traoré offers an example of the latter (Mutibwa, 1992; Azam *et al.*, 1999). Both examples have given rise to a rebellion, leading to the overthrow of the exclusive elite. Azam and Djim-toingar (2004) show that the Chadian civil war resulted from a similar failure of the Tombalbaye government to leave a fair share to the northerners.

The triangular redistribution system described, whereby the state buys some loyalty from the social base via the remittances and other kinds of redistributive flows delivered by the urban-based workers to their folks remaining back in the village, is rarely the cause of political violence, apart from the examples discussed below. It is usually a well-enforced mechanism, founded on the initial endowment of ethnic capital, which mostly ensures compliance with the rules of the game. It usually forms an almost exhaustive partition of the people of the country, with very few people remaining out of it, with the exception of some migrants of foreign origin. Nevertheless, the study of some recent African conflicts provides some examples of insurrection that were triggered by the discontent of the ethnic base with the fallout from the participation of their own elite in the state game.

A first instance is provided by the Tuareg movement in Mali and Niger in the early 1990s. Although this rebellion has been often presented as an ethnic problem between the Tuaregs and the other groups of Mali and Niger, a closer scrutiny shows that an important reason for this fighting was the discontent of the young jobless Tuaregs with their tribal rulers. The *Ishumar* (derived apparently from the French word *chômeur*, meaning unemployed), were former soldiers from the Libyan army that Colonel Khadafi had to fire when the oil money started to dry up. Returning to their homeland, these young Tuaregs realized that there was no opportunity for them, in particular because of the poor education that they had received, and the very poor infrastructure invested in their region by the Malian or Nigerien governments. General Moussa Traoré of Mali had purchased the quiescence of the Tuaregs by distributing some advantages to the members of the Tuareg traditional chieftaincy, with very little reward for the rest of the people. The north then witnessed an insurrection, which was initially directed as much against the feudal leaders as against the Malian and Nigerien states (Gaudio, 1992; Azam *et al.*, 1999). Another example of the breakdown of the redistribution system within an ethnic framework is provided by the insurgency in Sierra Leone in the early 1990s, described by Abdullah and Muana (1998) as a revolt of the *lumpen-proletariat*. Without any ethnic support, nor any national program, the Revolutionary United Front, formed from the underclass of Freetown and the illegal diamond miners, turned into a sort of bandit movement, committing atrocities against people from all groups. Another example is provided by Bates (1989), who presents an analysis of the *Mau-mau* insurgency in Kenya in the 1950s. He suggests that it was also triggered by a breakdown of the relationship between the *Kikuyu* elite and its ethnic base. These examples illustrate the fact that the ethnic group can fail to provide the required link between its members and the higher levels of the state, and in this case a type of political violence erupts that is particularly difficult to control.

Most of the time, however, a violent insurgency arises when the elite from one (or several) ethnic group(s) are excluded from the sharing of the state bounty, rather than when the remittance flow between the elite and the villagers is cut. It is fairly significant to notice that the insurgent groups are very much a reflection of the structure of the ethnic groups described above: the analysis of guerrillas presented in

Clapham (1998) shows that most insurgent groups are led by their most-educated members, and that the loyalty that they get from their followers depends to a large extent on their ability to secure and redistribute resources within the group. Among others, Pool (1998) for the case of the Eritrean People's Liberation Front, and Young (1998), for the Tigray People's Liberation Front, illustrate precisely how the educated elite members have organized the distribution of resources among their supporters, and how this has helped attract more of them. The cross-border relationships with each other, as well as with southern Sudan, played a crucial role. However, in the days of the Cold War it was relatively easy to get funding from one of the superpowers, so that looting was not necessary. Nowadays, absent foreign support which is more and more difficult to mobilize in the post-Cold War period, the looting of alien groups is often the only solution left. In some cases, looting allows some warlords to sustain long-duration insurgencies, which do not seem to aim really at toppling the government but at creating an enclave under the control of the insurgents, in a sort of partial secession. This is just an extension of the framework presented here, where the redistribution of wealth is made by conquest.

9.5 Conclusion

This chapter has shown how peaceful African societies are organized around an elaborate "triangular" redistribution system. The state and the rest of the urban formal sector collect or produce substantial resources that "delegates" from the different ethno-regional groups desire to control for the benefit of their own group of origin. This analysis does not assume any kind of "evil nature" on the part of the individuals involved, and assumes instead that they are mainly motivated by altruism. However, because the resources of the government, as well as other formal sector resources, are collected anonymously, no individual would do any good to his own ethnic group if he refrained from participating in the scramble; by so doing he would simply leave a larger share of the resources to the others. The collective behavior of all the participants in the political process results rationally, from the individual viewpoint, in the maximization of the resources collected by the state, at the maximum of the Laffer curve. Hence, even altruistic "delegates" will eventually inflict significant distortions on the economy, in order to extract collectively as many resources as possible. The villagers would in fact be better off if none of them sent any "delegates" to the capital city, at least in the short run. However, once the scramble is on, as it is in the transitional phase of political and economic development analyzed here, each group has an incentive to send its own "delegates" to the scrum.

The sharing rule among the different groups has been shown to depend crucially on the expected gains from a potential war that each group could secure. This is why the "shadow of conflict" lies at the heart of this complex redistribution system that is dissected here. If the government is credible enough, then redistribution will prevent war from erupting, and each group will get a share that depends in some way on its efficiency at fighting. If credibility is not sufficient, then the civil war will break out, as emphasized in Azam and Mesnard (2003) and Azam (2006), and the sharing of resources will be performed by wasteful means.

This line of analysis suggests that economic reform and structural adjustment should be designed in such a way that the most efficient ways of redistributing income between groups should be selected, while the most distortionary ones should be avoided (Coate, 2000). The aid community should avoid slashing the most conspicuous methods of redistribution between groups, as this would at best divert the collection of resources to more discrete, but probably more distortionary, methods. At worst, succeeding in repressing redistribution would in many cases eventually trigger civil war. Priority should be given to the fight against self-serving diversion, whereby the ruling group grabs resources for its own benefit only, while efficient redistribution policies that benefit the excluded groups should be favored. A broad-based education policy, which favors the future political participation of all groups while increasing the opportunity cost of soldiering, should thus be the mainstay of the strategy of political and economic development.

General conclusion

Much remains to be done to understand the macroeconomics of African economies. Nevertheless, this book has hopefully shown that some progress can be achieved. The method advocated here combines case studies, focusing on some salient events and policy changes, with analytical modeling and econometric testing, when possible. After all, the take-off of macroeconomics in the West was triggered by a similar concern, as Keynes was trying to understand why there was so much unemployment in Britain in the wake of the 1929 crisis; econometrics came later. Much relevant information is not captured by the statistician's net, and must be replaced by some kind of sophisticated guesswork, taking advantage of any available indirect observations. Equilibrium modeling is an important tool for self-discipline, and the validity of some of the assumptions made can be put to the test by evaluating how much of the available information can be accommodated in the story. The work of the macroeconomist is often akin to that of a detective, trying to find the relevant clues to choose among different possible models. There is not yet any better solution than going to visit the country that one wants to analyze, and trying to put the right questions to the right people. *Bon voyage*!

References

Abdullah, I. and P. Muana (1998). "The Revolutionary United Front of Sierra Leone," in Ch. Clapham (ed.), *African Guerrillas*, Oxford: James Currey, 172–93.

Acemoglu, D. and J. Robinson (2000). "Why Did the West Extend the Franchise? Democracy, Inequality, and Growth in Historical Perspective," *Quarterly Journal of Economics*, 115(4), 1167–99.

Adam, C. S., B. Ndulu, and N. K. Sowa (1996). "Liberalisation and Seignorage Revenue in Kenya, Ghana and Tanzania," *Journal of Development Studies*, 32(4), 531–53.

Ajayi, J. F. A. (1990). "Population Movements and Exchange in Precolonial West Africa," in *The Long-Term Perspective Study of Sub-Saharan Africa, Volume 4: Proceedings of a Workshop on Regional Integration and Cooperation*, Washington, DC: World Bank.

Alesina, A. and A. Drazen (1991). "Why Are Stabilizations Delayed?," *American Economic Review*, 81(5), 1170–88.

Allechi, M. and M. A. Niamkey (1994). "Evaluating the Net Gains from the CFA Franc Zone Membership: A Different Perspective," *World Development*, 22, 1147–60.

Anbarci, N., S. Skaperdas, and C. Syropoulos (2002). "Comparing Bargaining Solutions in the Shadow of Conflict: How Norms against Threats Can Have Real Effects," *Journal of Economic Theory*, 106, 1–16.

Ariyo, A. and M. I. Raheem (1991). "Enhancing Trade Flows Within the ECOWAS Sub-Region: An Appraisal and Some Recommendations," in A. Chhibber and S. Fischer (eds.), *Economic Reform in Sub-Saharan Africa*, Washington, DC: World Bank, 245–58.

Arrow, K. J. (1962). "The Economic Implications of Learning by Doing," *Review of Economic Studies*, 29, 155–73.

Aryeetey, E. and C. Udry (1997). "The Characteristics of Informal Financial Markets in Sub-Saharan Africa," *Journal of African Economies*, 6(1), 161–203.

Ayogu, M. D. (2000). "The Structure of Power and the Pattern of Public Spending in a Fiscal Federalism," paper presented at the ABCDE–Europe Conference, Paris, June, forthcoming in *Journal of Policy Modeling*.

Azam, J.-P. (1990). "Informal Integration through Parallel Markets for Goods and Foreign Exchange," in *The Long-Term Perspective Study of Sub-Saharan Africa, Volume 4: Proceedings of a Workshop on Regional Integration and Cooperation*, Washington, DC: World Bank, 48–51.

(1991a). "Cross-Border Trade between Niger and Nigeria, 1980–1987: The Parallel Market for the Naira," in M. Roemer and C. Jones (eds.), *Markets in Developing Countries: Parallel, Fragmented, and Black*, San Francisco: ICS Press.

(1991b). "Niger and the Naira: Some Monetary Consequences of Cross-Border Trade with Nigeria," in A. Chhibber and S. Fischer (eds.), *Economic Reform in Sub-Saharan Africa*, Washington, DC: World Bank, 66–75.

(1991c). "Marchés parallèles et convertibilité: analyse théorique avec références aux économies africaines," *Revue économique*, 42, 75–93.

(1993). "The 'Côte d'Ivoire' Model of Endogenous Growth," *European Economic Review (Papers & Proceedings)*, 37, 566–76.

(1994). "The Uncertain Distributional Impact of Structural Adjustment in Sub-Saharan Africa," in R. van der Hooven and F. van der Kraaij (eds.), *Structural Adjustment and Beyond in Sub-Saharan Africa: Research and Policy Issues*, London: DGIS, James Currey and Heinemann, 100–13.

(1995a). "L'Etat auto-géré en Afrique," *Revue d'économie du développement*, 1995/4, 1–19.

(1995b). "How to pay for the Peace? A Theoretical Framework with References to African Countries," *Public Choice*, 83(1/2), 173–84.

(1996). "Savings and Interest Rate: The Case of Kenya," *Savings and Development*, 20(1), 33–44.

(1997). "Public Debt and the Exchange Rate in the CFA Franc Zone," *Journal of African Economies*, 6(1), 54–84.

(1999a). "Dollars for Sale: Exchange Rate Policy and Inflation in Africa," *World Development*, 27(10), 1843–59.

(1999b). "Unrecorded Cross-Border Trade and Regional Integration: A Welfare Analysis," in Ademola Oyejide, Ibrahim Elbadawi, and Stephen Yeo (eds.), *Trade Liberalisation and Regional Integration in Africa, Volume 4*, Basingstoke: Macmillan, 281–304.

(2000). "Predation and Markets," paper presented at the World Bank Summer Workshop in July 2000; unpublished.

(2001a). "Inflation and Macroeconomic Instability in Madagascar," *African Development Review*, 13(2), 175–201.

(2001b). "Macroeconomic Reforms in the CFA Franc Zone," chapter 11 in Ibrahim Elbadawi and Benno N'Dulu (eds.), *Economic Development in Sub-Saharan Africa*, London: Macmillan, 308–40.

(2001c). "The Redistributive State and Conflicts in Africa," *Journal of Peace Research*, 38(4), 429–44.

(2004). "Poverty and Growth in the WAEMU after the 1994 Devaluation," *Journal of African Economies*, 13(4), 536–62.

(2006). "The Paradox of Power Reconsidered: A Theory of Political Regimes in Africa," *Journal of African Economies*, 15(1), 26–58.

Azam, J.-P., J.-C. Berthélemy, and S. Calipel (1996). "Risque politique et croissance en Afrique," *Revue économique*, 47(3), 819–29.

Azam, J.-P. and T. Besley (1989a). "General Equilibrium with Parallel Markets for Goods and Foreign Exchange: Theory and Application to Ghana," *World Development*, 17, 1921–30.

(1989b). "The Case of Ghana," in J.-P. Azam, T. Besley, J. Maton, D. Bevan, P. Collier, and P. Horsnell, *The Supply of Manufactured Goods and Agricultural Development*, Development Centre Studies, Paris: OECD.

Azam, J.-P., B. Biais, M. Dia, and C. Maurel (2001). "Informal and Formal Credit Markets and Credit Rationing in Côte d'Ivoire," *Oxford Review of Economic Policy*, 17(4), 520–34.

Azam, J.-P. and C. Bonjean (1995). "La détermination du prix du riz: théorie et application au cas d'Antananarivo (Madagascar)," *Revue économique*, 46(4), 1145–66.

Azam, J.-P., C. Bonjean, G. Chambas, and J. Mathonnat (1993). *Le Niger: La pauvreté en période d'ajustement*, Paris: L'Harmattan.

Azam, J.-P. and G. Chambas (1999). "The Groundnuts and Phosphates Boom in Sénégal (1974–1977)," in P. Collier and J. W. Gunning (eds.), *Trade Shocks in Developing Countries, Volume 1*, Oxford: Oxford University Press.

Azam, J.-P., P. Collier, and A. Cravinho (1994). "Crop Sales, Shortages and Peasant Portfolio Behaviour: An Analysis of Angola," *Journal of Development Studies*, 30(2), 361–79.

Azam, J.-P. and C. Daubrée (1991). "La détermination des taux de change parallèles en Afrique: modèle macro-économique et test économétrique (Nigeria, Zaïre, Ghana)," *Economie et Prévision*, 97, 105–15.

Azam, J.-P. and C. Daubrée (1997). *Bypassing the State: Economic Growth in Kenya, 1964–90*, Development Centre Studies, Paris: OECD.

Azam, J.-P. and A. O. Diakité (1997). "Macroeconomic Policies and Exchange Rate Management in African Economies: The Guinean Case," paper presented at the Macroeconomic Policies and Exchange Rate Management in African Economies Workshop, Nairobi: AERC, May.

Azam, J.-P. and N. Djimtoingar (2004). "Cotton, War and Growth in Chad (1960–2000)," AERC "Explaining African Economic Growth Experience" Project, Nairobi: AERC, unpublished.

Azam, J.-P. and F. Gubert (forthcoming). "Migrants' Remittances and the Household in Africa: A Review of Evidence," *Journal of African Economies*, forthcoming.

Azam, J.-P. and A. Mesnard (2003). "Civil War and the Social Contract," *Public Choice*, 115(3), 455–75.

Azam, J.-P. and Ch. Morrisson (1994). *The Political Feasibility of Adjustment in Côte d'Ivoire and Morocco*, Development Centre Studies, Paris: OECD.

Azam, J.-P., Ch. Morrisson, with S. Chauvin, and S. Rospabé (1999). *Conflict and Growth in Africa, Volume 1: The Sahel*, Development Centre Studies, Paris: OECD.

Azam, J.-P. and O. Samba-Mamadou (1997). "La dévaluation des francs CFA et le cours parallèle de la naira," *Revue économique*, 48(3), 461–9.

Azam, J.-P. and W. Wane (2001). "The 1994 Devaluation and Poverty in the WAEMU," Washington, DC: World Bank, unpublished.

Banerjee, A., J. Dolado, J. W. Galbraith, and D. F. Hendry (1993). *Co-Integration, Error-Correction, and the Econometric Analysis of Non-Stationary Data*, Oxford: Oxford University Press.

Barad, R. (1990). "Unrecorded Tansborder Trade in Sub-Saharan Africa and its Implications for Regional Economic Integration," in *The Long-Term Perspective Study of Sub-Saharan Africa, Volume 4: Proceedings of a Workshop on Regional Integration and Cooperation*, Washington, DC: World Bank, 102–8.

Barro, R. J. (1990). "Government Spending in a Simple Model of Endogenous Growth," *Journal of Political Economy*, 98, S103–S125.

(1991). "Economic Growth in a Cross Section of Countries," *Quarterly Journal of Economics* 106(2), 407–43.

Bates, R. H. (1989). *Beyond the Miracle of the Market: The Political Economy of Agrarian Development in Kenya*, Cambridge: Cambridge University Press.

(2000). "Ethnicity and Development in Africa: A Reappraisal," *American Economic Review*, 90(2), 131–4.

Bates, R. H., A. Greif, M. Levi, J.-L. Rosenthal, and B. R. Weingast (1998). *Analytic Narratives*, Princeton: Princeton University Press.

Becker, G. S., K. M. Murphy, and R. Tamura (1990). "Human Capital, Fertility, and Economic Growth," *Journal of Political Economy*, 98(5), part 2, S12–S37.

Benhabib, J., S. Schmitt-Grohé, and M. Uribe (2002). "Avoiding Liquidity Traps," *Journal of Political Economy*, 110(3), 535–63.

Benjamin, N. C., S. Devarajan, and R. J. Weiner (1989). "The 'Dutch' Disease in a Developing Country: Oil Reserves in Cameroon," *Journal of Development Economics*, 30, 71–92.

Berg, A. and C. Pattillo (1999). "Are Currency Crises Predictable? A Test," *IMF Staff Papers*, 46(2), 107–38.

Berg, E. (1989). "The Liberalization of Rice Marketing in Madagascar," *World Development*, 17, 719–28.

Berthélemy, J.-C., J.-P. Azam, and J.-J. Faucher (1988). *The Supply of Manufactured Goods and Agricultural Development (Madagascar, Mozambique)*, Development Centre Papers, Paris: OECD.

Berthélemy, J.-C. and F. Bourguignon (1996). *Growth and Crisis in Côte d'Ivoire* Washington, DC: World Bank.

Berthélemy, J.-C., A. Seck, and A. Vourc'h (1996). *Growth in Senegal: A Lost Opportunity?*, Development Centre Studies, Paris: OECD.

Bevan, D., P. Collier, and J.W. Gunning (1990). *Controlled Open Economy*, Oxford: Clarendon Press.

   (1992) "Nigeria, 1970–1990," Country Studies, 11, International Center for Economic Growth, San Francisco: ICS Press.

   (1993). "Trade Shocks in Developing Countries," *European Economic Review (Papers & Proceedings)*, 37, 557–65.

Bhagwati, J. and B. Hansen (1973). "A Theoretical Analysis of Smuggling," *Quarterly Journal of Economics*, 87, 172–87.

Blanchard, O.-J. and S. Fischer (1989). *Lectures on Microeconomics*, Cambridge, MA: MIT Press.

Blanchard, O.-J. and P.-A. Muet (1993). "Competitiveness Through Disinflation: An Assessment of the French Macroeconomic Strategy," *Economic Policy*, 16, 12–56.

Bolton, P. and M. Dewatripont (2005). *Contract Theory*, Cambridge, MA: MIT Press.

Boone, C. (2003). *Political Topographies of the African State: Territorial Authority and Institutional Choice*, Cambridge: Cambridge University Press.

Bruno, M. (1991). *High Inflation and the Nominal Anchor of an Open Economy*, Princeton Essays in International Finance, 183: Princeton: Princeton University Press.

Bruno, M. and S. Fischer (1990). "Seigniorage, Operating Rules, and the High Inflation Trap," *Quarterly Journal of Economics*, 105, 353–74.

Burnside, C., M. Eichenbaum, and S. Rebelo (2001). "Prospective Deficits and the Asian Currency Crisis," *Journal of Political Economy*, 109(6), 1155–97.

Cagan, Ph. D. (1956). "The Monetary Dynamics of Hyperinflation," in M. Friedman (ed.), *Studies in the Quantity Theory of Money*, Chicago: University of Chicago Press, 23–117.

Casella, A. and B. Eichengreen (1996). "Can Foreign Aid Accelerate Stabilisation?," *Economic Journal*, 106, 605–19.

Chambas, G. and A.-M. Geourjon (1992). "The New Industrial Policy in Sénégal: A Highly Controversial Reform," in R. Adhikari, C. Kirkpatrick, and J. Weiss (eds.), *Industrial and Trade Policy Reform in Developing Country*, Manchester: Manchester University Press, 135–49.

Chhibber, A. and Shafik, N. (1991). "The Inflationary Consequences of Devaluation with Parallel Markets: The Case of Ghana," in A. Chhibber and S. Fischer (eds.), *Economic Reform in Sub-Saharan Africa*, Washington, DC: World Bank, 39–49.

Clapham, Ch. (ed.) (1998). *African Guerrillas*, Oxford: James Currey.

Coate, S. (2000). "An Efficiency Approach to the Evaluation of Policy Changes," *Economic Journal*, 110, 437–55.

Cohen, D. (1993). "Low Investment and Large LDC Debt in the 1980s," *American Economic Review*, 83, 437–49.

Collier, P. and J. W. Gunning (1999). "Explaining African Economic Performance," *Journal of Economic Literature*, 37(1), 64–111.

Corbo, V. and de Melo, J. (1987). "Lessons from the Southern Cone Policy Reforms," *World Bank Research Observer*, 2, 111–42.

Corden, W. M. (1993). "Exchange Rate Policies for Developing Countries," *Economic Journal*, 103, 198–207..

Dan Maradi, (Elhadji) B. (1994). "Monnaie CFA/Naira: Retour à la case départ?," *Le républicain*, November 10, Niamey: Nouvelle Imprimerie du Niger.

Dasgupta, P. S. and G. M. Heal (1979). *Economic Theory and Exhaustible Resources*, Welwyn and Cambridge: James Nisbet & Co. and Cambridge University Press.

Daubrée, C. (1994). "Analyse microéconomique des marchés parallèles et de la fraude documentaire, avec références aux économies africaines," *Revue économique*, 45, 165–92..

(1995). *Marchés parallèles et équilibres économiques: Expériences africaines*, Paris: L'Harmattan.

(1996). "Fraude documentaire, corruption et contrebande: modèle théorique et test économétrique sur le cas du Sénégal," Clermont-Ferrand: CERDI, mimeo.

Deardorff, A. V. and W. F. Stolper (1990). "Effects of Smuggling under African Conditions: A Factual, Institutional and Analytic Discussion," *Weltwirtschaftsliches Archiv*, 126, 116–41.

Deaton, A. (2001). "Counting the World's Poor: Problems and Possible Solutions," *World Bank Research Observer*, 16(2), 125–47.

de Grauwe, P. (1992). *The Economics of Monetary Integration*, Oxford: Oxford University Press.

Delgado, C. L. (1992). "Why Domestic Food Prices Matter to Growth Strategy in Semi-Open West African Agriculture," *Journal of African Economies*, 1, 446–71.

Demery, L. (1994). "Côte d'Ivoire: Fettered Adjustment," in I. Husain and R. Faruqee (eds.), *Adjustment in Africa: Lessons from Country Case Studies*, Washington, DC: World Bank, 72–152.

Demery, L. and L. Squire (1996). "Macroeconomic Adjustment and Poverty in Africa: An Emerging Picture," *World Bank Research Observer*, 11, 39–59.

Devarajan, S. (1999). "Cameroon's Oil Boom of 1978–85," in P. Collier and J. W. Gunning (eds.), *Trade Shocks in Developing Countries, Volume 1*, Oxford: Oxford University Press.

Devarajan, S., C. Jones, and M. Roemer (1989). "Markets under Price Controls in Partial and General Equilibrium," *World Development*, 17, 1881–93.

Devarajan, S. and J. de Melo (1987a). "Evaluating Participation in African Monetary Unions: A Statistical Analysis of the CFA Zone," *World Development*, 15, 483–96.

(1987b). "Adjustment with a Fixed Exchange Rate: Cameroon, Côte d'Ivoire, and Sénégal," *World Bank Economic Review*, 1, 447–87.

(1991). "Membership in the CFA Zone: Odyssean Journey or Trojan Horse?," in A. Chhibber and S. Fischer (eds.), *Economic Reform in Sub-Saharan Africa*, Washington, DC: World Bank, 25–33.

Devarajan, S. and D. Rodrik (1992). "Do the Benefits of Fixed Exchange Rates Outweigh their Costs: The CFA Zone in Africa," in I. Goldin and L. A. Winters (eds.), *Open Economies: Structural Adjustment and Agriculture*, Cambridge: Cambridge University Press, 66–92.

Diamond, J. (1997). *Guns, Germs, and Steel*, New York: Norton.

Dornbusch, R. (1976). "Expectations and Exchange Rate Dynamics," *Journal of Political Economy*, 84, 1161–76.

(1987). "Collapsing Exchange Rate Regimes," *Journal of Development Economics*, 27, 71–83.

Dornbusch, R., D. V. Dantas, C. Pechman, R. de Rezende Rocha, and S. Simoes (1983). "The Black Market for Dollars in Brazil," *Quarterly Journal of Economics*, 98(1), 25–40, reprinted in R. Dornbusch, *Exchange Rates and Inflation*, Cambridge, MA: MIT Press, 1991.

Dornbusch, R. and S. Fischer (1993). "Moderate inflation," *World Bank Economic Review*, 7, 1–44.

Drugeon, J.-P. and B. Wignolle (1996). "Continuous-Time Sunspot Equilibria and Dynamics in a Model of Growth," *Journal of Economic Theory*, 69, 24–52.

Duruflé, G. (1988). *L'ajustement structurel en Afrique (Sénégal, Côte d'Ivoire, Madagascar)*, Paris: Karthala.

EAIOC (1993). *Les Etats d'Afrique, de l'Océan indien et des Caraïbes*, Paris: Ministère de la Coopération.

Eastwood, R.K. and A.J. Venables (1982). "The Macroeconomic Implications of a Resource Discovery in an Open Economy," *Economic Journal*, 92, 285–99.

Eaton, J. (1993). "Sovereign Debt: A Primer," *World Bank Economic Review*, 7, 137–72.

Edwards, S. (1983). "The Demand for International Reserves and Exchange Rate Adjustments: The Case of LDCs, 1964–1972," *Economica*, 50, 269–80.

(1988). "Real and Monetary Determinants of Real Exchange Rate Behavior: Theory and Evidence from Developing Countries," *Journal of Development Economics*, 29, 311–41.

(1997). "Exchange Rate Issues in Developing and Transitional Economies," *Journal of African Economies*, 6(3), 37–73.

Egwaikhide, F. O., L. N. Chete, and G. O. Falokun (1992). "Exchange Rate Depreciation, Budget Deficit and Inflation: The Nigerian Experience," Final Research Report, Nairobi: AERC.

Eichengreen, B., A. Rose, and C. Wyplosz (1995). "Exchange Market Mayhem: The Antecedents and Aftermath of Speculative Attacks," *Economic Policy*, 21, 249–312.

Faruqee, R. (1994). "Nigeria: Ownership Abandoned," in I. Husain and R. Faruqee (eds.), *Adjustment in Africa: Lessons from Case Studies*, Washington, DC: World Bank, 238–85.

Fernandez, R. and D. Rodrik (1991). "Resistance to Reform: Status Quo Bias in the Presence of Individual-Specific Uncertainty," *American Economic Review*, 81(5), 1146–55.

Fielding, D. (1995). "Investment in Cameroon 1978–1988," *Journal of African Economies*, 4, 29–51.

Findlay, R. (1991). "The New Political Economy: Its Explanatory Power for LDCs," in G. M. Meier (ed.), *Politics and Policy-Making in Developing Countries*, San Francisco: ICS Press, 13–40.

Fischer, S. (1983). "Seigniorage and Fixed Exchange Rates: An Optimal Inflation Tax Analysis," in P.A. Armella, R. Dornbusch, and M. Obstfeld (eds.), *Financial Policies and the World Capital Market: The Problem of Latin American Countries*, Chicago: NBER and University of Chicago Press, 59–69.

Foroutan, F. (1993). "Regional Integration in Sub-Saharan Africa: Past Experience and Future Prospects," in J. de Melo and A. Panagariya (eds.), *New Dimensions in Regional Integration*, Cambridge: Cambridge University Press, 234–77.

Foster, G., J. Greer, and E. Thorbecke (1984). "A Class of Decomposable Poverty Measures," *Econometrica*, 52, 761–6.

Franco, R. G. (1981). "The Optimal Producer Price of Cocoa in Ghana," *Journal of Development Economics*, 8, 77–92.

Garba, P. K. (1997). "The Nigerian Foreign Exchange Market: Possibilities for Convergence in Exchange Rates," Research Paper, 55, Nairobi: AERC.

Gastellu, J.-M. (1989). *Riches Paysans de Côte-D'Ivoire*, Paris: L'Harmattan.

Gaudio, A. (1992). *Le Mali*, 2nd edn., Paris: Khartala.

Ghanem, H. (1999). "The Ivorian Cocoa and Coffee Boom of 1976–79: The End of a Miracle?," in P. Collier and J. W. Gunning (eds.), *Trade Shocks in Developing Countries, Volume 1*, Oxford: Oxford University Press.

Greene, J. (1989). "External Debt Problem of Sub-Saharan Africa," in J. A. Frenkel, M. P. Dooley, and P. Wickham (eds.), *Analytical Issues in Debt*, Washington, DC: International Monetary Fund, 38–74.

Grégoire, E. (1986). *Les Alhazai de Maradi (Niger)*, Paris: Editions de l'Orstom.

  (1995). "Niger et Nigeria: l'impact de la dévaluation du franc CFA," *Afrique contemporaine*, 173, 20–5.

Grimm, M. (2001). "Macroeconomic Adjustment, Sociodemographic Change, and the Evolution of Income Distribution in Côte d'Ivoire," Helsinki: WIDER, unpublished.

Grootaert, C. (1996). *Analyzing Poverty and Policy Reform*, with contributions from Lionel Demery and Ravi Kanbur, Aldershot: Avebury.

Grootaert, C. and R. Kanbur (1995). "The Lucky Few Amidst Economic Decline: Distributional Change in Côte d'Ivoire as Seen Through Panel Data Sets, 1985–88," *Journal of Development Studies*, 31(4), 603–19.

Guillaumont, P. and Guillaumont, S. (1984). *Zone Franc et développement africain*, Paris: Economica.

Harris, J. R. and M. P. Todaro (1970). "Migration, Unemployment, and Development: A Two-Sector Analysis," *American Economic Review*, 60, 126–42.

Hashim, Y. and K. Meagher (1999). *Cross-Border Trade and the Parallel Currency Market – Trade and Finance in the Context of Structural Adjustment: A Case Study from Kano, Nigeria*, Research Report, 113, Uppsala: Nordiska Afrikainstitutet.

Herrera, J. (1994). "Sur l'inconvertibilité du F. CFA au Cameroun," *Politique africaine*, 54, 47–65.

Herrera, J. and B. Massuyeau (1995). "L'influence du Nigeria sur l'évolution des prix, taux de change et flux transfrontaliers des pays voisins de la zone franc: le cas du Bénin et du Cameroun," Paris: DIAL, mimeo.

Hill, P. (1963). *The Migrant Cocoa Farmers of Southern Ghana: A Study in Rural Capitalism*, Cambridge: Cambridge University Press.

IMF (2000a). "Côte d'Ivoire: Selected Issues and Statistical Appendix," Washington, DC: IMF, mimeo.

(2000b). Senegal: Recent Economic Developments, Washington, DC: IMF, mimeo.

Jamal, V. and J. Weeks (1993). *Africa Misunderstood or Whatever Happened to the Rural–Urban Gap?*, Basingstoke: Macmillan.

Johnson, O. E. G. (1987). "Trade Tax and Exchange Rate Coordination in the Context of Border Trading," *IMF Staff Papers*, 34, 548–64.

Kamin, S. B. (1993). "Devaluation, Exchange Controls, and Black Markets for Foreign Exchange in Developing Countries," *Journal of Development Economics*, 40, 151–69.

Kanbur, R. (1990). *Poverty and the Social Dimensions of Structural Adjustment in Côte d'Ivoire*, SDA Working Paper, 2, Washington, DC: World Bank.

Kaufman, D. and S. A. O'Connell (1992). "Fiscal and Monetary Effects of the Parallel Premium: Theory and the Tanzanian Case," paper presented at the Macroeconomics of Parallel Foreign Exchange Systems in Developing Countries Conference, Oxford: St Antony's College.

Kharas, H. and Pinto, B. (1989). "Exchange Rate Rules, Black Market Premia and Fiscal Deficits: The Bolivian Hyperinflation," *Review of Economic Studies*, 56, 435–48.

Kidane, A. (1993). "Exchange Rate Policy and Economic Reform in Ethiopia," Interim Report, Nairobi: AERC.

Komolafe, S. (1998). "Methodological Issues in Currency Convertibility for Developing Countries: Nigeria," Final Report presented at the AERC biannual meeting, Nairobi.

Kouadio, A. K., M. N'Zi, D. N'Guessan, and I. Ouattara (2000). "Ajustement monétaire et pauvreté alimentaire en Côte d'Ivoire," rapport d'étape révisé, CREA–AERC, Cocody: Université d'Abidjan.

Kouassy, O. and B. Bohoun (1994). "Fiscal Adjustment and Growth in Côte d'Ivoire," *World Development*, 22, 1119–28.

Krueger, A. O. (1974). "The Political Economy of the Rent-Seeking Society," *American Economic Review*, 64, 291–303.

Krugman, P. (1979). "A Model of Balance of Payments Crises," *Journal of Money, Credit, and Banking*, 3, 311–25.

(1989). *Exchange Rate Instability*, Cambridge, MA: MIT Press.

(1997). "Are Currency Crises Self-Fulfilling," *NBER Macroeconomics Annual 1996*, Cambridge, MA: MIT Press, 345–78.

LARES (1995). *Commerce informel et dévaluation du franc CFA*, Notes & Etudes, Paris: Caisse française de développement.

Leonard, D. K. and S. Straus (2003). *Africa's Stalled Development: International Causes and Cures*, Boulder and London: Lynne Rienner.

Lewis, W. A. (1954). "Economic Development with Unlimited Supplies of Labor," *Manchester School*, 22, 139–191.

Lipton, M. (1977). *Why Poor People Stay Poor: A Study of Urban Bias in World Development*, London: Temple Smith.

Lizondo, S. J. (1987). "Exchange Rate Differential and Balance of Payments under Dual Exchange Markets," *Journal of Development Economics*, 26, 37–53.

Lucas, R. E., Jr. (1988). "On the Mechanics of Economic Development," *Journal of Monetary Economics*, 22, 3–42.

Mahamadou, S. G. and O. Boukary (1995). "Estimation des échanges commerciaux Niger –Nigeria," Niamey: PASPE, mimeo.

Manchuelle, F. (1997). *Willing Migrants: Soninke Labour Diasporas, 1948–1960*, Athens, OH: Ohio University Press.

May, E. (1985). *Exchange Controls and Parallel Market Economies in Sub-Saharan Africa*, Staff Working Paper, 711, Washington, DC: World Bank.

McIntire, J. and P. Varangis (1999). "Reforming Côte d'Ivoire's Cocoa Marketing and Pricing System," Policy Research Working Paper, 2081, Washington, DC: World Bank.

McKinnon, R. I. (1979). "Foreign Trade Regimes and Economic Development: A Review Article," *Journal of International Economics*, 9, 429–52.

Mutibwa, P. (1992). *Uganda since Independence: A Story of Unfulfilled Hopes*, London: Hurst & Co..

Naylor, R. T. (1999). *Economic Warfare: Sanctions, Embargo Busting and their Human Cost*, Boston: Northeastern University Press.

Ndung'u, S. N. (1996). "Monetary and Exchange Rate Policy in Kenya," Final Report, Nairobi: AERC.

Neary, J. P. (1984). "Real and Monetary Aspects of the 'Dutch Disease'," in D. C. Hague and K. Jungenfeld (eds.), *Structural Adjustment in Developed Open Economies*, London: Macmillan, 357–80.

N'Guessan, T. (1995). "Comparative Analysis of Traditional and Bureaucratic Reaction Functions of the BCEAO in Côte d'Ivoire," *African Journal of Economic Policy*, 2(1), 47–58.

Nkurunziza, J. D. (2002). "Exchange Rate Policy and the Parallel Market for Foreign Currency in Burundi," Research Paper, 123, Nairobi: AERC.

North, D. C. (1990). *Institutions, Institutional Change and Economic Performance*, Cambridge: Cambridge University Press.

Obstfeld, M. (1994). "The Logic of Currency Crises," *Cahiers économique et monétaires de la banque de France*, 43, 189–213.

O'Connell, S. (1992a). "Short and Long Run Effects of an Own-Funds Scheme," *Journal of African Economies*, 1(1), 131–50.

(1992b). "Uniform Commercial Policy, Illegal Trade, and the Real Exchange Rate: A Theoretical Analysis," *World Bank Economic Review*, 6, 459–79.

Odubogun, K. (1994). "The Nigerian Foreign Exchange Market: Possibilities for Convergence in Exchange Rates," Interim Report, Nairobi: AERC.

(1995). "Institutional Reforms and the Management of Exchange Rate Policy in Nigeria," Research Paper, 36, Nairobi: AERC.

Ogiogio, G. O. (1993). "The Behaviour of Foreign Exchange Rates in Nigeria: Determinants and Market Efficiency," Interim Research Report, Nairobi: AER.

Oji, O. G. (2005). "ECOWAS Common External Tariff and Differential Efficiency of Lagos and Cotonou Ports: Implications for Firm-Level Productivity and Competitiveness of Nigerian Ports," Final Report, Nairobi: AERC.

Ouattara, I. (1997). *Profil de pauvreté en Côte d'Ivoire 1993 et 1995*, résultats définitifs, Abidjan: Institut national de la statistique.

Patinkin, D. (1965). *Money, Interest and Prices*, 2nd edn., New York: Harper & Row.

Pegatienan, H. J. (1988). *Stabilization Policy in an Agricultural Dependent Economy: An Econometric General Equilibrium Model of Côte d'Ivoire*, Boston University, PhD dissertation.

Persson, T. and G. Tabellini (1990). *Macroeconomic Policy, Credibility and Politics*, Chur: Harwood Academic.

(1993). "Designing Institutions for Monetary Stability," *Carnegie-Rochester Conference Series on Public Policy*, 39, reprinted in T. Persson and G. Tabellini (eds.), *Monetary and Fiscal Policy, Volume 1: Credibility*, Cambridge. MA: MIT Press, 1994, 279–310.

Pinto, B. (1987). "Nigeria During and After the Oil Boom: A Policy Comparison with Indonesia," *World Bank Economic Review*, 1, 419–45.

(1989). "Black Market Premia, Exchange Rate Unification, and Inflation in Sub-Saharan Africa," *World Bank Economic Review*, 3, 321–38.

Pitt, M. (1981). "Smuggling and Price Disparity," *Journal of International Economics*, 11, 447–58.

(1984). "Smuggling and the Black Market for Foreign Exchange," *Journal of International Economics*, 16, 243–57.

Plane, P. (1994). "La zone franc sous le choc de la dévaluation monétaire: faits et arguments," *Reflets et perspectives de la vie économique*, 23, 203–13.

Pool, D. (1998). "The Eritrean People's Liberation Front," in Ch. Clapham (ed.), *African Guerrillas*, Oxford: James Currey, 19–35.

Rama, M. (2000). "Wage Misalignment in CFA Countries: Were Labour Market Policies to Blame?," *Journal of African Economies*, 9(4), 475–511.

Randa, J. (1999). "Economic Reform and the Stability of the Demand for Money in Tanzania," *Journal of African Economies*, 8(3), 307–44.

Ravallion, M. (1985). "The Performance of Rice Markets in Bangladesh during the 1974 Famine," *Economic Journal*, 95, 15–29.

(1987). *Markets and Famines*, Oxford: Clarendon Press.

Rebelo, S. (1991). "Long-Run Policy Analysis and Long-Run Growth," *Journal of Political Economy*, 99, 500–21.

Ridler, N. B. (1988). "The Caisse de Stabilisation in the Coffee Sector in Côte d'Ivoire," *World Development*, 16, 1521–6.

Robertson, J. W. (1992). "The Process of Trade Reform in Nigeria and the Pursuit of Structural Adjustment," in C. Milner and A. J. Rayner (eds.), *Policy Adjustment in Africa*, London: Macmillan, 173–95.

Robson, P. (1987). *The Economics of International Integration*, 3rd edn., London: Unwin Hyman.

Roemer, M. (1987). "The Simple Analytics of Segmented Markets: What Case for Liberalization?," *World Development*, 14, 429–39.

Rogoff, K. A. (1985). "The Optimal Degree of Commitment to an Intermediate Monetary Target," *Quarterly Journal of Economics*, 100, 1169–89.

Rouis, M. (1994). "Sénégal: Stabilization, Partial Adjustment, and Stagnation," in I. Husain and R. Faruqee (eds.), *Adjustment in Africa: Lessons from Country Case Studies*, Washington, DC: World Bank, 286–351.

Samuelson, P. A. (1957). "Intertemporal Price Equilibrium: A Prologue to the Theory of Speculation," *Weltwirtschaftliches Archiv*, 93, 181–219, reprinted in J. Stiglitz (ed.), *The Collected Scientific Papers of Paul A. Samuelson*, chapter 73, Cambridge. MA: MIT Press.

Sargent, T. J. and Wallace, N. (1973). "Rational Expectations and the Dynamics of Hyperinflation," *International Economic Review*, 14, 328–5.

Schaffer, F. C. (1998). *Democracy in Translation: Understanding Politics in an Unfamiliar Culture*, Ithaca and London: Cornell University Press.

Schiller, C. (1989). "The Fiscal Role of Price Stabilization Funds: The Case of Côte d'Ivoire," *Journal of International Development*, 1, 297–320.

Sen, A. (1981). *Poverty and Famines*, Oxford: Clarendon Press..

Shigoka, T. (1994). "A Note on Woodford's Conjecture: Constructing Stationary Sunspot Equilibria in a Continuous Time Model," *Journal of Economic Theory* 64, 531–40.

Shleifer, A. and R. Vishny (1998): *The Grabbing Hand*, Cambridge. MA: Harvard University Press.

Sidrauski, M. (1967). "Rational Choice and Patterns of Growth in a Monetary Economy," *American Economic Review*, 57(2), 534–44.

Stark, O. (1991). *The Migration of Labor*, Oxford: Basil Blackwell.

Stiglitz, J. (2002). *Globalization and its Discontents*, New York: Norton.

Tanzi, V. (1987). "Quantitative Characteristics of the Tax System of Developing Countries," in D. Newbery and N. Stern (eds.), *The Theory of Taxation for Developing Countries*, Washington, DC: World Bank, 205–41.

(1992). "Structural Factors and Tax Revenue in Developing Countries: A Decade of Evidence," in I. Goldin and L. A. Winters (eds.), *Open Economies: Structural Adjustment and Agriculture*, London, Paris, and Cambridge: CEPR, OECD, and Cambridge University Press, 267–85.

Tirole, J. (2002). *Financial Crises, Liquidity, and the International Monetary System*, Princeton and Oxford: Princeton University Press.

Todaro, M. P. (1976). "Education and National Economic Development in Kenya," document submitted to the National Committee on Educational Objectives and Policies, reprinted in T. Killick (ed.), *Papers on the Kenyan Economy*, Studies in the Economics of Africa, Nairobi: Heinemann Educational, 1981.

Van de Walle, N. (1991). "The Decline of the Franc Zone: Monetary Politics in Francophone Africa," *African Affairs*, 90, 383–405.

Walsh, C. E. (1995). "Optimal Contracts for Central Bankers," *American Economic Review*, 85, 150–67.

Woodford, M. (1986). "Stationary Sunspot Equilibria in a Finance Constrained Economy," *Journal of Economic Theory*, 40, 128–37.

Working, H. (1949). "The Theory of the Price of Storage," *American Economic Review*, 39, 1254–62.

World Bank (1987a). *The Cote d'Ivoire in Transition: From Structural Adjustment to Self-Sustained Growth*, Report, 6051-IVC (4 vols.), Washington, DC: World Bank.

(1987b). *World Development Report 1987*, Washington, DC: World Bank.

(1995a). *World Debt Tables 1993–94*, Washington, DC: World Bank.

(1995b). *World Tables 1995*, Washington, DC: World Bank.

(1996). *World Development Report 1996*, Washington, DC: World Bank.

(1997). *African Development Indicators*, Washington, DC: World Bank, diskette.

(2005). *Senegal: Poverty and Human Development*, Report, 26189-SN, Washington, DC: World Bank.

Yao, J. Y. (1988). "Education et salaire en Côte d'Ivoire," *Cahiers ivoiriens de recherche économique et sociale*, 15, 11–34.

Young, J. (1998). "The Tigray People Liberation Front," in C. Clapham (ed.), *African Guerrillas*, Oxford: James Currey, 36–52.

Younger, S. D. (1992). "Testing the Link between Devaluation and Inflation: Time Series Evidence from Ghana," *Journal of African Economies*, 1(3), 369–94.

Zagré, P. (1994). *Les politiques économiques du Burkina Faso*, Paris: Karthala.

Zartman, I. W., with T. D. Bakary, A. A. Boahen, A. Gboyega, and D. Rothchild (1997), *Governance as Conflict Management*, Washington, DC: Brookings Institution Press.

Index

Page numbers in **bold** refer to illustrations.

Abacha, General, 18, 21, 89, 131
Abdullah, I., 236
Abidjan, 187, 191
Accra, 126
Acemoglu, D., 223
Adam, C. S., 85, 102
ADF test, 94
African Economic Research
    Consortium (AERC), xiii
"African goods," 117, 160–166, 169,
    191
Ajayi, J. F. A., 199
Akan, 191, 201, 214–216, 218, 219
Alesina, A., 175
Algeria, 38
Allechi, M., 105
Amin, Idi, 15, 235
Angola, 139–140
Angolan Coffee Board, 140
Antananarivo, 145–146
arbitrage, 49
Ariyo, A., 108
Aryeetey, E., 181
Asian crisis, 79, 134, 154, 156
"auto adjustment," 120
"authorized dealers," 70
Ayogu, M. D., 228, 230
Azam, J.-P., 12–17, 27, 29, 46, 50–51,
    58, 60, 62–64, 72–73, 77–78, 80–
    81, 91–92, 95–96, 102, 107–108,
    112, 117, 122–123, 126, 136–137,
    139–140, 142, 145, 147, 158–160,
    173, 175–176, 178, 182, 185–186,
    210–211, 214–215, 219, 221,
    223–226, 228–230, 234–236, 238

Babana, 19
Badagri, 18, 20
Banerjee, A., 54, 77, 167, 211
Banque Centrale des Etats de l'Afrique
    de l'Ouest (BCEAO), 17, 53, 54,
    105, 125–127, 176
Banque des Etats de l'Afrique Centrale
    (BEAC), 17, 53, 54, 61, 105,
    125–127
Bantu, 216
Barad, R., 27
Barro, R. J., 199, 207, 209
Bates, R. H., 236
Baule cocoa, 234
bauxite, 70, 91
Becker, G. S., 199, 206
Bedié, President Konan, 219
Besley, T., 27, 29, 58, 60, 62, 64, 73,
    77
Benhabib, J., 5, 100, 136
Benin, 15, 18–23, 54, 109, 125, 158,
    176–178
Benjamin, N. C., 107
Berg, E., 145, 147, 154
Berthélemy, J.-C., 46, 197, 210
Bertrand, 30
Besley, T., 14, 15, 27, 29, 46, 58, 60,
    62–64, 72, 77
Bété, 227, 234
Bevan, D., 46, 72, 76, 107
Bhagwati, J., 27, 31
Bohoun, B., 122
Bonjean ,C., 140–142, 144–145, 147
Boone, C., 223, 227
Boukary, O., 15, 19

Bourguignon, F., 197
"brain drain," 203
Bretton Woods institutions, 14, 36, 88,
    106, 111, 113, 120, 122, 124, 130,
    147
Bruno, M., 73, 83
Burkina Faso, 15, 19, 106, 108, 109,
    110–113, 120, 127, **129**, 177–179,
    198, 215, 219
  gold mining, 106
  migrant workers, 108, 198
  SAP, 106
Burnside, C., 154, 156
Burundi, 81
Busia, K. A., 214

Cagan, Ph., 82
Caisse de stabilisation, 198–199
CAISTAB, 12
Camdessus, Michel, 129, 174
Cameroon, 1–2, 12, 15–17, 20–22,
    53–54, 106–107, 110, 112–114,
    120, 123, 127–128, 132, 137, 139,
    178–179
"*candongeiros*," 146
Casamance, 227
Casella, A., 175
cedi, 159
CEMAC, 47, 71, 105, 131, 157, 175,
    179
Central African Republic, **109, 178,**
    179
CFA Franc, 5–6, 15, 17–18, 21, 41, 52,
    71, 94, 105–106, 110–111,
    117–118, 157–169
  devaluation, 106, 124–133, 135,
    137, 139, 165–167, 173–179,
    196–197
  DM, 175, 176
  US dollar, 47, 87, 110, 122, 127,
    157, 159, 166–167, 197
CFA Zone, xiii, 5–6, 15, 17, 40, 45–47,
    53, 65, 105, 106, 114–119, 122,
    125–128, 157–169, 173–180, 185,
    195
  formal sector wages, 175
Chad, 1–2, 17, 21, 53–54, 111, 178–
    179, 211, 213–216, 220, 235
Chambas, G., 107, 123
Chhibber, A., 73

Chow-breakpoint test, 167
Clapham, Ch., 237
Coate, S., 238
cocoa, 14–15, 173, 198, 214, 218, 223
  see also Ghanaian Cocoa
    Marketing Board
Cocoa Marketing Board (Cocobod), 15
Cohen, D., 114
Cola nut, 6
  effect, 136–137, 156–169
Collier, P., 46, 72, 76, 107, 139
commodity crash 1987, 119, 197
Common External Tariff (CET), 11
  see also tariffs
Conakry, 138
Congo, 109, 178
Consumer Price Index, 77–78, 95–96
contract theory, 24
"convergence hypothesis," 200
Corbo, V., 87
Corden, M. W., 41
"core capital good," 200
"cover" effect, 30, 35
corruption, 1, 23–26
Côte d'Ivoire, 7, 12–15, 58, 106–109,
    112–114, 120, 122–124, 127, 128,
    131–132, 173–174, 176–180, 182,
    186–187, 190–192, 195, 197–199,
    201, 207, 209, 212–216, 218–220,
    223, 227, 234–235
  poverty and socio-economic groups,
    186–192
Cotonou, 18, 20–21, 23, 125, 158
Cotontchad, 211
cotton, 211, 213
Coulibaly, Gbon, 227
Cravinho, A., 139
currency, 1, 4–6, 69–104
  see also cedi, naira CFA Franc
convertibility, 45–66
  foreign, 13, 16
currency crisis, 124–133, 134–169
  foodstuffs, 139–147
  models, 147–156
  national currency convertible, 5
  self-fulfilling, 134, 152–154

Dakar, 192
Daubrée, C., 12, 14, 16, 56, 60, 27, 31,
    46, 72, 78, 80–81, 91–92, 136, 210

de Melo, J., 45, 87, 106–107, 111
Deardorff, A. V., 31, 32, 44
Deaton, A., 195
Delgado, C. L., 117, 160
Demery, L., 114, 122, 173, **174**
Derg regime, 146
deterrence, social peace through, 224–227
Devarajan, S., 27, 31, 35, 41, 45, 106–107, 111, 173
Diakité, A. O., 91, 95–96
Diamond, J., 147, 216
Dickey–Fuller (DF) test, 77, 91–92, 95
Diola, 227
Djimtoingar, N., 211, 235
Djulas, 214, 216
Domar, 199, 204
Dornbusch, R., 3–4, 71–73, 76, 83, 109, 137, 147, 155, 165
Drazen, A., 175
Drugeon, J.-P., 85
Dupuit–Laffer effect, 204, 209

East Forest, 191
Eastwood, R. K., 168
Eaton, J., 114
economic stabilization, 21
education, 199, 209–210
Edwards, S., 71–72, 127, 138
Egwaikhide, F. O., 72
Eichenbaum, M., 154, 156
Eichengreen, B., 134, 154, 175
"enclave production," 220
Equalization Fund Management Board, 20
Equatorial Guinea, 109, 111, 178
Eritrean People's Liberation Front, 237
ESAM, 192
Ethiopia, 36, 71, 174
ethnic rent, 217–218, 220, 222
ethnicity,
    and wealth, 216–221
    see also geography
European goods, 117, 160–164, 169
exchange rates, 13, 16–17, 43–44, 50, 79, 69–104, 117–118
    see also naira, CFA Franc
    CPI, 95–96
    inflation, 72–78, 108–111

nominal anchor policy, 73, 85–87, 91, 108
export crops, 200–212, 229

Faruqee, R., 72, 77
Faucher, J.-J., 46
Fernandez, R., 175
FGT (Foster, Greer, and Thorbecke) measure, 188
Fielding, D., 107
Findlay, R., 205
Fischer, S., 72–73, 76, 83, 85, 106, 109
foreign exchange market, 4, 16–17, 18, 35, 38, 69–104
    see also currency
Forest Zone, 199
Foroutan, F., 40
Foster, G., 188
"*franc fort*" policy, 111
France, 105, 124–126, 128, 129, 168, 175
Freetown, 236
FTA, 4, 27, 39–40, 44
    see also trade liberalization

Gabon, 106, 109, 178
Gambia, 14, 15, 178
Garba, P. K., 50–51, 69–70
Garoua, 17, 127
Gastellu, J.-M., 199, 201, 218
Gaudio, A., 236
Gbagbo, President of Côte d'Ivoire, 13
GDP, 54, 70, 97–98, 106, 109, 115, 122, 132, 157, 177, 179, 180, 194, 199, ,206, 208–209, 212
geography,
    and wealth, 213
Geourjon, A.-M., 123
Ghana, 14–15, 18, 46, 58, 73, 126, 174, 178, 198, 201, 214, 218
Ghanaian Cocoa Marketing Board, 58
Ghanem, 107, 197
Gniagbé, Bété Kragbé, 234
gold, 91
government intervention, 49
Granger non-causality test, 74, 79–80, 92–93
Greene, J., 114
Grégoire, E., 15, 17, 127, 132
Grimm, M., 195

Grootaert, C., 173–175, 186–187
groundnuts, 107, 109
Gubert, F., 228
Gueï, General, 215
Guillaumont, P., 45, 199
Guinea, 5, 74, 90–97, 136, 157, 169, 178
Guinea-Bissau, 70
Gunning, J. W., 46, 72, 76, 107

Hansen, B., 27, 31
Harambee movement, 210
Harberger triangle, 218
Harris, J. R., 181, 191, 194
Harrod–Domar model, 199, 204
Hashim, Y., 18, 157
Hausa, 16, 126, 213
Herrera, J., 15, 17, 22, 127
"Hicksian week," 52
Hill, P., 201, 218
Hotelling's Lemma, 58–59
Houphouët-Boigny, President, 124, 173, 198, 213, 215, 219, 223, 227, 234–235
human capital, 200–206

IMF, 26
Ibadan, 19–20
inflation, 22, 74–98, 108–111, 123
   food as an inflation-proof asset, 139–140
   tax, 87, 98, 106
inflation Laffer curve, 102–104
informalization of the economy, 185–186
international financial institutions (IFI), 4, 124, 128, 136, 176
International Monetary Fund (IMF), 51, 176

Jamal, V., 181
Johansen Cointegration Test, 91
Jones, C., 27, 31, 35
Johnson, O. E. G., 26

Kamin, S. B., 27
   model, 31
Kanbur, R., 173–175, 187, 199
Kandi, 19

Kano, 16, 127, 157
Kaufman, D., 72
Keita, Modibo, 214
Kent, Laurence, 144
Kenya, 5, 15, 73, 78–81, 92, 97, 102, 136, 174, 210, 235–236
Keynes–Ramsey formula, 182
Khadafi, Colonel, 236
Kharas, H., 71–72
Kidane, A., 15
Kikuyu, 236
Komolafe, S., 51, 159
Kouadio, A. K., 187, 195
Kouassy, O., 122
Kru, 214
Krueger, A. O., 14
Krugman, P., 137–138, 147–150, 152–153, 155, 161

labor, 180–186, 217
Laffer, 204, 209, 237
Laffer curve, 83, 98, 102–104, 154, 232
Lagos, 18–19, 20, 23, 157
Lagrange multiplier, 101
Leonard, D. K., 220
Lewis, W. A., 199, 212
Libyan army, 236
Lipton, S. J., 181
Lizondo, M., 71–72
Lomé, 53
Lucas, R. E., 199

macroeconomics,
   applicability to developing countries, xi
Madagascar, 6, 46, 141–142, 144–146, 157
   currency crisis, 137–139, 146
   Malagasy, 136, 145
Mahamadou, S. G., 15, 19
Malagasy Franc (FMG), 146, 168–169
Mali, 109, 131, 177–179, 198, 213–214, 219–220, 235–236
Manchuelle, F., 219
Mande, 191, 215
Maradi, 16, 20, 54, 132
markets, parallel, 1–5, 15–17, 56, 66, 70–71, 73, 82, 97

exchange rate, 15, 74, 79, 86–87, 89
  Naira, 16
Massuyeau, B., 15, 17,22
Mau-mau, 236
Mauritania, 178
McIntire, J., 12–13, 15, 198
Meagher, K., 18, 157
Mengistu regime, 15
Mesnard, A., 214, 221, 223–225, 238
migration failure, 218–220
Mitterrand, President, 198
monetary integration, 40–43
money function, 99–104
money-less model, 56
Morrisson, Ch., 12, 107–108, 112,
  122–123, 173, 186, 234–235
Mozambique, 46, 70, 146
Muana, P., 236
Mugabe, President, 3
Murphy, 199, 204
Muslim, 214, 223
Mutibwa, P., 235

Naba, Moro, (Mossi Emperor), 215, 219
naira, 4, 16–18, 21–22, 47–48, 51–53,
  127, 136, 157–167
  US dollar, 158–159, 164, 166–167
Nash equilibrium theory, 88–90, 229,
  231
Naylor, R. T., 3
Ndulu, B., 85, 102
Ndung'u, S. N., 92
Neary, J. P., 91, 160, 164
N'Guessan, T., 125
"New Forces," 15
New Guinean Franc (NGF), 91, 92
"New Industrial Policy," 123
Niamey, 16, 29, 185
Niamkey, M. A., 105
Niger, 12, 15–17, 19, 21, 29, 47–48,
  51–55, 61, 112, 126, 176, 177,
  178, 185–187 191, 195, 213, 236
  poverty and socio-economic groups,
  191–193
  SAP, 14, 17
Nigeria, 4–5, 11, 13, 15–23, 29, 43,
  46–52, 69–72, 74–79, 85–87, 89,
  90, 92, 97–98, 105, 114, 125–127,
  131, 136, 157–167, 174, 178,
  213–214

re-export fertilizer, 38
subsidized fertilizer, 1
trade with Benin, 18–23, 158
trade with the CFA Zone, model of,
  160–166
trade with Niger, 21, 29
Nkurunziza, J. D., 81
nominal anchor policy, 85–98, **100**,
  108
  credibility, 87–90
non-tariff barriers (NTBs), 14
North, D., 223

Obasanjo, O., 214
Obote, M., 15, 235
Obstfeld, M., 152
OCA, optimum currency area,
  40–41
O'Connell, S., 27, 29, 31, 45, 72
Odubogun, K., 13, 50–51, 69–70, 72
oil, 11–13, 20, 50, 69, 76, 106, 109,
  159, 175, 179
Oji, G. O., 23
Ouattara, I., 187

paddy, rice, 138, 141–142, 145
Pareto, V., 218
Patinkin, D., 56
Pattillo, C., 154
peace, price of, 221–227
peaceful cone, 222
Pegatienan, H. J., 198–199
Persson, T., 87, 90
"Peso effect," 131
Phillips curve, 137
phosphates, 107, 109, 113
Pinto, B., 69, 71–72
Pitt, M., 30, 32, 34–35
  model, 35
Plane, P., 45, 123
Pontryagin's Maximum Principle, 5,
  60, 101, 182
Ponzi-game trajectory, 119–120,
  129–130, 132
Pool, D., 237
poverty, 174–175
  measures of, 188–190
  socio-economic groups, 186–194
private production, 200–204
public debt, 114, 116–119

public sector production of human
  capital, 204–206

quantitative restriction (QR), 14, 22,
  28, 35, 41, 44–45, 56, 63–65, 73,
  77, 117
  see also non-tariff barriers,
  smuggling

Raheem, M. I., 108
Rama, M., 178–180
Rand Zone, 40
Randa, J., 102
Raparson, Emilienne, 144
Ravallion, M., 140–141, 143
Rawlings, Jerry, 214
real exchange rate, 116–119
real-side adjustment strategy, 120–124
Rebelo, S., 154, 156, 199–200, 207
redistribution of wealth, 222–238
  aid, 238
  triangular game, 228–229
redistribution syndrome, 215–216
Revolutionary United Front, 236
Ricardo, David, 198, 201 223
rice, 138–147
Ridler, N. B., 70, 198
Robertson, J. W., 72
Robinson, J., 223
Robson, P., 27
Rodrik, D., 41, 45, 173, 175
Roemer, M., 27, 31, 35
Rogoff, K. A., 74, 90, 98
Rose, A., 134, 154
Rouis, M., 122–123

Sahelian countries, 113, 135, 213, 216
Samba-Mamadou, O., 159
Samuelson, P. A., 140–141
San Pedro harbor, 234
SAP, 14, 17, 46, 76, 78
Sargent, T. J., 71
Savannah, 191, 199
Schiller, F. C., 12, 70, 198
Schmitt-Grohé, S., 5, 100, 136
Seck, A., 210
sector, formal and informal, 6
seigniorage 83, 120, 134
  foreign, 117

Sen, A., 143
Senegal, 1, 14, 106–110, 112, 120,
  122–124, 127, 128, 157, 177–178,
  178, 180, 192, 194, 210, 219, 223,
  227
  "New Industrial Policy," 123
  trade shock, 107
Senghor, Léopold Sédar, President, 210
  223–224, 227
Senufo, 214, 217, 227, 234
Serer, 223
"shadow transfer," 51
Shafik, N., 73
Shaki, 19
Shigoka, T., 85
Shleifer, A., 51
Sidrauski, M., 5, 100
Sierra Leone, 220, 235, 236
smuggling, 27–30, 35, 44, 53–63, 117,
  123
  cost of, 31–32
  monetary integration, 40–43
  official trade, 30–37
  regional integration, 39–40
  welfare cost of trade distortion,
    23–27, 32
  welfare effect of, 22, 32–39, 43
Solowian Harrod–Domar model, 199
Sonacop, 20
Soninke, 219
Sowa, N. K., 85, 102
Squire, L., 173–174
stabilization funds, 12, 13, 20, 36, 223
Stark, O., 201
Stiglitz, J., 129, 134, 136
Stolper, W. F., 31, 32, 44
Straus, S., 220
structural adjustment programs (SAP),
  14, 70, 185
  Burkina Faso 1991, 113
  Madagascar 1994, 147
  Niger, 55
  Nigeria, 72, 76, 78, 85, 98
  Senegal (1979–1980), 113
Sudan, 237

Tabellini, G., 87, 90
tablita, 87, 97
Tamura, R., 199, 204
Tanzania, 70, 174

Tanzi, V., 116
tariffs, 2, 33, 35, 60–63
  tariff-driven smuggling, 60
  trade distortions, 22–27, 32
taxes, 11–13, 204, 206–209, 222, 223,
  229, 230, 232–233
"Taylor rule," 136, 144
Tigray, 146, 237
Tirole, J., 154
Todaro, M. P., 181, 191, 194, 210
Togo, 19, 48, 176–178
Tombalbaye, F., 213, 235
Touré, Samory, 216
Touré, Sékou, 90
tradable goods, 42–43, 117, 160
trade, 1–4, 11, 12,
  "cover" effect, 30, 44
  cross-border, 11–44
  distortion, 23–27, 46
  liberalization, 33–35, 37, 62,
    65–66
  parallel, 15, 27, 45–66
Traoré, Moussa, 214, 235–236
Tuareg, 236

Ubangui Shari territory, 215
Udry, C., 181
UEMOA, 157
Uganda, 235
Uribe, M., 5, 100, 136

Van de Walle, N., 175, 178
Varangis, P., 12–13, 15, 198
Venables, A. J., 168
Vinerian analysis, 3, 27, 39, 43
Vishny, R., 51
Vourc'h, A., 210

wages, 179–186, 199, 201–203
Wallace, N., 71
Walras's Law, 63
Walsh, C. E., 90
Wane, W., 178, 186
Wapa market, 157
war veterans, 3
"Warehouse State," 18
weak formal institution, 1
Weeks, J., 181
"Weimar republic," 151
Weiner, R. J., 107
West African Economic and
  Monetary Union (WAEMU), 11,
  44, 53, 94, 175–176, 179–180,
  192, 194
West Forest, 191
White, 49
Wigniolle, 85
Woodford conjecture, 85, 152
Working, H., 140–141
World Bank, 51, 70, 114, 122, 124,
  176, 187–188, 194, 197
Wyplosz, C., 134, 154

Yansané, Kerfalla, 5, 91, 137
Yao, J. Y., 199
Young, J., 237
Younger, S. D., 73

Zagré, P., 105–106, 108, 120
Zaire, 46, 105, 126, 178
Zartman, I. W., 214
Zimbabwe, 3, 14, 48, 63, 71, 220
Zimbabwean (Zim) dollars, 48
Zinder, 19, 53, 54